The Dealmakers of Downstate Illinois

THE DEALMAKERS

of Downstate Illinois:

Paul Powell, Clyde L. Choate, John H. Stelle

Robert E. Hartley

Southern Illinois University Press
Carbondale

Southern Illinois University Press

www.siupress.com

Cover illustrations (clockwise from top): Representative Paul Powell (*left*)
with Southern Illinois University president Delyte Morris (Abraham
Lincoln Presidential Library and Museum [ALPLM]); Governor John
Stelle on a mule presented to him by Sam Plant of Murphysboro (ALPLM);
and Staff Sergeant Clyde L. Choate receiving the Medal of Honor from
President Harry S. Truman (National Archives; 111-SC-210881).

Library of Congress Cataloging-in-Publication Data
Names: Hartley, Robert E., author.
Title: The dealmakers of downstate Illinois : Paul Powell,
Clyde L. Choate, John H. Stelle / Robert E. Hartley.
Other titles: Paul Powell, Clyde L. Choate, and John H. Stelle
Description: Carbondale, IL : Southern Illinois University Press,
[2016] | Includes bibliographical references and index.
Identifiers: LCCN 2015034220| ISBN 9780809334742
(pbk. : alk. paper) | ISBN 9780809334759 (e-book)
Subjects: LCSH: Illinois—Politics and government—1951– |
Legislators—Illinois—Biography. | Illinois. General Assembly—
Biography. | Powell, Paul, 1902–1970. | Choate, Clyde L., 1920–2001. |
Stelle, John H., 1891–1962 | Politicians—Illinois—Biography. | Illinois—
Politics and government—1865–1950. | Southern Illinois (Ill.)—Politics
and government—20th century. | Southern Illinois (Ill.)—Biography.
Classification: LCC F546.2 .H33 2016 | DDC 328.73/0922—
dc23 LC record available at http://lccn.loc.gov/2015034220

Printed on recycled paper. ♻

This paper meets the requirements of
ANSI/NISO Z39.48-1992 (Permanence of Paper) ∞

For the readers: Mary, Bud, and D. G.

Contents

Gallery of illustrations beginning on page 85

Acknowledgments

Writers of Illinois political escapades, I among them, depend on background sources for leads, anecdotes, trivia, rumors, and facts. During my work on this book the universe of writers' helpers lost three gifted men who had guided me through the political thicket for several books and history articles. I have paid tribute to them before, and I must do it again, for they have left me with a treasury of material that I will continue to use. David Kenney and I wrote two books together. David also served as a valuable editor of manuscript drafts. My files of Gene Callahan information are overflowing. Encounters with Gene date to the late 1970s. Alan Dixon, who served forty-two years in Illinois elective offices, never failed to return my calls and faithfully added his special flavor to my research. Contributions from all three sources are represented in this book. Thank you, gentlemen.

Research about Clyde Choate presented special challenges. Coming to my rescue was journalist, author, and longtime friend Taylor Pensoneau. He made available many documents from his Choate file, accumulated while working in Springfield for the *St. Louis Post-Dispatch*, and after. Taylor's keen journalistic eye was at work during Choate's years as a Democratic Party leader in the state House. He shared recollections of those times, so important to this story. Taylor's excellent books about Dan Walker, Russell Arrington, and Richard B. Ogilvie contain valuable information about Choate's activities during the 1960s and 1970s, which

Taylor graciously gave me permission to use. His contributions enrich the Choate story, as do his books on Illinois politics.

I learned early that official U.S. Army service records for Clyde L. Choate were destroyed in the 1973 fire at the National Archives Record Center (NARA) in St. Louis. NARA employee Karen Cooper discovered overlooked records that helped reconstruct critical pieces of his service. The Maryland offices of NARA made available unit records for Choate during the time he fought the battle that earned him the Medal of Honor. The U.S. Military Institute at Carlisle, Pennsylvania, added copies of rare documents for the Choate story.

The helpers with this book are many. It is evidence of the varied voices that are necessary in writing political history. They include John Reinhardt at the Illinois State Archives; Gwenith Podeschi, on staff at the Abraham Lincoln Presidential Library (ALPL); Steve Kerber, who keeps watch over archives at Southern Illinois University (SIU)-Edwardsville; Claire Fuller Martin, who has provided critical research for many of my projects; Bob Fallstrom, who reaches back to my time as editor of the *Decatur Herald and Review*; Bryan G. Huff, expert on oil production at the Illinois Geological Survey; Mark DePue, writer, editor, military veteran, and oral history expert at ALPL, for many contributions; Walter Ray, overseer of political documents at SIU's Morris Library; Beverly Warshawsky, for her "loan"; Mike Lawrence, whose vast knowledge of Illinois politics is a precious resource; Melissa Hicks of the Brazil, Indiana, public library; research helpers at the Eldorado, Illinois, Memorial Public Library District; and James M. (Jim) Wall, an invaluable source for 1970s presidential politics. D. G. Schumacher and Fletcher Farrar again saved me many times with their edits of the manuscript. I reserve special thanks for the work on images by Mary Michal (now retired) and Roberta Fairburn in audiovisuals at the ALPL, and Gary Hacker of Vienna. Editor in chief Karl Kageff and the team at SIU Press deserve my highest praise.

I always save my superlatives for Mary Hartley's comments, edits, and patience.

The Dealmakers of Downstate Illinois

Introduction

This book is about a golden era of legislative action in Illinois political history and many of the men who made it so. Specifically, it explores the post–World War II period from 1947 to 1977 and describes the bipartisan behavior of members in the Illinois General Assembly. Moreover, it identifies a list of critical issues debated and passed by the legislature, many of which favored downstate Illinois, and the means by which that was accomplished.

Yes, there are many stories from that time of tomfoolery, corruption, greed, and sleight of hand. Not many of the characters who served deserve a bronze statue for bravery and courage. Their ethical shortcomings aside, the principal characters produced a body of work that deserves recognition for its progressive reach into every corner of the state. The members fought on the floor of each chamber, stabbed backs behind the scenes, traded special favors for votes, and pulled every legislative trick in the bag. Such is the history of making laws most anytime. Stalemates occurred, but few prevailed. In all, it was a political circus with results. The record looks positively uplifting when compared to periods before and after in Springfield.

Also reflected in this tale is a graphic picture of evolving regional politics at a time when the arena featured more than just Chicago against the rest of Illinois or an emphasis on factions of only one political party. During the three decades, three Republicans (Dwight Green, William

Stratton, and Richard Ogilvie) and four Democrats (Adlai Stevenson, Otto Kerner, Samuel Shapiro, and Dan Walker) served as governor. With few exceptions Republicans controlled the state Senate and House. For much of the thirty years Democratic politicians from southern Illinois initiated deals, big and small. Politicians all over the spectrum had critical roles in passing and defeating the proposals, but it took dealmakers to get things started and finished.

Times were different. Compared to today's legislative activity, conditions were primitive. Until the 1960s, the General Assembly met every two years for six months, with an occasional special session thrown in. If the leadership could not squeeze the business in during that time period, it did not come up again for two years. Members of the House and Senate had no staffs, and the modest pay required most to have a second or third job at home. Campaign costs, remarkably small even when adjusted for inflation, came out of the candidate's pocket for the most part. Without laws for financial disclosure, dollars flowed from all manner of influential interests. That might explain why many legislators walked around Springfield with their hands out. However, the part-time nature of state government did not inhibit the introduction of grand ideas or huge expenditures. Toward the end of the three decades, the cumulative effects of policies and annual legislative sessions created pressure for more sources of revenue, which changed the dynamics of governing substantially.

Who were the persons who made things happen in Springfield and across downstate Illinois? Paul Powell, Clyde Choate, and John Stelle were principal players in the huge stage show. They developed coalitions that cut across regions and parties. They fueled outcomes with money—especially Stelle, who had substantial personal wealth, and Powell and Choate, men of more modest means. They all knew who had the money and how to bring them to the action. In order to get something done in public policy, interests had no choice but to work with those for whom ethical standards were loosely applied. This was not a simple case of good guys against bad guys. You dealt with those who had the power and votes. Legislation enriched many, especially Powell, who accumulated millions of dollars for personal use. He declared much of it on tax returns in order to avoid the wrath of the Internal Revenue Service. However, only Powell knew about the rest, and no records exist for all the money he poured into campaigns for his friends.

By the consensus of Powell's contemporaries—friends and foes—he was a near-genius in skills required to produce legislative results. That alone explains his record as Speaker of the House three times and minority leader at most other times. Uneducated beyond high school, untrained for political leadership except by experience in local dogfights, and a gifted orator complete with spicy vocabulary and cornpone humor, he was one of a kind. Choate rode Powell's coattails through the legislative muck and learned carefully. He became as close to a clone of Powell as possible, and they liked and respected each other. After Powell left the legislature, Choate carved his own impressive niche by building on what he learned from Powell, combined with his own tough-minded personality. Often placed well behind Powell and others in terms of impact on legislative affairs, Choate in his full story is quite impressive.

Meanwhile, Stelle, full of ideas, bluster, high-octane risk taking, and plenty of money, worked closely in political adventures with Powell. Stelle's career in elective office ended poorly with a short-lived term as governor in 1940. But many of the contacts he made during that time paid off in later years. It was during the two decades after he left office that Stelle worked deals as a partner with Powell, Choate, and others to form a strong base of support with the county fair crowd from rural areas, and with military veterans. Despite the disappointing outcomes in public office, Stelle never gave in to his enemies.

THESE THREE—AND THEIR CLOSE associates throughout southern Illinois and scattered across other downstate locales—had more in common than the quest for power and money. They were small-town natives who thrived during their early years in a southern Illinois economic environment that gave the term *hard luck* fresh meaning. In McLeansboro (Stelle), Vienna (Powell), and Anna (Choate) they had totally different experiences and opportunities. But they shared a deep-seated ambition and value system that honored hard work and ethical flexibility. Their strong sense of loyalty was paid and repaid countless times. In political battles they were tough guys with a strong instinct for survival who also knew the right time to compromise. They were sons of southern Illinois who understood their constituencies, and that background held them together. Without the many friends and compatriots who climbed aboard for the ride to financial and political success, they would not have been extraordinary.

Horse racing and Southern Illinois University (SIU) were two of their favorite causes, and they receive emphasis in this narrative. Powell and Stelle were unchallenged leaders in racetrack development and stock ownership, and they spread the financial benefits among those who could be relied on for support of other issues. When it came to providing SIU with the money and clout to grow from a small state teachers college to a major university with two large campuses, Powell and Choate delivered the goods and earned the eternal thanks of Carbondale, Edwardsville, and many southern Illinois citizens.

An explanation of the playing field on which the political games occurred is critical as background to all that occurred in the decades after World War II. Regardless of efforts over the years to reapportion legislative districts to comply with population shifts and federal decisions, some of which succeeded, the method of electing members to the General Assembly, especially members of the House, remained the same. The procedure was a provision of the 1870 Illinois Constitution called cumulative voting. Every Senate district, no matter its boundaries, elected three representatives. Almost always the district elected two from the dominant political party and one from the minority. This occurred because every person with a ballot had three votes. The choices were one vote for each of three candidates, one and a half for two candidates, or three for one, called the "bullet." The minority party candidate prevailed by asking supporters for the "bullet."

Mark DePue, associated with the Abraham Lincoln Presidential Library, explained the consequences of cumulative voting in a history paper entitled "The Cutback Amendment of 1980." In summarizing the impact of cumulative voting, he wrote, "As a result, once the members arrived in Springfield, party unity in legislative battles was harder to achieve, and working across the aisle was common. It made for a much more collegial environment, claimed its many supporters. The system fostered politicians who could be independent of the party's leadership; it resulted in some colorful political mavericks." That is a concise description of the legislative world from 1947 to 1977.

His paper also tells how Illinois voters rejected cumulative voting for single-member districts in the 1980 election. The immediate outcome was one-party rule of the General Assembly and a change in strategies and tactics for passage of legislation. Chicago and Democratic Party domination of the General Assembly, long delayed by a refusal to acknowledge the reality of demographics, became the new normal. It also increased the rapid demise of downstate influence in Springfield.

Powell, Stelle, Choate, and friends could not have worked their "magic" without the partisan political balance afforded by cumulative voting. When that opportunity prevailed, they and their allies prospered.

Inevitably, the demographics of growth took over, ending the decades of progress propelled from southern Illinois. Surprisingly, the predictable outcome was delayed. The story laid out in this book is a slice of Illinois political history that today's residents of Illinois will find hard to believe. But it happened when an incredible mixture of issues, determined legislators, and constitutional opportunities came together.

READERS WILL COME ACROSS REFERENCES to "Egypt" and "Little Egypt," which may be unfamiliar. There are a dozen stories of how Egypt (in southern Illinois) got its name, but historian Robert Howard offered an explanation that rings true with other Illinois historians.

In his one-volume history of Illinois, he first disposed of various unfounded theories, one being that the area resembled the delta of the Nile—which it does not. Howard wrote that the naming occurred after an incident during the deep snows and low temperatures of northern regions in 1830. Suffering was widespread and food was scarce in the north parts, but the people were relieved by supplies of meal and feed transported from the older and milder southern counties. He wrote, "The people remembered the account in Genesis of a Mediterranean famine in which the people of the north received help from Pharaoh's court in Egypt." Howard said the name *Egypt* for southern regions of Illinois began to appear in print about 1843.

1.
Common Ground in Small Towns

A Lifelong Love Affair with Vienna

Throughout Paul Powell's career in Illinois politics, reporters made special trips to Vienna to grasp the local flavor about Powell and size up the home ground of a powerful man. One such scribe, Chris Vlahoplus, a writer working in Springfield, made his journey to deep southern Illinois in 1961.[1] He wrote articles for United Press International, one centered in Vienna, one in Harrisburg, and one in Springfield. Vlahoplus called the town a hamlet, the region the "Bible belt," and Powell's house a "tiny kingdom by the square." Vlahoplus recounted basic biographical information and watched Powell greet local people who wanted to talk and ask for a job before he headed back to the state capital. He described Powell as bearing a "striking resemblance to movie actor Wallace Beery." Oversimplified perhaps, but typical of press characterizations of Powell in his prime, and likely dismissed by the subject.

That treatment by Vlahoplus—who later became a press spokesman for Governor Otto Kerner—is one of the reasons why Powell's friends and enemies in Vienna rushed to his defense. They resented outsiders coming by to pass quick judgment for audiences outside southern Illinois, harmless or not.

A chip on the shoulders of many Vienna residents was apparent when I visited the town in February 1998. A highlight was my meeting with residents and conversations with the Powell faithful, who wanted to make the case for Powell without dwelling on outsiders who demeaned the town as well as its resident. They seemed determined to provide a counter story to what they considered the shortcomings of articles based on little understanding of people in southern Illinois. These resentments had a long history, not all of them related to Powell.

FROM HIS EARLIEST AGE—HE was born in Vienna on January 21, 1902— Paul Taylor Powell was known by almost everyone in Vienna. The town had a population of about 1,200. His father had a high profile as a drugstore owner and operator. The family lived in a large Victorian house a half block from the town square. While the Powells did not reach the status of wealthy and powerful, they had a strong presence in Vienna's upper middle class. Many years after Paul's death in 1970, townsfolk who gathered around a table at the Powell house remembered him almost from infancy. For them, Paul's life was well lived.[2]

The Powell home—referred to as the Thomas Powell home—sits north of the town square. Given the proximity to the square, the Powell family's business ventures were close at hand. Paul Powell had money from his estate set aside in trust to keep the home available for public visitation, much like one would expect to find for governors or presidents. While that arrangement remains in the present day, funds have diminished due to investment challenges.[3]

You can tell much about a person from the personal space in a home. The Powell house is a memorial to the man, a museum, open to the public and managed by the local historical society. Powell had two personal spaces on the first floor of the two-story Victorian building. One was a small office near the front door. Speculating about what might have been is a favorite pastime of visitors to houses of great men (or women). Office files probably once held many personal documents that were confiscated by the Internal Revenue Service after his death in 1970, leaving behind scrapbooks from his secretary of state days and copies of his obituaries.[4] One can imagine him sitting behind the desk.

Powell spent most of his time in an addition to the original house that might be called a family room. However, that description does not fit the image of Powell, who had two wives and no children. It was a man-cave before modern culture coined the term. This room held mementos and gifts presented to Powell over the many years of his public service. Other items included overstuffed chairs, books, personal photographs on a wall, fancy (empty) liquor bottles, and television sets. One person remembered seeing Powell in his lair on a Saturday afternoon with three different football games playing on TV sets and Powell, always the politician, talking on his telephone.[5] Telephone, of course, because in his day that was the primary method of communicating beyond a face-to-face conversation. Here is where Powell conducted business, entertained guests, and greeted old friends living in Vienna. The rest of the house was laid out in a traditional manner, with living room, sitting room, and kitchen downstairs, and three bedrooms and a bath upstairs.

The Vienna square, like that found in older communities of southern Illinois, once thrived as the town's commercial center. By 1998 commercial development was scattered on the outskirts of the town, and the square had suffered as a result. Dominating the square with center position was the courthouse and government offices for Johnson County. Thomas Powell, whose Illinois roots reached back into the late 1800s, owned a drugstore for many years on the northeast corner of the square, and the building still stood. At one time a restaurant managed and operated by Paul had been in the same building. Neighbors remembered several locations where Paul operated businesses: three different locations where he ran his restaurant (Powell's Café); a grocery store Powell managed for a short time; and a dry cleaning establishment, which he operated as a teenager in the back of a barbershop. An advertisement for the cleaning business, reportedly from a school playbill stated, "Take your clothes to Powell's Pantatorium for cleaning, pressing and repairs." The budding entrepreneur sold out after graduating from high school, in what might have been Powell's first major "deal" for money. Before that investment, Powell earned spending money hustling papers, shining shoes, washing collars—anything to make money.[6]

In Powell's time, and for years afterward, the square became the center of political talk and gossip for Republicans and Democrats. A worthy participant who carried on the tradition at the square was C. L. McCormick. His visibility in Vienna increased after World War II, when Powell had taken near-permanent residence in Springfield, with occasional visits to Vienna.

McCormick, a Republican, and his brother operated a restaurant and taxi service for several years after the war. McCormick's political history began on the Vienna city council, progressed to the Johnson County clerk's office, and in 1956 he was elected to the state House of Representatives, where he watched and learned from friends Powell and Choate. He occasionally voted with them in the prevailing mood of bipartisanship. The Vienna political hotspot on the square escalated when he started a general store named C. L. McCormick and Sons Little Big Dollar Store.[7] As well as a place of business, the store became McCormick's district office, where he received telephone calls from across the state. If out-of-town visitors or locals wanted to talk politics directly with McCormick, they had to do it in competition with customers at the dollar store.

The store chatter was bipartisan, reflecting local interests and friendships. Michael McCormick, C. L.'s son, described his father's political relationships: "[T]hose guys would get together and in elections they might cuss a little bit of the party, and they might say, 'The Democrats are better; the Republicans don't care about this or that.' But there wasn't the personal nature of this. These guys liked each other."[8] McCormick carried on the legacy of Powell with a welcoming handshake and talk of all kinds at the dollar store on the square.

As with most small communities, the main cemetery—some towns had more than one—hints at the town's history, etched in stone of various sizes. The large Paul Powell headstone states proudly, "Here Lies a Lifelong Democrat" and "A Great American." It acknowledges his years as mayor of Vienna and years as a member of the school board. Also buried in the cemetery are his father, mother, two wives (Violet, born 1901, and Daisy, born 1897), and his brother Hartwell who died in a gun accident in 1914. The cemetery preserves names and dates that made up a significant portion of Powell's personal story in Vienna.

The day's conversation I had with Vienna residents in 1998 started around a table in the Thomas Powell house. Available for reminiscences of Paul were Royce Hundley, a longtime dentist in town and classmate of Paul, and Edith Brown and Delbert Brown—all well-known residents. Also available was an oral history on tape made by Levi Locke. These were the first of several who remembered the man that day. Others included Gary Hacker, in charge of the local historical society and keeper of the Powell house, and Jim (Stud) Walker, a close friend of Powell. They characterized the Powell they knew and mostly skipped over the tales and mythology that made up the rest of his life. Nevertheless, they spoke of the environment that shaped Powell's personality and attitudes, all of which influenced his later history.

Among the stories told were about Paul's father, Thomas, and his two wives. With his first wife, Rosa, he had four children. She died and Thomas remarried. Thomas and his second wife, Vinna, had two boys named Hartwell and Paul. Paul's mother originally was from Pulaski County but had attended schools in Vienna. Powell's friends talked about Hartwell, referring to him as easygoing, good-natured, and well liked. He had gone on an outing east of Vienna with a friend to knock apples out of trees using the butt end of a rifle.[9] As he crossed a fence, the rifle accidentally discharged and shot Hartwell, who was fourteen. He bled to death.

The reminiscences turned to Paul Powell's two wives, whose personalities had left indelible and quite different impressions in Vienna. Hundley recalled Powell's first wife, Violet Price, in glowing terms: "She was one of the sweetest girls that ever grew up in Vienna. And she had a soprano voice that was beautiful."[10] Memories of Violet included the contributions she made to entertain customers at Powell's Café, where she played the piano while people danced. Mrs. Levi Locke added this to remembrances of the couple: "He was such a nice-looking young man, who didn't like to part his hair. He was very mannerly and very much in love with Violet, who was a beautiful, quiet-spoken brunette."[11] Her school friends called her "Piggy." Hardly anyone had a harsh word about Violet, or the couple's time together.

Life in Vienna seemed almost perfect for Paul until 1924. That is when Thomas Powell died, leaving his survivors including his widow and Paul and Violet, and not much money in the bank. Years later, Powell offered a reason for his father's financial issues: "I can remember when I was in [the drugstore] as a small boy, men would come in and say, 'Uncle Tom I need some pills for the bellyache, but I haven't got any money.' There wasn't anybody who walked out of there without pills for the bellyache. The reason my father was a man of humble means was because he signed his name on too many notes that he had to pay off, and I have many of them in my lock box today. But they were friends of his and he tried to help them."[12]

Following that personal setback, a second even more devastating tragedy occurred on March 18, 1925. On that day the infamous Tri-State Tornado slashed from Missouri through southern Illinois and into Indiana, killing 695 persons, injuring as many as 13,000, and causing unbelievable destruction. Violet chose that day to visit her parents in Murphysboro, one of the hardest hit communities in the tornado's path. She died in the storm. According to friends, Powell may have never fully recovered from the personal tragedy. Hundley said to me, the visitor, "I think Paul's life would have been a lot different if she had lived, because she was so sweet."[13] That was no idle comment.

On June 13, 1929, just more than four years after Violet's death, Powell married Daisy Butler, whom he had met at the county courthouse, where she worked as a court reporter. His friends were quick to point out that Daisy was not a native of Vienna but had come from Villa Ridge, Illinois, in Pulaski County. They added that she had a good education. Just prior to the marriage Powell had been elected to the school board, his first venture into elective politics.

That started him on an elective public service career in which he won every election including two contests for secretary of state in 1964 and 1968. Of the fifteen election contests for the House, starting in 1934, he had no primary competition in three. In the others he had mostly token opposition as he won primary contests by margins of as much as 10 to 1.[14] On at least ten occasions the voters of his district had no choice but to vote for Powell and the two Republican candidates. Powell never forgot what he owed to cumulative voting. In Republican-dominated Johnson County, it was highly unlikely Powell would have been elected if the district had only a single member in the House.

The coincidence of the marriage to Daisy and election to public office cannot be underestimated in terms of Powell's career. He enjoyed politics, and she encouraged his ambition and advancement, and in the early years acted as his personal secretary. However, unlike Violet she did not work at the restaurant. When he took her political advice, she complimented him for being smart. When he did not take her advice, she cursed him. Until she died in 1967, they carried on a domestic war that occasionally went public. Mrs. Levi Locke of Vienna remembered, "She was nice, but she had a temper and was just the opposite of his first wife. She'd stand right there and tell you just what she thought."[15]

The source of Daisy's crisp public comments often related directly to her husband's social activities with other women, several of whom worked with him in Springfield. During his state government career, which stretched for thirty-six years, the two grew about as far apart as possible while remaining married. He flagrantly brought women to the house in Vienna, and they accompanied Powell to public events in southern

Illinois. His activities increased as Daisy's health declined and she spent much of her time in Chicago for medical treatment. The dentist Hundley recalled, "She stopped me over at the drugstore one day. She cussed every breath. 'You know he brought that bitch down to the Du Quoin State Fair. Why didn't he leave her in Springfield?'"[16]

One of the more memorable clashes between Paul and Daisy rose to the surface in Vienna for all to observe, including a thousand friends and political celebrities from across the state. In 1961, Powell's close friends Clyde Choate and Stud Walker planned a "This Is Your Life" party in Vienna to honor Powell, who had been elected Speaker of the state House for a third time. Shortly before the program, Walker encountered Daisy in Vienna. She was mad about Powell and his social life and threatened to expose it all at the celebration. Walker told Powell, who then made arrangements for Daisy to be in Chicago at the time of the party. Powell's only reference to Daisy at the event was "Daisy is not here tonight. She tried to stay, but had to go to Chicago."[17] The local newspaper's only mention of Daisy's absence in a lengthy account of the party appeared in the last paragraph. But everyone in town knew the full story.

Few in Vienna knew as much about Powell's life, in town and in Springfield, as Stud Walker. In spite of that familiarity, Walker remained an admirer who at the drop of a hat would recite all that Powell had done for him personally, and for others in Vienna. Walker, twenty-one years younger than Powell, in some respects may have been the older man's "son." Powell counseled him in personal matters and in political ventures. Walker was a Republican, but that mattered little in their relationship. When Walker sought election as city clerk on the Republican ticket, Powell told his Democratic friends in town to vote for Walker, who won. Walker told of an encounter afterward with Daisy Powell: "I saw Daisy after the election and she said 'I voted for you, you Republican son-of-a-bitch and I've been sick ever since.'" Walker added, "That was Daisy for you. I took what she said with a grain of salt and talked back to her. She liked me."[18]

In summarizing his experiences with Powell, Walker echoed comments from around the kitchen table: "He had to excel in whatever he did. He liked to be complimented. He was a man of his word. You couldn't help but like Paul Powell. I trusted him. He was my hero because he was a self-made man. He struggled. He was not the most polished man in the world, but he talked the language of the common man."[19]

Stories abound about Powell's entry into the 1934 election contest for state representative at age thirty-two. One who claimed firsthand knowledge was Paul O'Neal, a Vienna presence. He said, "He really didn't have much interest in politics but did it because it was the right thing to do and his mother would be proud of him . . . Paul and I were in this cabin, actually a still, when I asked him to run for the House. He told me that he didn't have any money, but I answered that we could make up a batch of liquor and he could have the first hundred or two hundred bottles. I gave him some money, too."[20] Mel Lockard, a longtime friend of Powell and native of southern Illinois, said Powell considered taking a job in Springfield, but decided to run for the House instead.

The people around the table in Vienna and others who counted themselves special friends left a deep impression that Powell led two distinct lives: one in Vienna and Johnson County, and another in Springfield and Chicago. They could see the differences, even if others could not, and tried in their own words to speak in a local context of his integrity, honesty, loyalty, compassion for others, and labors for improving life in southern Illinois. They wanted others to know that the two lives had little connection with each other.

When among friends in Vienna, Powell could wink and grin. In his remarks at the appreciation dinner in 1961 he talked about attending the Christian Church as a young boy. "My brother Hartwell and I put 50 cents in the plate each Sunday, but they never let me pass the collection plate."[21]

PAUL TAYLOR POWELL, 68, DIED during the night of October 9 or early morning of October 10, 1970, at a hotel in Rochester, Minnesota. He was there for medical treatment. Staying in the same hotel room was Margaret Hensey, Powell's close friend. His death set off a frenzy surrounding his financial holdings. At the center of the controversy was a discovery of cash totaling more than $800,000 in various locations, but mostly in a Springfield hotel room. His total estate in 1970 dollars amounted to $3,292,959.[22]

Reflecting his two separate lives, a memorial service was held in Springfield on Tuesday, October 13, and a funeral service and burial in Vienna two days later. Powell's bequests, listed in his will, included a handful of causes and people in his hometown, although the bulk of money went to friends and associates elsewhere. The local gifts: a trust fund to keep his home site available for public visitation; $25,000 to the First Christian

Church of Vienna; $5,000 to the First Methodist Church of Vienna; $10,000 to the Vienna Cemetery Association for blacktopping the road to the cemetery; and $10,000 for poinsettias to shut-ins in Johnson County at Christmas, with the flowers to be purchased from Bellamy Floral in Vienna.[23] Powell owned shares of bank stock in these southern Illinois towns: Marion, Harrisburg, Metropolis, Cobden, and Carbondale.

Notably, his estate also recorded a "cancellation." Before revising his will, Powell had intended to establish a $50,000 memorial trust fund for political studies at Southern Illinois University. However, he deleted that from his will because of his anger and unhappiness with antiwar protests on campus in 1968 and 1969.[24]

A Growing Family Stays on the Move

In the 1970s when Clyde Lee Choate competed for the elite position of Speaker of the Illinois House of Representatives, a reporter wrote: "Clyde Choate is a legacy from the days when a coal miner's son could rise to a first floor corner suite of offices in the State Capitol building."[25]

There is much more to the story. Not all coal miners' sons held public office for thirty years. As far as his father working in the mines, those jobs had unintended consequences, such as layoffs, plant closings, on-job deaths, and living in a "company town."

The reporter added, "He is a throwback to the days when a war record was almost a necessary stepping stone for a young man seeking public office." As a means of bringing Choate's incredible military service into his achievement, the reporter struck gold. For fifty years after World War II, veterans reached the heights of public office. Presidents Dwight D. Eisenhower, John F. Kennedy, and George H. W. Bush come to mind.

The fact remains that Choate's journey took many turns, and they provide light and perspective on his political career. He was a product of southern Illinois, its culture and financial deprivations, and an example of those who struggled to escape by taking advantage of opportunities. During his political days, urban elitists liked to make fun of Choate's countrified ways, until they tried—and failed—to get the best of him in Springfield.

Clyde Choate's family roots are deeply imbedded in the southern part of the state. His father, James Isaac Choate, was born April 28, 1876, at

Anna, Illinois, in Union County to Isaac and Hanna Choate. Isaac was born in Illinois and Hanna was born in Kentucky.[26] The 1880 census listed no children other than James Isaac. The likelihood is that James's parents were descendants of families that came to southern Illinois from southern or border states as was the case with most migrants to the area in the nineteenth century. Original settlers were primarily subsistence farmers who found agriculture a poor way to make a living. They sought other means of providing for a family, but the pickings were slim.

The first pioneer settlers of the vicinity now comprising Union County arrived in the early 1800s, following the Ohio and Mississippi rivers. According to written histories, those early arrivals were "delighted with the land of plenty," both the game and the excellent water. In the early years of the Illinois Territory, clashes between settlers and Indian tribes added an element of risk and fear, resulting in the establishment of small forts for protection.[27] By 1815 the danger of clashes with Indians had passed.

Until statehood in 1818, there were only a handful of counties in the Illinois Territory. After statehood, the large counties were divided. On January 2, 1818, Union County was established by carving the area out of Johnson County.[28] The town of Jonesboro came first on donated land. Slowly the county added residents, and by 1835 a census showed the population at 4,417, evenly divided between male and female. A local history stated, "An industrial survey showed five shoe-makers and saddlers, one tailor, two wagon makers, two carpenters, one cabinet maker, two hatters, eleven blacksmiths, three tanyards, twelve distilleries, two threshing machines, one cotton gin, one horse and ox sawmill, eighteen horse and ox grist mills and five water grist mills."[29]

Often the development of small towns in southern Illinois came about and grew because of men who had opened the first businesses, had acquired land, and had served in government offices. That was the story of Anna. The town site was laid out in 1853 on land owned by Winstead Davie on either side of the soon-to-be constructed Illinois Central Railroad.[30] The community was named for Davie's wife, the child of early Jonesboro settlers. A written history described Anna as a "well developed little community with homes, stores, mills, churches and schools. We see them in the center of a farming community located near a river where the settlers and traders exchanged their products for the articles necessary for some comforts of life."[31]

There were four buildings on the early Anna town site. In the fall of 1855 the first passenger train on the Southern Division of the Illinois Central Railroad passed through Anna, bringing change and growth opportunities few people could imagine. The town's first election of a mayor and council occurred in 1872. As with many growing communities in the late nineteenth century, life presented a number of challenges. Major fires in 1877 and 1879 destroyed many buildings and set back the local economy temporarily.[32] National recessions such as in 1893 had an impact as well. But Anna and Union County prevailed, thanks in large part to its founders.

Davie oversaw much of the early development of Anna and earned the unofficial title of "Father of Anna." Born with physical challenges, he required the use of crutches throughout his life.[33] He came to Illinois in 1817 and started a school near Jonesboro. Davie eventually opened a general store that provided him with funds to acquire substantial acreages of land. He also served as recorder, county and circuit clerk, and probate judge. In 1857 Davie left public office and enlarged his business interests. He built the first steam mill in Anna, gave property for church and school sites, and constructed business buildings. Anna Davie died in 1880 and he died in 1885.

Clyde Choate's ancestors were part of those early experiences of Union County and Anna. In that small community environment his father, James, married Ester (one census referred to her as Easter) E. Womack, a native of Kentucky, on April 1, 1894, in Union County.[34] By 1900 the couple and three children, the oldest aged five, lived in Anna, where James worked as a day laborer. Ten years later James and Ester continued to live in Anna, with James employed as a teamster (handling horses) at a coal mine. They had six children by that time.[35] Serious changes occurred in the family in the following years. Ester died, leaving James with a house full of children. He met and married a widow, Grace Ellen Brown, a native of Kentucky who had been living with her three children at Jonesboro.[36] By 1918 the new blended family lived in West Frankfort, Franklin County, Illinois, where James worked at an Old Ben Coal Company mine. They began adding more children to the family.[37] When finished, they had sixteen children of his, hers, and theirs combined.

Coal had been dug out of hillsides of southern Illinois for decades before commercial mining came with the twentieth century. Wealthy speculators and corporations centered mine development in Saline, Williamson, and Franklin counties. The Old Ben Coal Company maintained several mines, most of them in Franklin County, some as recently as 2000. As with many mines in the region, the company's underground operations were plagued by methane gas, which led to numerous explosions and deaths.

Tensions between the United Mine Workers of America union and mine operators began late in the 1800s and early 1900s. Strikes were violent, nasty affairs with National Guard troops often called in to keep the peace. With corporate mining came company towns where houses were little more than shacks. Grim living conditions were a reality of company town life. Work underground was dangerous. In 1905 at Zeigler No. 1 mine, fifty-one men and boys died in a gas explosion. At the same mine in 1909 an explosion killed twenty-six.[38] These were representative of occurrences in Saline, Williamson, and Franklin counties during the time James and his children were present.

Despite conflict among workers, unions, and companies, the coal business grew, as did employment. By 1920 more than one hundred mines operated in the three counties. The population of the coal towns altogether reached 41,000. The whole structure of economic growth and existence was built on coal, which meant increased activity for savings and loans, banks, and real estate firms.

In 1920 the Choate family lived on Logan Street in West Frankfort, Denning Township, in the heart of mining territory.[39] James listed his work as "labor top coal mine," indicating he worked aboveground at a mine. James and Grace had seven children at home, while the two oldest children from the 1910 census were not listed. On June 28, 1920, Grace Choate gave birth to Clyde Lee.[40] Four more children were born after Clyde.

Migrants from southern portions of the United States in the early 1900s brought a tolerance for violence and lawlessness to southern Illinois. They influenced bloody eruptions during the 1920s in Williamson, Franklin, and Saline counties. As Paul M. Angle wrote in *Bloody Williamson*, his classic account of murder and mayhem connected to mining, "Almost without exception they [migrants] were hot-blooded, proud, obstinate, jealous of family honor, quick to resent any insult . . . They could kill with little compunction."[41] The book referred largely to the Herrin Massacre, but included tales of other violence, gang activities of the Shelton brothers, and the uprising of the Ku Klux Klan. Violence that led to the shocking murder by striking mine workers of nineteen strikebreakers at the Southern Illinois Coal Company occurred in June 1922. Only six persons were indicted for the slaughter. In two trials during 1922 and 1923, juries acquitted them all. The 1920s in southern Illinois, some of which the Choate family lived through, featured violence connected to gambling, illegal booze, and gang fighting.

The Choate family was on the move again in the 1920s, leaving deep southern Illinois and its mining business for a time in Nameoki, Illinois, Madison County, across the Mississippi River from St. Louis.[42] The family lived at 2812 Myrtle Avenue. James's occupation was as laborer. They moved back to Anna within a year, with his occupation listed as general farm laborer. There were seven children living at home, with three older than Clyde. James's mother, Hannah E. Choate, was living with the family at that time. Mrs. Choate, eighty-two, died in 1931 after being bedridden for most of a year.[43]

As an adult, Clyde often gave glimpses of his childhood in media interviews. During the 1930s when he moved into his teenage years, the family lived in Anna and also on a farm near the town. He left an impression that they owned the farm, because they "lost" it during the Depression and moved back to Anna, where James worked as a self-employed laborer.[44] Six children, including Clyde, lived at home in 1940.

Compared to farmers working land farther north that consistently produced a bounty of corn and soybeans for decades, farmers in the south scrambled to produce enough goods to bring to market, including fruits and vegetables. One manufacturer made tomato baskets, strawberry boxes, and strawberry crates. Each town seemed to have a harness shop in the early years of the twentieth century, and organizations such as the Odd Fellows provided entertainment and a social life for many citizens. It was not until the 1920s that hard-surface roads, called "hard roads," made getting around a bit easier and accommodated automobiles. They brought change to a part of Illinois that had not changed much in decades.

Mel Lockard, whose family came to Union County from Tennessee in 1837, wrote a memoir late in life in which he talked about rural life in the time of the Choate family.[45] He became a successful banker and served eighteen years as a trustee of Southern Illinois University, and later on the Illinois State Board of Higher Education. In his book, Lockard described life as a young driver on primitive roads: "You started out on a Sunday and you never knew whether you were gonna get back or not. You'd take a little drive—you had to take along a water bucket so if you ran out of water you'd get some water out of the creek to put in the radiator—and you'd stop several times. They were rough riding and they were dusty and dirty and the first people who had enough money to buy an automobile wore a white duster and a lot of them had people to drive them." Before cars, Lockard said, young people walked, rode freight cars on the railroad, and took an occasional passenger train for short distances to Carbondale and Murphysboro.

Choate told of milking eighteen cows, slopping hogs, and attending to vegetable crops on the farm. He said they grew sweet potatoes, cucumbers, cantaloupes, and peppers for the market, a reflection of small-farm living in the region. He told an interviewer, "Know how you plant cucumbers? You plow, you disc, you hoe. You make a hill, you put in a little manure, you put in your seed and cover it."[46] After he had milked the cows, Choate walked four miles to school, where he took out the clinkers and ashes and built a new fire in the coal-burning stove so the chill would be gone when the teacher and other pupils arrived. He also swept the room after school. The teacher paid him a dollar a week out of her own pocket.[47]

Choate told an interviewer, "When I got my first month's pay, I was rich. I had to walk past the poor farm to get home and I stopped to talk to the superintendent. When I got home, I was leading a goat and carrying a rabbit. I spent the whole pay for them. I asked my father, 'I made a good buy, didn't I Dad'? My father smiled and said, 'Yes, son, you made a good buy.' My father was a very kind man. In those days they were worth about a dime for the rabbit and 50 cents for the goat."[48]

While attending Anna-Jonesboro Community High School in the late 1930s, Choate played football, although he weighed only about 140 pounds. He won a school letter for each of three years. Choate talked about lean years on the football field, too: "One year we lost to Carbondale 77 to 0. We had a different coach each of those three years. My last coach, Paul Houghton, was a good coach. He said if we had had our squad for three years we would have been winners."[49]

Boxing was a favorite sport for participating in, watching, and listening to on the radio. Clyde fought in the popular Golden Gloves program as a welterweight. He said the Anna Jaycees organization sponsored fights every Friday night and he got involved. The winner got $5 and the loser $3. There was more than physical risk involved, as he explained:

"It almost cost me my football eligibility. Somebody protested that I was a professional. But one of the Jaycees made an affidavit that I hadn't taken any money, so I kept my eligibility."[50]

After the United States declared war against Germany and Japan, Choate decided to join the military. He and a friend, Carroll P. Foster, hitchhiked to Marion, Illinois, to volunteer for the U.S. Army. Choate failed the physical examination, but his friend passed and was accepted. Carroll served in the Pacific and was killed early in that theater of the war. The Anna American Legion post was named for him. Choate didn't give up after one rejection: "I tried three times to volunteer, but when my draft notice came, they took me the first time with no hesitation. When I left home my father shook hands and said, 'Son, I'll never see you again.' He was right. He died [March 7, 1945] on my way [home] from France."[51]

A Hero's Story

Clyde Lee Choate, twenty-one years old, a lean five feet eight inches tall and weighing less than 180 pounds, entered active duty with the U.S. Army at East St. Louis, Illinois, on April 25, 1942.[52] The nation had wars to fight in Europe and Asia, with inadequate weaponry, inexperienced soldiers and sailors, and an anxious citizenry waiting for news of a victory. Any victory. Choate was assigned to a unit for tank destroyers.

Prior to World War II the U.S. military had no antitank vehicles. The idea for a tank destroyer (TD) blossomed in 1940 and 1941 when officials watched with trepidation as Germany marched across Europe with panzer divisions leading the way and leveling everything in their paths.[53]

Choate served in the army for almost three years, including thirty-one months in combat zones—Tunisia, Sicily, Naples-Foggia, Rome, southern France, the Rhineland—fighting against the Germans as a member of an antitank battalion.[54] Considering the hundreds of thousands of soldiers who died, were injured, or went missing during their military service in the Mediterranean and western Germany combat zones during those three years, it is nothing short of remarkable that Choate lived not only to tell his story, but to receive the Medal of Honor in person from President Harry S. Truman.[55]

Choate was assigned to the 601st Tank Destroyer Battalion, formally organized in 1941, one of the first TD outfits in the army. TD units were formed as stand-alone battalions assigned to fight with infantry divisions.

TD soldiers were trained not only to fight with their mounted guns but also to conduct "dismounted tank hunting." In other words, if TD vehicles were unable to operate in certain terrain or were stopped cold by German defenses, the soldiers operating them were expected to ambush enemy tanks and raid tank parks using small arms, grenades, mines, and improvised weapons. As described in a history of the TDs, trainees underwent "a grueling schedule that included conducting night reconnaissance crossing deep streams, climbing slippery barbed-wire-covered banks, scaling steep walls, detecting booby traps, street fighting and mastering demolitions."[56] This training served Choate well as his time in combat unfolded.

In actual combat the 601st operated often in those foot-soldier situations. In the written history of the Third Infantry Division, to which the 601st was attached during much of its combat life, flexibility was reality in the mission: "The 601st went far beyond normal expectation in its performance of duty in combat. The Standard Operating Procedure for tank destroyer units was to destroy enemy tanks. The 601st was called upon, in addition, to attack various other ground targets such as pillboxes and other enemy fortifications or possible strong points in close support of the attacking infantry. Enemy infantry was also considered a prime target."[57]

The army struggled to design and outfit the TD before the first units saw combat. It revised the design frequently in hopes of providing the battalions with greater firepower and protection for personnel. No matter what design prevailed at any time, the soldiers' nickname stuck: "Purple Heart Box." A 601st veteran described the TD in these understandable terms: "What it was was a tank vehicle with an open turret that had a big gun mounted on it. You went to do battle with tanks and you were constantly having somebody deposit a grenade down the open turret. They used to talk about us as the guys who rode around with the top down like a convertible."[58]

When ready for its initial taste of combat, the 601st was attached to the First Infantry Division, known as the "Big Red One." On August 2, 1942, less than four months after becoming an army private, Choate and his battalion were headed to Europe on the *Queen Mary*, and eventually to North Africa and the tedious, bloody, and frustrating road to Rome.[59]

The 601st began training at Tidworth Barracks, an old British cavalry facility about sixty miles from London.[60] The first taste of warfare for Choate's unit began on December 21 at Souk el Khemis, Tunisia, one of the favorite attack sites for German fighter planes known as "Stuka Alley."

The Ju-87 Stuka was a two-man German dive-bomber and ground-attack aircraft. At that location men of the 601st experienced their first enemy air attack that left one soldier dead. According to TD history, the enraged outfit shot down its first German Spitfire fighter in retaliation.[61]

As the Tunisian fighting continued into February 1943, the intensity of the battles meant that each inch of ground gained was hard to win and harder to retain. One such occasion involved the 601st at Sbeitla, Tunisia, and nearby Kasserine Pass, where pressure from German forces caused panic. At midday on February 17 elements of the 601st reported being under attack by fifty German tanks and infantry, and began falling back. The 601st informal history commented on the situation: "Confusion was king that day. There was no communication between units, no traffic control, no organization, and no order. It was every man for himself... It was a sad day for the new, inexperienced American Army."[62] Pressured by advancing Germans, U.S. units retreated through Kasserine Pass. Historian Rick Atkinson wrote, "Kasserine may fairly be considered the worst American drubbing of the war."[63]

No matter how successful a single battle became, Americans learned that the enemy always had another attack ready, and it occurred in the battle at El Guettar, Tunisia, on Tuesday, March 23. The battlefield stretched along a ridge for fifteen miles, with the First Infantry Division in prime position and preparing for an offensive attack of its own.

Holding a part of the ridge out in front of artillery were three companies of the 601st anchoring the American line. At dawn, American troops discovered thirty German tanks in rectangular formation with infantrymen behind. The panzers attacked with such fury that one company of the 601st fell back with heavy losses. Another company fought until its ammunition ran out. Historian Atkinson described the scene and the TD role: "German tanks poured into the gap and had nearly broken through to turn the American flank when Company A opened fire at 2,200 yards; the 75mm volley staggered the panzers . . . Fire intensified from both the tank destroyers and artillery." By midmorning the panzers had retreated. Atkinson continued: "Twenty-four of thirty-six guns from the 601st were lost. Collectively, the battalion had fired nearly 3,000 75mm shells and almost 50,000 machine-gun rounds. The unit commander . . . survived to notify division general Terry Allen that his battalion no longer existed."[64] But Choate and many of his colleagues survived to fight another day.

For its gallant performance, the 601st Tank Destroyer Battalion, including Choate, received a Presidential Unit Citation, in an order issued May 9, 1945. The citation said in full,

> The 601st Tank Destroyer Battalion is cited for outstanding performance in combat on 25 March 1943 near El Guettar, Tunisia. Filling a two and one half mile gap in the American lines, the battalion absorbed the shock of an all-out onslaught by the German 10th Panzer Division, and materially assisted divisional and attached artillery units in definitely stopping two successive, determined enemy tank attacks, launched in great strength. Although greatly outnumbered and outgunned, the Battalion traded shot for shot with the overwhelming enemy force. Doggedly holding its ground, harassed by enemy dive bombers, and long-range artillery, with ammunition running dangerously low, the Battalion prepared to hold out to the end despite the loss of twenty-seven of its thirty-seven guns. The German tanks approached to within one hundred yards of its positions only to be thrown back with heavy losses. When the enemy reformed for a second assault, the Battalion placed such intense fire on the advancing German soldiers that the attack was stopped before it could get well under way. The 601st Tank Destroyer Battalion contributed to this outstanding victory of the First Infantry Division, wherein, with other units of the Division, it fought with such ferocity and intense determination that at least four hundred enemy casualties were left on the field, thirty-seven enemy tanks destroyed, and numerous other enemy armored vehicles evacuated in a disabled condition.[65]

After the North Africa campaign, Sicily was the next Allied beachhead, but the 601st saw little action. Allied forces captured Sicily rather quickly, setting the stage for the first assault on Italian soil. German units were waiting. The next battleground for the 601st was the landing at Salerno. The battalion landed at Salerno on September 9, 1943, with the Thirty-sixth Infantry Division and remained with that division until September 30, when it was attached to the Third Infantry Division. While not all problems facing the 601st were solved by assignment to the Third, that unit for the most part figured out how to use the TD battalion effectively.

In the Allied breakout from Salerno, the drive north began in earnest. The challenge, among others, was to confront high mountains and the

German army emplacements. A key location in the Allied strategy was the town of Mignano, ninety miles from Rome.[66] The fight for Mignano had deep meaning for the Third Division and for Clyde Choate.

The battle began on November 5 and lasted more than two weeks before U.S. troops could claim a measure of victory. During the fight for Mignano, Clyde Choate was wounded in action on November 15, just days before the Thirty-sixth Division relieved the exhausted Third Division. Military records provide little official detail about the episode, except to state, "Wounded in action near Mignano, Italy, 15 November 1943."[67] Anecdotal information published years later had the incident at a different location and added, "He was awarded the Purple Heart after receiving a severe leg injury, which left him hospitalized for several weeks."[68]

The worst was yet to come for the Third Division and the 601st. In name, it was Anzio. American and British units landed in force at the Anzio beach in Operation Shingle on January 22, 1944. Anzio was the battalion's third beachhead landing in the Mediterranean war zone. Before Anzio, the battalion had just received new Greyhound armored cars, which replaced the light tanks.[69] The 601st, according to plan, could expect to find the flat territory around Anzio more conducive to tank and antitank warfare than battling through Italy's mountains.

The 601st had little rest after the first few days beyond the beachhead. In an attempt to take control of Cisterna, a strategic town on the highway to Rome, the Third Division found German forces organized and on the offensive. A written history of TDs provided this explanation of the 601st support positions for the embattled division when the German defense line held: "They [the 601st] encountered a tough defensive line that exploited stone houses, ruins, and the natural cover offered by canals, stream beds, and draws as positions for strong points. Gunners dueled with German antitank guns at ranges of 1,000 to 1,700 yards and knocked out three. Third platoon of Company B engaged a tank at only 300 yards and destroyed it by firing shells through two walls of the house behind which it was lurking."[70] In another firefight, 601st tank killers knocked out four panzers in two days. A month later during another of the pitched battles during the stalemate, the 601st stopped twenty-five panzers and guns during a single thrust. The Third Division history gave the battalion overall credit for destroying forty-two enemy tanks and killing a large number of enemy personnel while losing only two TDs to enemy fire.[71]

Choate, who had recovered sufficiently from injuries to participate in the Anzio operation, was awarded the Bronze Star in action with Company C near Isola Bella, Italy, on March 2, 1944.[72] Existing military documents give no specifics for Choate's award.

The community of Isola Bella, an island in Lake Maggiore, was near a critical battle zone where Allies and Germans fought for vital ground. The TDs' informal history stated that Isola Bella "was constantly shelled, mortared, dive bombed . . . There was no rest, no break and no sleep except the sleep that comes with complete exhaustion."[73]

The informal history of the 601st said this about the battalion's combat-veteran status after Anzio: "The 601 that broke out of the Anzio beachhead was a tough, experienced, battle-hardened, confident battalion. The men had 'got' forty-three Kraut tanks on the beachhead for the loss of three, and they weren't afraid of anything the Kraut had, or made, or manned."[74]

Much fighting remained before American troops, including the 601st, liberated Rome on June 5, 1944. Although there was a cloak of secrecy about the next assignment, in a short time the Third Division and 601st Battalion learned of the destination: southern France. The mission was named Operation Dragoon, an offensive thrust with the prime target to capture ports at Toulon and Marseille. Beginning August 15, 1944, it was primarily a military venture of U.S. and French troops. Operation Dragoon, which lasted until September 15, was one of the most successful and least contested battles fought by U.S. soldiers in Europe.[75] Weak German resistance to the Third Division and the 601st made the landing much easier than expected. Within a week or two of the Allied landing, the ports of Toulon and Marseille were secured.

When Operation Dragoon officially ended, the Third Division and 601st Battalion were prepared for what was called the Rhineland Campaign. In barely a month Allied forces had liberated two-thirds of France. The relatively easy times were over, however.

Soldiers of the United States and France looked directly at the Vosges Mountains in southern France near the border with Germany, anticipating winter fighting on unfriendly terrain on which Germans had installed devilish devices to thwart the allies. Never in the history of modern warfare had an army fought its way successfully through the Vosges. Historian Atkinson described the challenges: "Ahead lay the granite and gneiss uplands of the Vosges, a primordial badland of cairns, moors, peat bogs, and hogback ridges rising above four thousand feet."[76]

This introduced a phase of the battle with German troops that taxed the patience and resources of the Allies from October 1944 to March 1945. The 601st Battalion that had faced the German army from North Africa to southern France with Allied combat units would be attached to infantry units throughout the frustrating six-month ordeal. Choate, in Company C of the 601st, was involved much of the time. As the battle heated up at the beginning of October 1944, Company C was attached to the Thirtieth Infantry Regiment of the Third Division.

The weather plagued both Allies and Germans during October 1944 as the mountains and lowlands began to change toward winter conditions. According to 601st Battalion headquarters records there were seven days of rain, six of showers, eleven that were cold and cloudy, and seven under fair skies.[77] The rains made mud a constant hazard. These were the circumstances under which Choate and his battalion teammates struggled.

In the first week of October, Company C with Choate included was detached from the Third Division and assigned to the 179th Infantry Regiment of the Forty-fifth Division. Company C would remain in that assignment until it was attached again to the Third Division, Thirtieth Infantry Regiment, on October 25.

Although Company C reported to the 179th command, its movements and encounters continued to be recorded on operations reports at the 601st headquarters. That is how the 601st first heard of action involving a Company C TD and a Mark IV German tank. The unit journal recorded at 8:35 A.M. that the battalion commander received a telephone call from a different battalion attached to the Forty-fifth Division.[78] The report was that the Company C commander had suffered a head wound at the forward command post that morning. The report added, "Also we lost 1 M-10 [TD] last night due to enemy action." This was an encounter involving Staff Sergeant Choate, although his name was not mentioned until later dispatches. The company commander was hospitalized and replaced.

The 601st operations report for the same day stated that Company C's first platoon lost one M-10 TD "due to enemy action." The report continued by stating that the first enemy tank shell broke the M-10 traversing mechanism, thus disabling the TD. When a German Mark IV tank was approximately ten yards from the TD, the crew was ordered to abandon the TD. The report declared, "Thereupon, platoon Sgt, C Co, and Inf[antry Lieutenant] manned bazooka and KO'd said [enemy] MK [Mark] IV, dispersing [enemy] crew by firing 3 clips, 45 cal pistol."[79] In an 18:15 hours report the unit journal stated, "BN [Battalion] Motor Off[icer] arrived at the BN CP [Command Post] with information that 'C' Co's destroyer (S/Sgt Choate's) was retrieved and found to be of no further value. Will have to be salvaged."[80] Thus was the first mention of Choate in the 601st official record of the day's encounter.

It took time and subsequent reports to determine exactly what happened that day involving Staff Sergeant Choate. During combat, initial reports often were hurried and failed to capture the precise story. For example, the first battalion report cited was dated October 13, 1944. The unit's informal history did not mention the date. Final U.S. Army records stated that the incident involving Choate occurred on October 25, 1944.

A detailed account of Choate's bravery appeared in the official history of the Third Infantry Division.[81] It stated,

It was in th[e] vicinity north of Les Rouges Eaux, on October 25, that S/Sgt. Clyde L. Choate, Company C, 601st TD Battalion, engaged a German Mark IV tank in a one-man battle, with Choate stalking the tank until he finally destroyed it just as it was about to break through to an infantry battalion CP [Command Post] area.

"The Germans had launched a surprise attack on densely wooded positions on a hilltop occupied by our forces," related Lt. Col. Walter E. Tardy, commanding officer of the 601st, "and the enemy struck with force and decision. The only tank destroyer available in this sector was knocked out before it could open fire. The German tank proceeded straight down a wagon road, slashing through the infantry positions and shooting the soldiers in their foxholes."

"Sergeant Choate couldn't find all of our crew and he believed the driver was trapped in the burning TD. Choate ran through a rain of enemy fire to the M-10 which was empty. Kraut infantry followed the Mark IV as it headed toward the infantry battalion CP about 400 yards to our rear," added Sgt. Thomas L. Langan who was a gunner in the ill-fated TD.

"The German tank cruised through the woods, firing down into foxholes of the doughboys and crushing soldiers to death under its tracks. Grabbing a bazooka from one of the foxholes, Choate immobilized the enemy tank, which the Germans then converted into an armored pillbox.

"Choate ran back to our infantrymen again, got another rocket and closed in on the tank to within ten yards, always under heavy enemy fire. The shot was a bull's eye and Germans began piling out of it, with Choate shooting them with his revolver."

T/4 [Technician Four] Jay W. Shively, who also witnessed the event, said that Choate "winged" at least two Krauts and threw a hand grenade into the tank to be certain there were no more live ones in it.

Losing their tank, the German infantry became disorganized and the melee ended with thirty Germans killed, wounded or captured.

How Sergeant Choate "got his man" and stopped enemy armor without a tank destroyer is legend in the 601st Battalion.

Elsewhere in the division history Choate was cited for his "conspicuous gallantry and intrepidity at risk of life, above and beyond the call of duty."

The 601st informal history stated simply, "While the Battalion minus 'C' company was resting, Clyde Choate did a pretty good imitation of Superman, KO'd a Kraut tank single-handed and earned a C. M. H. [Congressional Medal of Honor]."[82] Of the more than 1,800 men who fought through eight campaigns with the 601st, made four D-day assaults, and spent 546 days in actual combat, Choate was the only member to receive the Medal of Honor. He was twenty-four years old when the battle occurred.

Some of the most intense combat in the history of the 601st and Clyde Choate occurred after October 25 in the northeast portion of France. With their backs literally to the Rhine River, German troops fought tenaciously to keep Allied units from crossing into Germany. The nasty winter weather of 1944–45—during the Battle of the Bulge—in the Vosges Mountains provided U.S. troops with some of the war's worst combat conditions. The 601st fought sometimes in knee-deep snow that masked acres of densely sown German mines.[83]

During heavy action that continued into February 1945 the 601st destroyed eighteen enemy tanks and was among attached units of the Third Division that later received a Presidential Unit Citation for bravery. In part, the citation said, "Fighting incessantly, from 22 January to 26

February 1945, in heavy snow storms, through enemy-infested marshes and woods, and over a flat plain crisscrossed by numerous small canals, irrigation ditches, and unfordable streams, terrain ideally suited to the defense wall on the northern perimeter of the Colmar bridgehead, [the units] drove forward to isolate Colmar from the Rhine."[84]

Just as the Third Division and other Allied units prepared to take the war to the German homeland in March, Clyde Choate received a thirty-day rest and recuperation leave to the United States. He left Europe on March 12 and arrived in the United States on March 19.[85] As he prepared to report for duty at the end of his leave, Choate was hospitalized at the veterans hospital in Marion, Illinois, with a fever. World War II for Staff Sergeant Clyde L. Choate had ended. He was discharged May 26, 1945, at Fort Sheridan, Illinois. He had been on combat duty in North Africa, Italy, and southern France for thirty-one months.

The Medal of Honor

Clyde Lee Choate's Medal of Honor citation reads,

> He commanded a tank destroyer near Bruyeres, France, on October 25, 1944. Our infantry occupied a position on a wooded hill when, at dusk, an enemy Mark IV tank and a company of infantry attacked, threatening to overrun the American position and capture a command post 400 yards to the rear. S/Sgt. Choate's tank destroyer, the only weapon available to oppose the German armor, was set afire by 2 hits. Ordering his men to abandon the destroyer, S/Sgt Choate reached comparative safety. He returned to the burning destroyer to search for comrades possibly trapped in the vehicle risking instant death in an explosion which was imminent and braving enemy fire which ripped his jacket and tore the helmet from his head. Completing the search and seeing the tank and its supporting infantry overrunning our infantry in their shallow foxholes, he secured a bazooka and ran after the tank, dodging from tree to tree and passing through the enemy's loose skirmish line. He fired a rocket from a distance of 20 yards, immobilizing the tank but leaving it able to spray the area with cannon and machinegun fire. Running back to our infantry through vicious fire, he secured another rocket, and advancing against a hail of

machinegun and small-arms fire reached a position 10 yards from the tank. His second shot shattered the turret. With his pistol he killed 2 of the crew as they emerged from the tank; and then running to the crippled Mark IV while enemy infantry sniped at him, he dropped a grenade inside the tank and completed its destruction. With their armor gone, the enemy infantry became disorganized and was driven back. S/Sgt. Choate's great daring in assaulting an enemy tank single-handed, his determination to follow the vehicle after it had passed his position, and his skill and crushing thoroughness in the attack prevented the enemy from capturing a battalion command post and turned a probable defeat into a tactical success.

On May 26, 1945, Clyde Lee Choate, a month short of twenty-five years of age, was an unemployed ex–army soldier like millions of other young people would be who had spent years on land and at sea in combat zones of Europe and Asia. Many struggled with recurring nightmares and were unable to find work, or hold a job. In short order they spent wages received when discharged from the service and leaned on relatives for room and board. For many, the road to recovery would be long and often disappointing.

There were exceptions, of course. Like others, Choate had no significant work experience or training as a civilian, and his education had ended with graduation from high school. However, upon discharge he received enough back pay to get him to a place where employment was possible.[86] After discharge at Fort Sheridan he traveled to St. Louis, where he lived with a sister. Soon he found work as an apprentice brakeman on the Missouri-Kansas-Texas Railroad, known widely as the "Katy." His experience with the railroad was brief, as Choate explained many years later: "I didn't last long as a railroader. I made one trip. I jumped off the train with my lantern and my old football knee gave way under me and I almost fell under the train. I quit when we got back to St. Louis."[87]

During the time living with his sister, Choate read in the *St. Louis Globe-Democrat* that he had been awarded the Medal of Honor for his bravery in France during October 1944.[88] He returned immediately to his mother's home in Anna, where he found a U.S. Army major looking for him. Choate recalled, "The major had already set in motion the plans for me, my mother and my sister to go to Washington to receive the medal."[89]

President Harry S. Truman had received official notice of Choate's honor, along with information about five other honorees in a letter from Secretary of War Henry L. Stimson on June 18. Shortly thereafter Truman signed the citations. The citation for Choate, on White House stationery, stated, "The President of the United States takes pleasure in awarding the Medal of Honor to Staff Sergeant Clyde L. Choate, Co. C, 601st Tank Destroyer Battalion, United States Army, for service as set forth in the following . . ." At the citation's conclusion President Truman signed the document on July 2, 1945.[90]

The presentation to Choate by Truman on August 23 remained an unforgettable personal moment for the veteran and his family, as well as part of Medal of Honor history. Choate described it this way: "President Harry Truman presented me with the medal. He leaned over and said, 'Sergeant, I would rather have earned this medal than be president of the United States.'"[91] For a newspaper article honoring Choate fifty years after the presentation, Choate talked of his respect for Truman: "I truly believe he'll be treated by history as one of the real great presidents this nation had. He was humble, brave—not at all afraid to stand up for what he knew was right. He had a definite effect on my life. I tried to follow his example and treat people with kindness and respect and never tell a lie."[92] Choate added, "The Medal of Honor made me better known than the average returning GI, but I never used it in my campaigns." He did not have to say a word about the honor. Almost every biographical news story and public event in his honor through the end of his life in 2001 did it for him.

Overwhelmed with ceremonies in Washington, Choate quickly faced reality: He needed a job. The opportunity arose to purchase and operate a restaurant in Anna. Choate bought the Southern Barbecue, a drive-in where he had worked as a carhop while in high school. The venture turned sour because of food and supply shortages after the war. He explained, "I had an awful hard time making any money at it because of a shortage of the necessary things it takes to run a restaurant."[93] It was especially difficult to get meat, condiments, and other items, he added.

Jobs were not all that plentiful in postwar southern Illinois even for a Medal of Honor recipient. Unknown to him, however, the political drums had sounded across the region and the state, catching the attention of familiar names in Democratic politics. Twenty-two miles east of Anna in Vienna lived a state representative who had served a decade in the Illinois

General Assembly and in the 1945 session was assistant minority leader. That representative, Paul Powell, could see the possibility for a young Medal of Honor veteran in the legislature, assuming he had the necessary personal attributes. Not far away in McLeansboro, Illinois, lived John H. Stelle, a former governor who maintained widespread political influence through his connections in the American Legion. He served as national commander of the Legion in 1945, and was instrumental in establishing organization posts throughout the state.

If someone with promise, or with a popular standing among citizens, needed work, those two men and their allies would see to it. In Springfield, the public official with the widest job opportunity reach outside the governor's office was Edward J. Barrett, secretary of state. A veteran of World Wars I and II and a major force with veterans across the state, Barrett, a Chicagoan long plugged in to southern Illinois politics, would be expected to come to the aid of Choate. Barrett and Stelle first worked the state's political venue together in 1930, and remained close through the years. No matter what office Barrett sought through the years—state treasurer, auditor, secretary of state, governor—Stelle led the cheers. Meanwhile, Powell and Barrett formed a powerful alliance in Springfield that connected them with downstate political forces. As one longtime state government official familiar with Choate's political story said, "Powell got him the job."[94] Choate was about to be surrounded by friends he did not know he had.

A political ally of Barrett from Anna, Robert Willis, contacted Choate about a job as license investigator in the secretary's Springfield office. Choate accepted and moved to Springfield. A career in public service had not occurred to Choate at that moment. He planned to study for a law degree while working for the secretary of state. As if that might have surprised some people, Choate said later, "I wanted to be a lawyer, believe it or not."[95]

As Choate was finding his way around the state capital, political events occurred that would alter the veteran's plans and career. On the heels of winning a second term as governor of Illinois in 1944, Dwight Green and Republican members of the legislature anticipated the end of World War II and the return of thousands of soldiers to the state. They created a commission for coordinating all veterans' affairs and appropriated $385,000 to pay bonuses.[96] Payments were to begin in 1947. Among legislators opposing Green's program was state representative Herbert L. Upchurch, the lone Democrat among three representatives for District 50, Choate's home area. Barrett was not happy with Upchurch's position and began planning to produce a candidate who could defeat the incumbent in the primary election of 1946.[97]

Meanwhile in Springfield, Barrett recognized that Choate had promise as well as cachet. Responding accordingly, the secretary "loaned" him to assist the American Legion in a statewide membership drive by giving speeches. Choate explained his reaction to the assignment: "Barrett thought I was very capable of making speeches, which I wasn't. Well, I'd never made a public speech in my life so I canned a little speech that was the same over and over again. He heard me make this speech up near his hometown in Cook County and the next day he called me into his office in Springfield and said, 'I want you to run for state representative.'"[98] Another version had Barrett announcing, "You're ready now."[99] Events in 1946 were about to change Choate's life story.

Upchurch was born in Benton, Illinois, on June 18, 1908. He attended Southern Illinois Normal College (later Southern Illinois University) and worked as a teacher and school official. He was elected to the legislature in 1940, along with two Republican representatives. In District 50, Republicans dominated. As the single Democrat from the district, Upchurch won reelection in 1942 and 1944.[100] He would not be a pushover.

To suggest that Choate did not have a clue about politics or service in the General Assembly sells him short. In a few months in Springfield he would have absorbed at least limited knowledge of life in state government. Even if Upchurch had won, Choate would have remained an employee of Barrett with a career in politics still possible.

Choate later explained his strange new surroundings: "I wasn't sure what a state representative did and I certainly didn't know what the job paid. I was working for the secretary of state as a license investigator. The job paid $250 a month [$3,000 a year] plus a car. I was elected to my first term and found out it paid $2,500 a year, with no car, no expense account. That was it."[101] He forgot to add that living expenses while the legislature was in session six months during the two-year term came out of his pocket and members had no paid staff help. Most House members had a job or business in the district to provide additional income, and that would become necessary for Choate. Eventually, he opened an insurance and real estate office in nearby Carbondale.

To underscore his humble political beginnings, Choate told of his first campaign speech at a meeting of Williamson County committeemen in Herrin: "The county chairman had a grocery store and they were all wait-ing for me in the backroom of the store. On the drive up from Anna I had been busy memorizing a speech but when I got there I couldn't remem-ber anything. I stood up and said, 'Well, I'm running for the legislature and I sure hope I win.' That was my speech."[102] That blunt talk combined with his reputation as a military hero was enough, although he needed help from savvy locals. Choate credited three people for key roles: Albert Carter and Bob Willis of Anna and Ray Hubbs of Herrin. "They were all World War I vets—and I really didn't know them before but they worked day and night for me."[103] There was no better recommendation for public office in 1946 than service in World War II.

Choate defeated Upchurch and with the 1947 session began a legisla-tive career that lasted thirty years. In Choate's first session his acquain-tance from Vienna, Powell, was chosen minority leader. Two years later Powell became Speaker of the House. Choate could not have had a more influential mentor. Choate outlived those who opened the door in 1946: Powell, Stelle, and Barrett. As for his law school ambition: "I ended up getting my education in the legislature."[104]

No sooner had Choate been sworn in for his first legislative term in 1947, he married Mabel Madonna Ross. They made Anna their home no matter how much acclaim Choate received. Clyde, his wife, Donna, and their two daughters seemed comfortable with headquarters at home. As countrified as Choate appeared to some so-called sophisticates from Chi-cago and Springfield, he never turned away from his southern Illinois roots.

Product of Landed Gentry

Hamilton County, Illinois, was more than a home to John Henry Stelle. It was home to a land-based family dynasty that embraced Stelle and pro-vided him with a well-funded platform for a lifetime of adventures in politics and business. From the small town of McLeansboro, Hamilton's county seat, Stelle's influence reached from Illinois and Indiana to cities, state capitals, and Washington, D.C.

During a lifetime of seventy-one years, Stelle enjoyed a staggering number of successes and almost as many stunning defeats. Many of them resulted from his commanding personality, his will to put an imprint on all that he touched, and his astonishing ability to attract enemies. Stelle worked overtime doing favors for his friends and seeking revenge for political slights. In almost all his pursuits he was a presence bigger than life. Even with high-profile escapades for three decades or more, many of Stelle's business and political ventures remain a closely guarded family secret. In personal affairs he preferred person-to-person contact without a mass of correspondence, and he left few public paper trails.

No matter how high he climbed or how far he fell, Stelle owed much to family members who preceded him. They were hardworking patriotic Illinoisans committed to building their place in the state's history during the first century of statehood.

Thompson Beverly Stelle Sr., of French Huguenot stock, and his wife, Elizabeth, came to the Illinois Territory from New Jersey in 1816, two years before establishment of statehood. Illinois was part of the Indiana Territory until 1809, when Congress established the Illinois Territory.[105] The Stelle family was among the earliest settlers in what became Hamilton County. As soon as land was cleared for farming, the crops were tobacco, wheat, corn, and oats, along with apple orchards and pastureland.

In all probability the Stelles traveled to the Illinois Territory on the Ohio River to its confluence with the Wabash River and nearby Shawneetown, the first white settlement in Illinois. Once they reached Shawneetown, they were perhaps twenty miles from their destination in White County. Hamilton County was carved from White County in 1821. The settlers usually took what was called the Goshen Road.[106]

In the 1818 census, taken to determine whether the territory had sufficient residents to become a state, the population of White/Hamilton County was said to be 3,832 persons in 572 families. Historian Solon Buck wrote that it was "doubtful there were 100 families in Hamilton county [in 1818]. The principal settlements appear to have been in the central township, in which McLeansboro is now located, and in Knight's Prairie."[107]

Looking for land to farm, the family settled in Knight's Prairie.[108] With sufficient water available from the Saline River, the Stelles worked hard to provide for a growing family that eventually numbered fifteen children, eleven of whom lived to maturity.

Thompson Senior lived almost fifty years in Illinois before dying on a farm four miles west of McLeansboro in 1864. His widow lived another nine years until 1873. In the course of their lives, they witnessed the growth of Hamilton County from its beginnings in 1821 through the incorporation of McLeansboro in 1840. In the second Illinois generation of Stelles, three boys lived to maturity among the eleven children, including Jacob, grandfather of John H. Stelle. Like his father, Jacob farmed land in Hamilton County and was said to be successful. He married Judith Farmer to whom nine children were born. Jacob and his brothers served in Illinois units during the Civil War, beginning a legacy of Stelle service in the military that continued through World War II.[109]

One of the sons born to Jacob and Judith was named Thompson Beverly Stelle II. He was born January 23, 1845.[110] He watched his grandfather Thompson B. Sr. and his father Jacob sustain a large family from the soil of Hamilton County. He continued the family ties to farmland but also received a substantial education and took a position of influence and leadership in McLeansboro.

Thompson attended McLeansboro public schools and Indiana Asbury University in Greencastle, a college started and supported by the Methodist Episcopal Church, and now called DePauw University.[111] He switched to McKendree College in Lebanon, Illinois, also a school supported by Methodists. In 1868 he received a bachelor's degree and law degree from McKendree. At age twenty-three Thompson began practicing criminal law. He quickly entered local politics and in 1869 was elected at age twenty-four to a four-year term as county judge. Ever after he was known in town as Judge Stelle.

Thompson later was elected to the McLeansboro school board and also served as mayor of the town. He married Laura E. Blades of Hamilton County, and they reared six children, the last of whom was John Henry Stelle, born August 19, 1891.[112] John had three sisters and two brothers. Thompson participated in a number of businesses, including a department store in McLeansboro. On his acreage west of town he farmed and raised livestock. On many fronts, Thompson Stelle prospered and retained wealth. His great personal achievement in that regard came from the accumulation of land in and near McLeansboro.[113] The 1905 plat map for McLeansboro Township listed properties totaling 913 acres along the western border of the town, concentrated in a broad band from north to south.[114] He also purchased several lots in town, and a gristmill and sawmill at Hoodville, in the southern part of the county. Stelle died in

1906 at the age of sixty. Published reports stated that his landholdings amounted to about 2,000 acres.[115]

John Henry Stelle grew up familiar with the chores and responsibilities of a complex agricultural operation. Respect for the land remained a huge part of his life until he died. Land was the source of experimentation with animals and crops, and his wealth included extraction of oil and coal. Stelle kept his hand in breeding horses for investment, racing, and use on ranches owned by others. His later ownership of stock in Illinois racetracks meant he could enjoy time at the track and tend to his horse stalls.

John was a husky young man and like many boys turned his attention to athletics. One biographer described Stelle as "broad-shouldered and virile."[116] His sport of choice was baseball. From about 1908 to 1913, he spent summers playing baseball while reading law with Judge Johnson H. Lane in McLeansboro, attending college, working on the farm, courting, and marrying.[117]

After graduation in 1908 from McLeansboro Township High School Stelle enrolled at Western Military Academy preparatory school in Alton. Later, he completed studies at Washington University in St. Louis. Meanwhile, he made the acquaintance of Wilma Wiseheart, who was reared on a farm near Shawneetown.[118] The young couple was not inclined toward a big wedding that might have been the course for someone of Stelle's stature. Instead, they headed for Evansville, Indiana, to get married. As Wilma said later, "They told us we weren't old enough, and we went to Henderson, Kentucky." They married on November 30, 1912.

Stelle continued to play semiprofessional baseball in the minor leagues after his marriage. However, a professional baseball career was not in Stelle's future. He graduated with a law degree from Washington University in 1916 and started a legal practice in McLeansboro. Stelle began to show the entrepreneurial streak that would bring him business fame and fortune. By 1915, Stelle had acquired sixty-four acres of land adjacent to the city limits on the west edge of town. He proposed to develop Stelle's Addition, and the city approved his housing plan on June 12, when he was twenty-three years old.[119]

By the time of Stelle's graduation with a law degree in 1916, World War I was ablaze in Europe, with the major combatants—Germany and its allies against France, Britain, and Russia—suffering staggering numbers of dead and wounded. President Woodrow Wilson and Congress declared war on April 6, 1917, and on April 17, John Stelle enlisted as a private in the Army National Guard.[120] Stelle's superiors recognized his leadership skills and promoted him to sergeant by August. He entered officer training at Fort Sheridan and was commissioned a lieutenant. In January 1918 he was sent overseas with the Seventy-seventh Infantry Division to train for combat and served on the front lines and in the deadly trenches. For his performance on the battlefield Stelle was promoted to captain in December 1918. He received an honorable discharge on May 19, 1919, and returned to McLeansboro. Along with thousands of fellow soldiers, Stelle had been wounded and gassed.

World War I changed many aspects of his life. He was emboldened in business affairs and eventually in politics. Also, a strong influence of the postwar days was his involvement in the formation of the American Legion in Illinois, a political gift that kept giving during four decades. Illinois had provided 351,000 soldiers for the war.[121] Even considering those who died, were injured, or moved to other locations, the number had instant political potential.

In the midst of organizing Legion posts across Illinois, Stelle staked his claim to placing them in every part of the southern half of the state.[122] In the quest to be a Legion leader in Little Egypt Illinois, Stelle encountered regional differences between Chicago and downstate communities. Frictions that developed were largely attitudinal, reflecting differences in expectations and demands for services in urban and rural areas. Thomas Littlewood, author of a book on the Legion in Illinois between the two world wars, stated, "The political dynamics of doing favors in Chicago were different from those in the more sparsely settled sections of the state. In small communities, residents were generally more reluctant to accept public charity. Not only was there little reluctance in the big city, but the dispensers of public assistance expected to be credited by the recipients."[123] Such urban-rural tensions would be a part of Stelle's political history. Almost every step of the way from Stelle's early activism with the Legion—he served as local post commander in 1924—until he died in 1962, veterans' affairs and friendships played major roles in his political life.[124]

John and Wilma eventually reared two sons, John Albert, born in 1917 shortly before his father enlisted in World War I, and Russell Thompson, born in 1922. They would become partners with their father in a myriad of business operations in Illinois and Indiana. Both sons served as officers in World War II. John A. died in 1999 at age eighty-one, and Russell in 2012 at ninety.[125]

In the period after his return from World War I, Stelle devoted much of his time to developing a portfolio of businesses to complement his growing farm operation east of town. He purchased the McLeansboro Shale Products Company, maker of brick, drain tile, and building blocks.[126] At any given time several hundred persons and in some cases thousands were employed on his farm, in businesses, and through investments in oil and coal.

Stelle helped organize the Hamilton County Fair Association and served as its president in 1923.[127] Throughout the state, county fair associations promoted harness racing, and many fair officials were influential political activists at the local and state levels. He ran for Hamilton County state's attorney and the state Senate but failed to win either.[128] The losses in local elections did not end Stelle's desire to hold public office. Throughout life, he never let defeats stall his ambition. Leaning on his knowledge of Legion affairs, Stelle organized the Democratic Serviceman's Club in 1928, and worked for party candidates across Illinois.[129]

During the 1920s Stelle had made the acquaintance of Edward J. Barrett, a young operative with a cherubic look about him who started at the bottom of the Chicago Democratic machine.[130] Their friendship was a match made in political heaven. Although Stelle was nine years older than Barrett, they shared the experiences of World War I. Barrett had enlisted at age seventeen and was wounded and gassed. He was one of the organizers of disabled American veterans in Illinois. Barrett grew up on Chicago's South Side and attended St. Rita High School. He went to Spaulding Institute and later graduated from Mayo College.[131] Attracted to politics, he began work as a precinct captain in an Irish ward and was employed as secretary to the leader of the Chicago Street Sweepers Union.

While their personal backgrounds differed, Stelle and Barrett found common ground in their ambitions for public office. Early in his political experiences Stelle realized that he could not reach political heights in Illinois without help. Later, he explained his dilemma: "There I was three hundred miles south of Chicago. I had to have a foothold in Chicago. Without it I would have been as dead as a mackerel."[132]

The next opportunity for Stelle occurred working with Barrett in the 1930 statewide elections. At age thirty, Barrett was a young man in a hurry.[133] He knew the score in Chicago and the statewide Democratic Party. He needed to be slated by top officials or he would fail. Anton Cermak, party organization leader in Chicago, was the Democratic boss with a reach throughout the state. For the 1930 elections Cermak slated Mike Zacharias for the position of state treasurer. Barrett decided it was time to challenge the machine, and he chose to run against Zacharias in the primary.

The only chance Barrett had to win the Democratic primary was to build support downstate to offset the presumed advantage Zacharias had in Chicago and Cook County. Stelle, working as downstate manager for Democratic candidates, signed up specifically to help Barrett's bid. Political operatives said Barrett had no chance to win, but he pulled an upset over Zacharias. Barrett followed that with a general election victory over longtime Republican activist Clarence F. Buck by 74,921 votes.[134] Barrett became the youngest state treasurer in state history.

Believing he had earned a job with Barrett, Stelle asked the new treasurer for work and was appointed assistant treasurer. In 1931, Stelle and his wife moved to Springfield for what would be a decade of some of the wildest and wackiest political moments in the history of Illinois. Stelle continued to make frequent trips to McLeansboro.

Stelle's next step to high office occurred in 1932 when he teamed with attorney Scott Lucas of Havana, Illinois, to coordinate Henry Horner's campaign for governor. Lucas sought the Democratic nomination for the U.S. Senate in 1932 but failed to get the party's nod.[135] As a supporter of Governor Horner, he was elected to the U.S. House seat from his home congressional district in 1934. After two terms in the U.S. House, in 1938 Lucas fought the Kelly-Nash Chicago organization for the party's nomination as U.S. senator. He won two terms as senator, and in 1949–50 he was Senate majority leader. Lucas remained an ally of Horner while the governor and Stelle fought a bitter battle. In spite of their cooperative venture in 1932, Lucas and Stelle would be at odds politically in the following decades.

Unable by state law to serve consecutive two-year terms as state treasurer, Barrett decided to run for state auditor in 1932. Barrett won that contest by 298,356 votes and appointed Stelle his assistant.[136] By 1934, Stelle had spent four years in Springfield carefully studying the political landscape. He put together his connections downstate with a growing reputation in Chicago as an effective campaign organizer and potential officeholder. With official support from the Chicago organization and Governor Horner, Stelle ran for state treasurer.

Stelle's opponent for treasurer in the 1934 general election was a tested government veteran, Republican William J. Stratton, father of William G. Stratton who would be governor of Illinois from 1953 to 1961. With full backing of the statewide Democratic organization, Stelle won easily by 270,783 votes.[137] Stelle and Barrett were, by 1935, individually on tracks to higher public office. They would remain politically and personally close allies for decades to come.

Meanwhile, political leadership in Chicago ended in the hands of Mayor Edward Kelly. He endorsed Stelle's run for treasurer in 1934. Kelly and his political partner, Patrick Nash, grew displeased with Horner and prepared to choose and support a different candidate in the 1936 primary. Meanwhile, Stelle began looking for the next step in his political career.

Hoping to hold onto downstate votes and placate members of the Democratic State Central Committee outside Chicago in 1936, Kelly sought a candidate for lieutenant governor, the only remaining opening on the party slate. The lieutenant governor was elected separately from the governor; however, it was assumed the lieutenant governor would be an ally of the governor. Official duties were few. Kelly picked Stelle for the position and forced him to choose between the machine in Chicago and the machine belonging to the governor.[138]

Realistically, Stelle had little choice. If Stelle wanted to leverage his downstate strength, the best opportunity was to stay with Chicago Democratic interests. That decision drove a final stake in the heart of Stelle's relationship with Horner. Further angering the governor was Kelly's choice of Barrett for state auditor.

During the primary campaign, animosity between Stelle and Horner thickened, and it carried over to Barrett. The governor called them the "two cherubs." In one speech downstate Stelle mentioned the surplus that existed in the treasury and could be spent to ease the impact of the Depression. Horner suggested that "he's not worrying about a surplus so much as he's worrying because he can't get his hands on it."[139] Keeping up his quarrel with Stelle and Barrett, Horner called them "self-serving politicians who are unfit for any office."[140]

Barrett and Stelle both defeated Horner's selections and cruised by Republican opponents in the general election. In an outspoken moment after the election, Horner told a confidant, "I'd cut off this finger if I could get Stelle out of that office."[141]

The period of Stelle's life from 1936 to January 1941 represents the high and low marks of his political career. Books and newspaper articles over the decades have labeled Stelle as the Antichrist, or more accurately the anti-Horner. Their clash became a classic drama of regional and personal politics. Stelle did not help his cause. He was not a sympathetic personality in state politics of the late 1930s. The tales, some of which have lived to this day, painted a dark and nasty picture of Stelle. They contained some facts, even some reasonable assumptions, along with lies.

The deterioration of their relationship is well documented. The story includes Horner's failing health that led to his death in October 1940 before completing the second term. Horner refused to step down due to illness and allow Stelle to become governor. Horner's hatred of Stelle led him to an agreement with Mayor Kelly and his political advisor Jacob Arvey to deny Stelle an opportunity to be on the ballot for governor in the election of 1940. They also dumped Barrett.[142] After Horner's death, the acrimony continued in Springfield as Stelle, now governor, cleaned house of Horner's appointees and aides, began a reorganization of targeted departments, and replaced almost all county chairmen with friends. He had only ninety-nine days to serve, and he cut a wide swath against anything and anyone associated with Horner.[143]

For years after 1940, Stelle kept a special place in his memory for the betrayal by Kelly and Arvey. There was not a forgiving bone in his body. He warred for two decades with Milburn (Pete) Akers, a journalist Horner hired for public relations and to besmirch Stelle. After resigning before Stelle fired him, Akers became an editor and columnist at the *Chicago Sun* and *Sun-Times*. He perpetuated a relentless anti-Stelle campaign in the pages of the newspaper.[144]

Two weeks after Horner's death, Stelle announced the appointment of George Edward Day, a Springfield paint dealer and friend, as state purchasing agent.[145] In the short time Day served, he managed to generate a quantity of rumors and newspaper stories about excesses. Stelle had become interested in traffic safety and watched an experiment in Minnesota with great interest. That state had designated areas of unsafe passing on state highways by painting yellow lines. Pursuing a similar program for Illinois, purchasing agent Day bought huge quantities of yellow paint, from paint dealer Day, for striping the highways. The program generated outcries of misuse of state funds and cronyism.[146] Day and Stelle remained friends and business associates for years.

Stelle also turned toward activities that in large part fed the legacy that he was a wastrel in Springfield, devoted mostly to having a good time at the expense of state taxpayers. A favorite story was that periodically Stelle was driven in a state-owned Cadillac to a private hunting preserve in southern Illinois. Stelle owned part or all of a 1,000-acre hunt club in the Cairo area. There were accusations of irregularities in official operations. Newspaper reporter and historian Robert Howard wrote years later, "Rumors of irregularities were never documented."[147]

Biographer Littlewood stated that Stelle had rooms in the mansion redecorated, and in the final days of his tenure spent $1,900 on repainting. Early in the ninety-nine days, reports proliferated about wild parties at the mansion for friends and political pals from southern Illinois. Stelle's son Russell told this author, "The mansion wasn't fit for parties. The only party held there was Christmas. Parties were held at Springfield hotels."[148] Regarding redecorating, Russell Stelle stated, "The mansion was falling apart."

Over the years, Stelle spent time assuring reporters and citizens that his quarrel in the 1930s was not with Horner, but with those around him who were "thieves." He told his son Russell, "I made a mistake breaking with Horner."[149] Almost any public official sent home without a job and blistered by newspaper columns and editorials would spend years licking his wounds and looking for less stressful work. Not John Stelle. As his son Russell said of his father, "He was a tough cookie. He didn't take any crap."[150] He left Springfield with no stated remorse.

The official role of a lieutenant governor in Illinois was small potatoes in terms of official commitments. Stelle had plenty of time to direct his farm near McLeansboro. He oversaw expansion of production on the farm and introduction of new techniques and experimental agriculture. He bought and sold cattle, building a nice profit. Using coal found on his properties, he engineered the making of electric power for the farm. During the late 1930s, Stelle dabbled in oil production that after World War II became a major success. Through all his apparent nonpolitical business affairs, Stelle made the most of his political friends and their interest in his ventures. Rather than sitting around enjoying accumulated wealth, Stelle, according to Russell, "Never got involved with money. He used it."[151]

John Stelle's interest in a business enterprise in Brazil, Indiana, reflected the close proximity of his home in McLeansboro to the state, his familiarity with the product and its potential, and most of all the opportunity to purchase the company for next to nothing. The venture also thrust Stelle into the politics of Indiana.

In his business interests outside of politics, Stelle's involvement often began as a legal adviser or in an unofficial role for a friend or acquaintances. That is what happened in Indiana. Stelle was a legal consultant to Clay Products Company in Brazil when it declared bankruptcy in 1937.[152] He saw the potential of ceramic tile in a growing market for commercial and personal home use. Stelle made the most of his insider situation—he also was a stockholder—with Clay Products and purchased its three manufacturing plants. With his attention focused on activities in Illinois as lieutenant governor, and on other business opportunities, Stelle took his time to rebuild what became Arketex Ceramic Corporation. The name, a play on the word *architect*, was developed with the company's ceramic engineer, George Shoemaker.[153]

At its peak in the 1950s and 1960s, Arketex had three plants with kilns operating twenty-four hours a day and employing more than a thousand workers who produced glazed tile in seventy different colors and hues. Employees at satellite operations and in foreign countries brought the employment total to nearly three thousand, according to Stelle's son, Russell. The business grew in the 1940s and 1950s beyond any estimates.[154] The Stelle family's profits soared. But Arketex's production began to decline in the 1960s. The Stelle family sold the business in the late 1960s, and it operated another decade before closing.

Stelle's Illinois friend Paul Powell was another person who benefited from Arketex connections. In 1945 Arketex began paying Powell an annual fee that continued for twenty-two years.[155] Payment started at $900, increased to $1,800 in 1946, and remained the same every year with the exception of two. Arketex also paid Powell's health care premiums, which helped ease Powell's large medical bills in the 1960s. There are no records indicating what, if any, services Powell provided for Arketex. Stelle also offered Powell opportunities to share in oil developments, primarily in Saline County near Eldorado, Illinois. Powell's income was modest from those investments. Son Russell said, when asked about the payments to Powell, that the two men were "horse traders." He also alluded to work by Powell on real estate transactions but provided no details.[156]

Exploration and production of oil became one of John Stelle's most financially successful ventures, with holdings concentrated in Illinois.

Stelle began his involvement in oil modestly by drilling first in 1939 and bringing in producing wells during 1940. The first oil in the Stelle family was produced from three wells near the small town of Hoodville, south of McLeansboro in Hamilton County. Those producing wells were established on the Louisville and Nashville Railroad right of way.[157] The wells were so close to the tracks that son Russell, who worked at the location, remembers having to get off the rigs when trains went by in order to feel safe.[158]

The total of Stelle's oil holdings are something of a mystery, or at least subject to question. According to family estimates and newspaper accounts, before Stelle's death in 1962 he and associates developed four hundred wells in southern Illinois, and he had oil holdings in West Texas, Kentucky, and Tennessee. On his own or in partnership with others—called a syndicate—Stelle had producing wells in the counties of Hamilton, Franklin, Gallatin, Madison, Montgomery, Perry, and Saline.[159] It also was stated that Stelle held an interest in fifteen to twenty wells in Hamilton County during the 1950s, although no records exist of those wells in Stelle's name. (Illinois State Geological Survey records for the period 1940 to 1959 are used here to document a partial picture of his oil pursuits.) Stelle's oil business progressed slowly through the World War II years and the rest of the 1940s, with one additional well investment in 1947. That was in partnership with George Edward Day.[160]

One of Stelle's Illinois oil bonanzas began in 1953, and production lasted through that decade. All of the documented well activity occurred in Saline County's oil-rich Eldorado Consolidated Oil Field, adjacent to Hamilton County, with much development concentrated near the town of Eldorado.[161] A syndicate was formed on December 10, 1953, by Stelle, attorney Ralph W. Choisser, businessmen J. Cecil Sullivan, Eugene Choisser of Eldorado, and Day for exploration, drilling, and production of oil.[162]

Stelle's relationship with the Choisser family, and especially Ralph, is an example of how personal associations from business and politics influenced many joint ventures throughout southern Illinois. Ralph Choisser was a Saline County judge, banker, oilman, politician, thoroughbred horse breeder, and friend of Stelle.[163] A veteran of World War II, Choisser was active in the Eldorado American Legion post. He purchased controlling interest in the First State Bank of Eldorado in 1953 and remained attorney and director of the bank until 1970. In 1952, because of longtime ties to horse breeding and racing, he was appointed a steward representing the

Illinois Racing Commission. By law, stewards were charged with regulating horse racing. They supervised racing meets by rules and regulations of the racing board and were empowered to investigate violations and to revoke or to suspend licenses. At one point he presided over all racetracks in the Chicago area. When Cahokia Downs racetrack, a primary investment of Stelle, opened in 1954 outside East St. Louis, Choisser was named steward for a season. Since he owned no Cahokia Downs stock, there was no apparent financial conflict of interest.

J. Cecil Sullivan had extensive business holdings in Eldorado and Harrisburg. He invested in the First State Bank of Eldorado, also, and owned a motel, construction company, and roofing company in Harrisburg. He was a representative of Midland Securities in Chicago. He also had interests in farming, cattle, and coal mining. Sullivan was a confidant of Republican governors Dwight Green and Richard B. Ogilvie.[164]

By the early 1940s Stelle had established his American Legion credentials in many ways, mostly political. But he also had earned a reputation among veterans as someone acutely attuned to their needs. When Legion leaders at the national level began conversations in the fall of 1943 about federal legislation that would create veteran benefits, Stelle, not otherwise consumed with public policy matters in Illinois, became a participant. The story is told that, in November, Stelle and other Legionnaires met in Salem, Illinois, to discuss a federal proposal. He is alleged to have written suggestions on a paper tablecloth as the ideas flowed from those gathered.[165] From that meeting onward Stelle assumed a key role in the effort, concentrated in Washington.

Late in November the push for an omnibus bill in Congress began, titled the Servicemen's Readjustment Act of 1944—better known as the GI Bill of Rights. Stelle headed a special Legion committee to press the case in Washington. By January 6, less than a month after the first committee meeting, a bill had been drafted.[166]

The Legion launched a nationwide publicity campaign, operated by state and local organizations down to the grassroots. A huge boost came from William Randolph Hearst and his chain of newspapers, including one in Chicago.[167] He provided funds to keep the committee and its workers going in Washington and assigned reporters to follow each step along the way. The order was not just to cover the news, but also to get the bill passed.

Stelle and two other members of the committee went door to door in the U.S. House and Senate to determine where every member stood on the issue. Passing the bill was no easy task. Opposition developed within Congress and among organizations known for lobbying on military bills. The Legion knew the bill would not pass without military support. Seeing the threat for what it was, Stelle took charge. He invited representatives of the services to meet with Legion officials, specifying that they should come prepared to approve a definite agreement on all disputed parts of the bill. After meeting for six hours with officers of the services, and without a settlement, the military people said they would have to confer with superiors. A Hearst reporter described Stelle's reaction: "His face purple, his fist pounding the table, he said 'Our understanding was you would come here with authority to reach a decision. If I had known that you didn't have that authority I wouldn't have wasted the time of my committee here tonight.'" Stelle's explosion worked. From that point on the military supported the bill as written. The reporter added, "Few men ever said no to John Stelle when he got his dander up. He was that kind of man."[168]

Legion interests also took their case directly to the White House in an effort to gain the backing of President Franklin D. Roosevelt. Meeting with the president were Stelle and Illinois U.S. senator Lucas, a former national Legion official. They confirmed the president's support. Stelle, working top congressional officials, declared at Legion headquarters, "By God, I got Alben Barkley, the majority leader, to sign it in his own handwriting."[169] Passage by the Senate was unanimous. The House dragged its heels for weeks before approving the bill 187 to 0.

After a difficult battle in conference, the full Senate approved the GI Bill on June 12, and the House on June 13, 1944. President Roosevelt signed the bill on June 22, precisely sixteen days after Allied troops invaded Europe on D-day.[170] Remarkably, Legion workers, with John Stelle in the forefront, had taken the outline of a bill through the entire legislative process to law in about seven months. Few would have given any odds of success.

Even Stelle's strongest foes in Illinois acknowledged his leadership role for a law that had profound impact on the history of postwar America. A final accolade came to Stelle and his family in 2004, forty-two years after his death. The Education Commission of the States, consisting of current governors, honored Stelle as the "Father of the GI Bill."[171]

Due largely to his leadership performance on the GI Bill, Stelle was elected national commander of the American Legion for a one-year term starting in November 1945. He took the oath of office flanked by his two sons, both combat veterans of World War II.[172] This job was no ceremonial position paid out of gratitude for his devotion to veterans. He took over during the flood of GIs returning home after years on battlefields across the world.

Veterans of World War I, World War II, and later the Korean War never forgot what they received from the GI Bill and government benefits for service, and they never forgot the man who worked for the programs through the decades. Whatever political clout Stelle had from the 1940s to his death in 1962 could be tied directly to American Legion members and veterans who rallied to his calls. Not all veterans were Democrats, not all were Republicans, but regardless of partisanship they remained loyal to Stelle. This kinship was essential to his political connections with Paul Powell, Edward Barrett, Clyde Choate, and a host of downstate Democrats and Republicans.

2.
Southern Illinois Power Brokers

Illinois political officials and observers often referred to Paul Powell in oral histories as a legislative magician. Discounting the pretense of not wanting to speak ill of a former colleague, there is a measure of truth in the accolades. There was nothing supernatural about his style. Instead, everyone could see what Powell was doing, or at least they had knowledge of what was to come. He was the master of practical regional politics in a time when party lines were easily bridged, coalitions worked, public disclosure was unheard of, and dominating personalities kept score. Many legislators loafed through the part-time business schedule of one session every two years. Powell and his allies were in motion full-time.

Leverage is how Powell assumed the heights of power and remained there for much of his thirty years in the House of Representatives. He knew the numbers. Often Democrats were in the minority, but their numbers remained close enough to a majority for deal making. That is when the small numbers of Democrats in southern Illinois occasionally worked with other downstate colleagues to make a statement against Chicago population growth and political clout. Powell also knew when to fold his cards and play along with the growing behemoth on Lake Michigan.

Powell recognized that issues often trumped partisanship, although he could always talk a good game at a party gathering. Proof of that strategy was his rank as No. 1 supporter of Southern Illinois University in the legislature. He never spent a day in college, nor apparently did he wish to.

He knew the powerful economic engine that the university could be in his home territory, and he filled a vacuum of political leadership by bringing Democrats and Republicans to the cause.

Powell demonstrated an uncanny sense of timing. Twice—in 1959 and 1961—he was chosen Speaker of the House, essentially with Republican votes and the complicity of the Republican governor, William Stratton. By doing so, he temporarily limited the growing strength of Chicago mayor Richard J. Daley. Powell's motivation was to rule. He lusted for power: to use it and lord it over his enemies.

Other issues that bridged partisanship were horse racing, state fairs, economic development, public welfare, and elementary and secondary education. Their appeal brought together lawmakers, special interests, and lobbyists of all stripes. Powell also knew the value of supporting veterans, although he never served a day in the military. For those who did, Powell was among royalty, primarily because veterans were some of his strongest supporters and the American Legion maintained a powerful political voice. He could thank his friend John Stelle for a lifelong connection to that constituency. When the legislature took up bonuses and other aid for World War II and Korean War veterans, Powell was a strong supporter.

He also knew how and when to toot his own horn, especially with newspaper editors and reporters. One of his strongest newspaper supporters was the *Springfield Daily Register,* which editorially leaned sharply toward Democrats. His friendship with editor V. Y. Dallman paid off with frequent applause for Powell's legislative heroics. The largest newspaper closest to his home in Vienna, the *Southern Illinoisan* in Carbondale, became a fierce editorial opponent. In order to get his story told, Powell wrote op-ed page columns for newspapers touting his accomplishments.[1] Mostly, he ignored the jibes of liberal editorial pages such as those of the *St. Louis Post-Dispatch,* which never found a sliver of evidence that Powell was worthy of being elected to any position.[2] He rarely received a plaudit from Chicago papers, but then again he was not on the ballot there during his legislative years. His friendly constituency in Vienna never believed those "outsiders" anyway.

In spite of opposition by individual newspaper editorial pages, Powell enjoyed reminding people of his recognition by legislative reporters. In an op-ed article for the *Southern Illinoisan* recounting his policy achievements, Powell added this touch: "Twice a poll was taken by the newspaper men who cover the General Assembly who honored me twice as an outstanding Legislator of Illinois, and in 1949 I was made an Honorary Member of their group, the Illinois Legislative Correspondents Association."[3] Periodically, reporters for wire services and metropolitan newspapers followed Powell for a day or a week and wrote about his activities at home and in Springfield, leaving a mostly positive impression.

In the far corners of Illinois, especially at the local community level, Powell enjoyed popularity most statewide officials only dreamed of. Why? Powell once said, "Don't ever turn down a drink or something to eat when you're campaigning. I don't care if they hand you a glass of muddy river water, you take a big gulp and tell em how good it is."[4] Paul O'Neal, a friend from Vienna, added another version of the answer: "He promised that if they voted for him, he'd always take care of them. And so long as I knew Paul Powell, he took care of them or anyone else who needed it."[5]

Powell's legislative achievements began when he first served in House party leadership during the session of 1945. The next session, 1947, he was minority leader. In 1949 he was named Speaker. He was chosen minority leader in 1951 and 1953. When the 1955 session was half-finished, Richard J. Daley was elected to his first term as mayor of Chicago. From that point, Powell dealt directly with the mayor's agenda in addition to his own. The sessions of 1951–57, with Republicans in the House majority, may have been Powell's most productive as he worked the capitol halls tirelessly with Democrats and downstate interests. Upon his resurrection as Speaker in 1959, Powell remained at the controls of issues he prized and the coalitions they required.

Redistricting of the House in 1955 favored the Chicago region with an increase in districts and over time showcased Daley's authority somewhat more in relationship to the city's population. One result of the increased number of legislative districts in 1955 and 1957 was the choice of Joseph L. De La Cour, a Chicago Democrat, as minority leader. Meanwhile, Republicans controlled both legislative chambers.[6] Normally, a downstate Democrat pushing against those odds would have taken a backseat in public policy matters. Not Powell. Both sides still needed the votes he controlled to get much done. No one knew that better than Republican governor William Stratton. Crafty in his own right, Stratton courted Democrats who were known to have been less than delighted with the previous governorship of Adlai Stevenson II. Powell was first on that list. Powell used his leverage effectively to cut deals with Chicago and Republican interests. Although he made no public announcement, Powell left an impression that he favored Stratton's reelection in 1956. The Democrat chosen to contest Stratton was Judge Richard B. Austin, a nominee not of Powell's choosing. When Stratton announced his bid for a third term in 1960, Powell said the governor would be tough to beat.[7] Stratton was defeated by Otto Kerner.

Powell's close friends from downstate listened to his advice even after he left the legislature. As secretary of state from 1965 to 1970, he commanded an extensive network of jobs in every corner of Illinois. He was known to withhold benefits and political dividends from his enemies or those persons who failed to listen to his advice. Those who remained in legislative leadership after he won the executive position, such as Choate, sought his ear on most major policy initiatives and maneuvers.

As a successful politician at the top of his game, Powell had more than a few officials and colleagues who wanted his scalp instead of his help. Some, notably Democrat representative Anthony Scariano, condemned virtually everything Powell did and questioned his every motive.[8] Through his career as state representative, state senator, and lieutenant governor, Paul Simon clashed with Powell in public and behind the scenes. Simon believed Powell was a crook, although he had done some positive things in public policy.[9] Representative Abner Mikva, another northern Illinois Democrat who often felt the political dagger of Powell, appreciated the Vienna resident's skill as a master legislator but fought him just the same.[10] C. L. McCormick, a Republican legislator from Vienna and special friend of Powell, offered this much quoted assessment of that opposition: "Powell comes from Johnson County, whose steep hills necessitate wearing thick heeled shoes. Sniping at Powell's heels won't hurt him a bit."[11]

Contending with those who would diminish his authority came with the territory, Powell claimed. Aside from differences over public policy matters, a fair share of the quarreling resulted from a belief by many that Powell used his position to feather his own nest. There is sufficient evidence that he accumulated personal wealth from deal making. The accusation went further, however, to paint a picture of illegal payoffs (bribes), underhanded campaign payments, and special favors paid for Powell's insider influence and access. Often verbally accused, Powell never was charged, indicted, or convicted. The lack of disclosure laws aided Powell's operations.

All of those considerations must be a part of assessing Powell's acquisition and use of power in state government, primarily during his thirty years in the legislature.

While many legislative members courted Powell's support and in turn helped him on critical votes, he acquired the loyalty of a few legislators who could be trusted to carry out orders and push public policy. First among many legislators were Clyde Choate of Anna and Clyde Lee of Mount Vernon. John Stelle, who never served a day in the legislature and whose family background differed markedly from Powell's and Choate's, must also be on the list of special friends who could generate General Assembly votes.

With Powell, these individuals helped make the period from 1949 to 1961 especially productive for southern Illinois projects and people—featuring Southern Illinois University—and also favored downstate interests. Choate worked as an understudy to Powell and eventually came into his own as a first-rate dealer in the legislature. Lee, less aggressive than Powell and Choate, provided a steady, orderly approach to public policy and coalition formation. Stelle contributed to coalitions of those interested in horse racing and veteran affairs. He often strayed from support of Democrats he disliked and pursued various means of support for Republicans. All of the men made jobs and patronage for people in their region first priorities of their efforts individually and as a team. Their lifelong roots in Little Egypt gave them faithful constituencies and connections across party lines.

Rather than coming together only when certain issues arose, these men constituted a special club. As such, they connected socially, stayed in contact when the legislature was not in session, and shared information from Chicago to the southern tip of Illinois. It made little difference which political party they favored, or what regional jurisdiction they represented. They worked together to protect their privileges as members of the General Assembly; reformers need not apply. Their reach extended to the state Senate, to Chicago interests, and to others with special interest legislation. In that respect they were inclusive, but club membership was extended to only a few. If club members gave something, they wanted something in return. Opportunities to make money ranked high. Club members contributed generously to campaigns of other members and those whose votes were available for critical issues. If they played, they stayed, for they received as much as they gave.

The supporting cast for working issues and ideas that benefited down-state interests included men with close personal ties to rural Illinois, who could keep a watchful eye on big-city political leaders.

Clyde Lee's family roots were on a farm six miles southwest of Mount Vernon, a location known by locals as "Long Prairie," on Big Muddy Creek. Born February 6, 1909, he was one of eight children.[12] His ancestors, like many southern Illinoisans, started from Virginia and stopped off in South Carolina and Tennessee before finding their way to Illinois Country. Except for a short time in the Marine Corps during World War II and several years in the Chicago area on racetrack business, his home was Mount Vernon. He spent twenty-four years in the Illinois General Assembly as a Democrat.

Lee won the office of city treasurer in 1933, and a year later was elected county treasurer. The county position was limited to one four-year term, which had him looking for work again in 1938. With name recognition as a city and county official, and a determination to campaign hard in the district precincts, Lee outpolled both incumbent House Democrats, sending one to "retirement."

Lee wasted little time in moving up another notch in the General Assembly. He ran for the state Senate in 1940 and won, with the important endorsement of the Illinois Agricultural Association. He was named to the Senate Agriculture Committee. Lee's four-year Senate term ended in 1944. By then he had waived his legislator's exemption from the Selective Service and was drafted at age thirty-four.[13] Upon return from military service he again took aim at a House seat. He defeated the incumbent Democrat and resumed a place in Springfield, with seniority.

Lee had earned credentials with the powerful county fair constituency that would influence his standing in the House and with Powell. Before entering the military, he had served as secretary of the Jefferson County Fair in Mount Vernon. The fair organization came upon hard times and folded. In 1947, Lee and others from the county bought the old fairgrounds facility in Mount Vernon and resurrected the county fair.[14] That activity led to membership in the state association of county fairs and paid off in establishing a friendship and longtime political association with Powell, who held county fair offices in Vienna and Metropolis. "I never knew Paul very well in the first sessions, but I got to know him better through the county fair association. That really was the beginning of our friendship. Over the years I would go down to Metropolis and help with harness racing down there."[15]

Because of his experiences in agriculture, Lee served on the House Agriculture Committee from 1947 until he retired. On three occasions during that time—1959, 1961, and 1965—he was chairman. However, in other sessions when Republicans led the committee, Lee still held a position of authority and power. During the years, Lee served in some capacity on all agriculture and fair organizations, keeping that coalition close.

As such, Lee had a front-row seat for legislative battles between rural and urban interests, and gained an appreciation for the differences between downstate legislators and those from Chicago. He observed, "Chicago members almost always voted as a unit, like their leader wanted them to. Where downstate we were elected on our own pretty much." In that environment, Powell had leverage. According to Lee, "Powell was a better operator than they were. He could get other Democrats as well as Republicans to vote for what he wanted." And what Powell wanted coincided nicely with Lee's priorities. "Powell wasn't a real educated man, but he was a very effective speaker. He was never at a loss of words . . . And he would answer any argument you gave him pretty quick and with a lot of enthusiasm."[16]

John Stelle brought an unusual mixture of money, politics, and horse racing to the picture of downstate activities. By the force of his personality, his "I owe nobody" attitude, and his willingness to produce payoffs for those who followed or helped him, Stelle ranked as the most controversial of the pack—Choate referred to him as "difficult." In spite of his liabilities he also knew how to count votes in the legislature and work effectively with coalitions. He understood the ways of Chicago politics and the importance of patronage. The legislators needed him, bluster and all.

The war years in Illinois provided Stelle minimal political opportunity. However, starting in 1945 Stelle, leaning on joint efforts with Powell and Edward Barrett, began weighing in on politics as if he had never been through the ordeal of 1940, during his term as governor. Stelle's first taste of victory in association with Powell occurred during the 1945 session of the legislature. The two men produced a bipartisan coalition of people with an interest in breeding horses and those tied to county fairs. This led to passage of the 1945 Harness Racing Act, which legalized pari-mutuel betting on harness races through the state.[17] The law opened the door to expansion of Illinois horse racing in the late 1940s, 1950s, and 1960s that enriched both men. One writer said of Stelle, "In horse racing circles he was the most influential downstater."[18]

As statewide political activity increased in 1947 ahead of the 1948 elections, both Stelle and Powell became aggressive in an attempt to influence the choice of party candidates for state offices. Knowing that the top of the party ticket would go to Chicago organization favorites—Adlai Stevenson, Paul Douglas, and Barrett—Stelle and Powell wanted a deal for downstate candidates to be slated for lieutenant governor, attorney general, treasurer, and auditor. The incentive for Stelle and Powell was the prospect of political jobs for southern Illinoisans, and a strengthening of downstate coalitions. Powell and Stelle got exactly what they wanted.[19] Party officials chose downstate people for state executive positions below governor and secretary of state. All of them won.

Neither Stelle nor Powell favored Stevenson as the gubernatorial nominee. Underlying the campaign efforts by Stelle and Powell for the Democratic ticket was a barely disguised contempt for Stevenson. The feeling was mutual from Stevenson and his soldiers. However, practical politics kept feelings below the radar. Regardless of Stevenson's overwhelming triumph, the attitudes of Stelle and Powell did not change. They would always view Stevenson as an inexperienced elitist.

Stelle's family tells a story that in part explains the attitude toward Stevenson. At a victory celebration breakfast at the governor's mansion in Springfield presided over by Stevenson, everyone was served pudding as dessert, while the new governor received strawberries, which were hard to find during the winter. Stelle said he might like some strawberries, too, causing Stevenson to say, "The governor eats strawberries, you eat pudding."[20] This confirmed for Stelle that Stevenson believed he was superior to all others.

That attitude may have contributed to Stelle's break with Stevenson, but there were other reasons for Stelle's subsequent rejection of some Democratic candidates for high office. As Illinois politics headed into the decade of the 1950s, Stelle demonstrated his independent nature, supporting many Republicans at the state and national levels. His choices provided evidence for critics' claims that Stelle was a "party-wrecker." He claimed to be a Democrat throughout.

Soon after the 1948 election Stelle found himself in the middle of the 1950 contest for the U.S. Senate between Lucas and Everett Dirksen, from

Pekin. Stelle broke with the Democratic Party and endorsed Dirksen over Lucas. During the campaign he met with veterans across the state in behalf of the Republican, saying, "As Americans rather than Democrats or Republicans you should vote for Dirksen."[21] With the help of votes by veterans, Dirksen won.

Stelle stayed at war with the Democratic Party as the nation and Illinois headed into the elections of 1952.[22] Stevenson's decision to seek the U.S. presidency caused a dilemma in the state Democratic Party just weeks before the general election. The party's central committee faced having to choose a candidate to oppose Republican William Stratton. Stelle and Powell, among many downstate party officials, regarded Edward Barrett as the logical choice to head the state ticket. Given Barrett's close ties to downstate politicians, including Clyde Choate, the support was not a surprise.

Stelle and Powell found themselves again opposing Stevenson, who gave his support for the nomination to Lieutenant Governor Sherwood Dixon. The Stevenson nod angered Barrett and his followers. Nevertheless, Barrett thought he had a good chance at the nomination.

A member of the state committee was newly elected East St. Louis mayor, Alvin Fields. While not a member of the inner circle of downstate Democratic leaders, Fields had every reason to support Barrett, notwithstanding his strong loyalty to Governor Stevenson. Before the central committee made its decision, Fields said he doubted that a downstate candidate could win, but he had an "open mind."[23]

Stevenson's endorsement of Dixon meant little without support from Chicago Democratic leaders. Among those was Jack Arvey, architect of the party's 1948 election sweep featuring Stevenson as governor and Paul Douglas as U.S. senator. Arvey, who remained close to Stevenson, pushed hard for the governor as presidential nominee. A final piece of the picture was Arvey's long-standing animosity toward Stelle and Barrett, going back to the fierce battles of the 1930s.

The central committee's votes were based on the number of Democratic votes cast in the last gubernatorial election as measured by congressional districts. Fields, representing the district that included St. Clair and Madison counties, had the largest number of votes to give outside Chicago and Cook County. Each congressional district's officials would cast the prescribed votes for Dixon or Barrett. Fields pointed out that if Chicago and Cook voted as a bloc, it would be enough to nominate a candidate.[24] Publicly, Fields had said he would not insist on any specific candidate, but that likely was political cover. Stelle, Powell, and Choate all were associated in the campaign to nominate Barrett, and they would be influential when Fields needed state government help for the survival of East St. Louis.

The Cook County party organization led a successful fight for Dixon. The Associated Press tally placed Fields among those voting for Barrett, but he argued with the information. Fields said, "It was unanimous for Dixon."[25] When reminded the vote was close, he added, "It was unanimous for Dixon on the last ballot." Undoubtedly, when the fight was over, everyone "voted" for the winner.

The vote illustrated the growing strength in voter numbers of the northeast portion of the state. In a showdown of that nature—outside of the legislature—Powell, Choate, and Stelle could not outvote the competition. After failing to get the nomination for Barrett, Stelle supported Stratton, whom he called "an honest man."[26]

Lost somewhere among legislative leaders whose lights shone brightly in the 1950s was the solid, quiet presence of Warren L. Wood, a longtime Republican Party servant in the Illinois House of Representatives. Importantly, during the period from 1935 to 1965—with the exception of two years for U.S. Navy service—Wood stood atop the Republican Party's House membership as Speaker during four consecutive legislative sessions from 1951–52 through 1957–58.[27] Coincidentally, those were some of the sessions of the 1950s during which Paul Powell built his reputation as a strategic legislative leader.

Wood, a native of Joliet, was born in 1910. He was a contemporary of Powell and other House leaders who devoted much of their lives to politics and to producing bipartisan legislation. The Wood family had a long history as Republicans.[28] After his graduation from the University of Illinois, Warren worked in the insurance business and managed the family's farm before and after his time in the legislature. His involvement in the family farm provided background for supporting agricultural interests and programs of importance to downstate Illinois, as well as the Republican Party.

Wood was first elected to the House in 1934 from a district that had produced two Republican members in the House. He was the youngest House member at age twenty-four.[29] In the same year, Powell won his first term in the House. They both left the legislature in 1965. For the balance of his thirty years in the House, Wood's party controlled both chambers of the legislature. Republicans had majorities of fifteen over Democrats in the 1951 and 1953 sessions. The margin over Democrats in the 1955 session was four, and in the 1957 session, after reapportionment of the House, it was eleven.[30]

His primary duty as Speaker was to push the agenda of Governor Stratton, but that often required getting help from downstate Democrats. Happy to be rid of the governorship of Adlai Stevenson, Powell found Stratton and Wood willing to listen and eager to get Democratic votes. Republicans as well as Democrats acknowledged the governor's political agility. Johnson Kanady, who served as press secretary during the second term, said Stratton "was young in years but very wise in politics."[31] Wood agreed, adding that the governor "knows Illinois like the palm of his hand." No wonder, then, that Powell and his soldiers felt at home working with Stratton and Wood, and included them in "The Club."

During the successes of downstate Democrats in the 1940s and 1950s, Clyde Choate received an education by the power brokers of southern Illinois. The youngest of the deal-making group, and initially the least politically savvy, he entered the state House in 1947. Choate's bravery on the battlefields demonstrated his personal fearlessness, but that counted for little in the bruising battles of the legislative process. He had Powell's eye from the beginning because of his heroism and the connections with Secretary of State Barrett. All Choate had to do was follow the leader and prove his willingness to learn and apply the lessons. Powell recognized the promise of the man from Anna and placed him where it counted.

Along with his reputation for bravery, Choate was an imposing physical specimen and had an engaging personality. Alan J. Dixon, who entered the House as a Democrat from Belleville in 1951, described Choate in his book *The Gentleman from Illinois*: "Choate was a strong, handsome man with thick sandy hair, a huge smile and an open and friendly manner. At the same time, he projected an image of 'devil may care' danger like a hidden canister that might explode at any moment . . . Clyde smoked Camels and usually lit one after another by using the stub of the discard. Yet, he was healthy and 'well met,' and could fight at the drop of a hat."[32]

Throughout his career of thirty years in the legislature, Choate offered a number of examples to fit Dixon's description. Describing the

Powell-Choate team, Dixon stated, "He [Choate] was Powell's 'man on the floor,' meaning he worked the votes after Powell established the objective in policy. You could tell when they were in business. They ran around the House floor gathering votes. When something major was on the table it took them more time to get things put together."[33]

Another observer of the legislature—but not a member—was Gene Callahan, who started his career as a Springfield journalist and became a close aide to both Paul Simon and Dixon. He said about Powell and Choate, "Choate and Powell were very, very close. In my view, he was closer to Choate than anyone ever in the House."[34]

Powell depended on Choate for the detail work so critical to rounding up votes, especially in a divided House. In that role Choate became critical to legislation favoring Southern Illinois University in the 1950s. As another of the southern Illinois cadre who never attended an institution of higher education, he followed Powell's lead in helping Southern Illinois University to blossom as the region's prime example of economic development. As matters turned out, Choate filled the position of chief promoter of the university twice as long as Powell, until his retirement from the House in 1977. Southern Illinois University then rewarded his loyalty with a job as lobbyist.[35]

Those legislative colleagues who spoke publicly of Choate in his prime did so with praise, in keeping with the tradition of offering silence rather than criticism of a colleague. In later years, some spoke more openly. One who did was George W. Dunne, a Chicago Democrat during the years of downstate clout. He said in an oral history, "I actually kind of thought that when I first met Clyde he was going to be a zoomer in the party, that he would ascend to great heights. But he and Paul [Powell] got to be very close working legislators. And I don't know, he just didn't aspire to any state office. And then surprisingly enough he resigned from the legislature and took on a job as lobbyist."[36] Choate always insisted that serving in the House for thirty years, much of it in leadership positions, was ambition enough.

3.
Groundwork for the Future

The 1949 General Assembly session offered promise for outcomes, especially for Democrats. For the first time in years the party controlled the House, Paul Powell assumed the position of Speaker, and a Democrat was governor. However, it would be no runaway for Democrats because Republicans controlled the Senate. When the session ended, downstate interests had done well, especially those connected to Southern Illinois University (SIU) and horse racing.

Neither of the outcomes was the work of one man, one party, or the governor. Having a maestro—Powell, in this case—helped, but the achievements resulted from creative coalitions that cut across parties and regions. Measured on a scale of importance, 1949 results on both subjects were modest. However, each opened a door to larger and more significant successes in following sessions.

SIU: Growing Up in Stages

Responsibility for the rise of SIU from little-known teachers college to widely recognized major university rested primarily in the hands of a few individuals, although hundreds or more dreamed of the day and added moral support. Well before achieving the leap to major university status with two campuses, a handful of leaders started the ball rolling. They included the following:

- Powell, in 1943, supported a bill in the House to change the name Southern Illinois Normal University to Southern Illinois University. The bill did not pass.[1] He helped pass a bill in 1947 changing the school's name to Southern Illinois University and permitting the school to offer a degree in liberal arts.
- Delyte Morris became president of SIU in 1948 and immediately put on a full-court press to elevate the school to university status and have its own separate board of trustees.[2] His energy and personality lighted up every SIU effort.
- State senator Robert G. Crisenberry, Republican from Murphysboro, had long been a promoter of increased significance for the school, and in 1949 he introduced a bill in the Republican-controlled Senate that put SIU in direct competition with the University of Illinois (U of I).
- Dr. Leo Brown of Carbondale, an avowed activist for SIU and graduate of the teachers college in 1932, pushed and prodded elected officials and rallied local citizens to apply pressure. They formed the volunteer team that brought SIU out of the higher education darkness, although Brown needed the assistance of Powell, Morris, and Crisenberry.[3]

The catalyst that put SIU on the legislative agenda in 1949 was the election of Powell as Speaker of the House. In an uncharacteristically modest comment, he said later, "I was in a position to guide Senate Bill 41 and 42 through the House, creating the Board of Trustees of Southern Illinois University."[4]

The Senate side was anchored by Crisenberry. He had entered the General Assembly a session before Powell and had been in the Senate since the session of 1937. Although Democrats swept state executive offices and reached a majority in the House as a result of the 1948 election, the state Senate remained in the control of Republicans. U of I supporters protected the school's interests in the Senate, but Crisenberry had significant seniority and a reputation for getting his way on southern Illinois issues. He began a career in education as a high school teacher in 1903 and in 1915 retired as superintendent of Carterville schools.[5] He became editor and publisher of the *Williamson County News* in Johnston City and in 1926 began his political journey as chief deputy sheriff of Jackson County and federal court bailiff. In 1932 he was elected to the state House.

In the case of SIU, political strength in the House meant little without a Senate partnership. The political challenge was crossing the partisan aisle and working on enough senators to pull the House into play. Having a senior member of the majority party in the Senate from southern Illinois meant potential public policy momentum. If Crisenberry could work his magic in the upper chamber, then Speaker Powell could take it from there. In that chamber Powell had moved quickly to get others loyal to him in critical places. For example, Clyde Lee sat on the House Education Committee. While junior in seniority, he could be eyes and ears for Powell and help generate support among others from the region.

Momentum for legislation to change the governance of SIU increased substantially in the wake of November 1948's general election returns. Having one of the two legislative chambers controlled by Democrats broke a stretch of Republican General Assembly domination dating back to 1939. During that time efforts to adjust the institution's status failed to get out of committees. Friends of the university and the alumni association were in high gear before January 1, 1949, when focus would be on the selection of a new Speaker and governor.

Although SIU gained "university" status and authority to grant a liberal arts degree through laws passed in 1947, supporters of the university chafed under an assortment of governing boards and committees that slowed implementation of decisions and placed SIU in the same category with teachers colleges.[6] First in line to regulate the school was the teachers college board of nine members appointed by the governor. Chairman of the board was director of the Department of Registration and Education, and secretary of the board was the state superintendent of public instruction, elected on a partisan ballot. If a proposal from SIU passed the college board, it still needed the approval of the registration department. Getting SIU "out of politics" was one of the goals of Senator Crisenberry: "I would favor a separate board, appointed by the governor, for Southern. A board of five members, I understand, has been suggested, with a tenure of 10 years, one member to be appointed every two years. That would make it impossible for any governor to control the board through his own appointments."[7]

Independence was a key word for those allied with SIU. Although governors rarely got involved in the appointment of faculty or administrators, they and regional politicians saw that patronage extended to nonacademic employees such as janitors, plumbers, clerks, and maintenance workers. The issue among politicians was not patronage per se but who got the jobs. The higher education arrangement called for patronage to start in Springfield and go down to party leadership at the local level.

Equality was another standard of interest especially when it came to the U of I, which had a separate board and workers who were employed under civil service laws. Crisenberry also stressed that SIU's needs were different from the four teachers colleges. "It is the only accredited four-year liberal arts college in Southern Illinois and it is growing so fast it has its own special problems," he observed.[8] As might be expected, the U of I and its political supporters did not see the issue as it was presented by Crisenberry. Early in the legislative session, after Crisenberry had introduced his bill in the Senate, politicians and administrators loyal to the U of I began mounting opposition to independence and equality for SIU. One argument centered on increased competition between large universities for limited resources. Rather than support the SIU plan, Senator Everett R. Peters, Republican from St. Joseph, called for a single board presiding over all state schools, saying, "Something will have to be done to stop the fight between schools over money."[9] Peters, whose district included the U of I, and Powell both served on the state budgetary commission, which had almost supreme control over the allocation of state funds.

While Powell awaited action in the Senate on SIU bills, he worked his magic in other ways. He and Peters agreed the budgetary commission would visit the SIU campus as part of its consideration of a $37 million request for new buildings on the campus. The visit also served as an opportunity for all members of the commission to be lobbied for other subjects. Powell also arranged quietly for President Morris of SIU and President George D. Stoddard of the U of I to meet and agree not to complicate the issue—at least publicly.[10]

As the session plodded along until May, or about six weeks before adjournment, Crisenberry's bill quietly gathered support in spite of some opposition. It finally made the Senate floor late in the month. Meanwhile, another attempt to stall the SIU plan surfaced in the House with a bill introduced by Representative Ora D. Dillavou of Urbana.[11] His plan was to put SIU under jurisdiction of the U of I board, much as the medical center in Chicago was. He claimed that U of I president Stoddard did not object to the plan. That meant only that the president chose not to get involved with a side play. As to whether Stoddard would try in any way to defeat the SIU proposal for a single board, he had assured SIU officials he would not be opposed. That meant the politicians could fight it out by themselves.

During the Senate floor debate, known opponents had their day publicly. Those included Peters, who continued to promote a single board for all colleges and universities. One southern Illinois senator, Democrat Kent Lewis from Robinson, spoke in opposition mainly to express concern for additional budgetary pressure if the SIU request were granted. William J. Connors, Republican minority leader from Chicago, sounded a solemn note when he mentioned that the Department of Registration and Education was opposed, as was Governor Stevenson. The final Senate tally spoke volumes for Crisenberry's hard work in the halls and offices of colleagues. The bill passed 28 to 9, calling for a board of seven individuals appointed by the governor for six-year terms. Not more than four of the members could be from one party.[12]

Through all these meanderings it became clear that two obstacles stood in the way of an SIU victory: the U of I and its friends in the legislature, and Stevenson. The governor never spoke explicitly about his reasons for opposition, but some kind of compromise would be necessary to get him on board. Meanwhile, Powell would take care of the U of I on his own terms and make sure SIU would get its separate board of trustees and a piece of the higher education pie.

In an attempt to get Stevenson's approval, a special subcommittee of the House Education Committee worked out an agreement with the governor that would give SIU permission to have its own board of trustees for a two-year trial period. At that time an assessment would be made of its operations by a special commission appointed by the governor. The agreement also included appointment by the governor of a seven-member board for the two years. Although no one expected the trustee plan to be reversed in 1951, it gave both the governor and SIU a temporary victory. Dillavou's proposal to put SIU under the control of the U of I trustees died in subcommittee. Recommendations were reported to the House Education Committee that approved the Senate plan 14 to 1, with two voting "present." The full House approved the board scheme 108 to 6. After the Senate approved the compromise, Stevenson signed the bill.[13]

Stevenson appointed the seven-member board after recommendations from community leaders. All but one member lived in southern Illinois, and the partisan breakdown was five Democrats and two Republicans. Leo Brown was chosen as chair of the trustees at the first meeting on July 18, 1949. Senator Crisenberry commented after the governor's action, "This marks the end of a long hard fight—probably not the end, either, because we must show in two years that this is the proper way to operate the institution."[14] Powell made no public statement, probably because he already knew about the likely fights ahead.

The payoff that began for SIU in 1949 benefited hundreds if not thousands of individuals connected to the school or dependent upon its expenditures. Politically, those who had attached themselves to SIU's future could claim at various times a share of the credit. The state's financial investment in SIU went directly to the school, and as far as is known today, little if any of it was diverted into special-interest pockets.

In one other major piece of legislation during the 1949 session that called for a different coalition of political interests, the fruits were more widely distributed into designated pockets.

Horse Racing's 1949 Jackpot

The Harness Racing Act of 1945 opened the door to pari-mutuel betting on a sport that had been the exclusive playground of horse breeders and county fairs. However, racetrack people, looking for investment money and larger purses, wanted more—more summer and fall dates, more opportunities for Illinois breeders' horses, and more prestige. About all the 1945 law had done was protect county fairs and thoroughbred racetracks and expand limited betting. Track interests could hardly wait to enlarge the harness racing landscape.

The horse racing floodgates opened in 1949, providing southern Illinois political interests an opportunity to ride the waves to personal riches. However, individuals did not receive all the money. Laws passed in 1949 also provided the state of Illinois with a fresh supply of revenue, badly needed to relieve state coffers from sales tax dependence. In all, institutional and personal beneficiaries collected much and often.

Illinois had a long history of horse racing dating to the 1800s. Laws regulating betting appeared in the 1920s.[15] In 1945 new laws provided expansion of harness racing. As is often the case with landmark legislation at the state or federal level, a critical mass of forces came together with the General Assembly session of 1949. The elements included a Democratic majority in the House, a Speaker committed to an expansion of racing, and interested parties across downstate such as county fairs, owners of racehorses, and speculators who could see prospects for growth. Combined with legislation affecting the future of SIU, the impact raised the region's political clout to new heights.

The precise timing of action leading to 1949 is difficult to pinpoint. Work behind the scenes had been done for years, anticipating a day when Democrats would control the House. Two of the key strategists were Powell and Representative Henry J. Knauf. When Powell became Speaker in 1949, Knauf was named chairman of the agriculture committee. Knauf's horse racing credentials were well known.[16] In 1949 he served as president of the U.S. Trotting Association, and he owned a large horse breeding farm. Knauf took the lead in convincing the county fair association to provide leadership. Powell placed Representative Clyde Lee on the agriculture committee where he could keep the Speaker informed of progress.

Quietly, these forces crafted two bills that met the needs of all interested parties. Reluctant interests, fearing that an expansion of harness racing might damage interest at county fairs, were targeted and convinced by forceful voices that expansion would benefit all. To help persuade hesitant groups, a separate bill was produced that increased the state subsidy for fairs by $1,000 each. Sponsors of the two racing bills were carefully chosen.[17] With Clyde Lee's name on the bill everyone was assured of Powell's support. The involvement of two key Republican House members, Clifford C. Hunter, from Taylorville, and W. P. Westbrook, from Harrisburg, sent the message that this was a bipartisan effort.

Five weeks before the June 30 legislative adjournment deadline, House Bill 1104, dealing with harness racing, and House Bill 756, increasing the allocation to county fairs, were introduced without fanfare. Hardly any press coverage occurred. House Bill 1104 provided these changes to the 1945 act:

- allowed harness racing between April 15 and November 15 and opened racing on the third Monday in July to the last day of August, which had been preserved for county and state fair racing only;

- eliminated prohibition on harness racing within five miles of any thoroughbred racing track licensed for the same date;
- gave the state racing commission authority to grant harness racing licenses to horse racing tracks where it served the best interest of the public and the sport.

This broad authority made it possible to license racing under any circumstances.

Movement of the bills in the House was guaranteed, but the state Senate remained in Republican hands. GOP senator Simon Lantz of Woodford County east of Peoria supported the bill but wanted it handled by a Democrat to provide bipartisan flavor. Powell and friends chose Senator John W. Fribley of Pana, who had served in the Senate since 1933.[18]

That lineup left only Governor Adlai Stevenson as the questionable link. His 1948 election campaign victory occurred in large part because Stevenson attacked gambling interests and accompanying corruption. With that background, would he sign laws expanding legal gambling across the state?

According to William (Smokey) Downey, who became an assistant to Governor William Stratton from 1952 to 1959, Powell took the issue directly to Stevenson. Downey stated, "The only reason he [Stevenson] signed it [was] Paul Powell . . . He [Stevenson] was against it. And Powell said, I heard him tell it myself, 'You're thinking about running for governor again. Have you any other ideas of running for office? Every county fair in the state of Illinois, they'll all be against you because this is going to help them.' And Powell was right about it. And that's how mutuel harness racing went on in the state."[19] Beyond Downey's account there is no evidence of such a meeting, but in the political context of 1949 the story makes sense.

With all hands on board, the harness racing bill moved quickly through the House. The House Agriculture Committee approved it 16 to 0, and the full House concurred 117 to 0. On the Senate side, the plan met no opposition. That chamber's agriculture committee signed on 11 to 0, and on June 27, the full Senate voted for it 45 to 0. In his message to the legislature Governor Stevenson voiced approval, describing the scheme primarily as likely to boost state revenue by $2.4 million. He made no mention of the impact on harness racing. Stevenson signed the bill into law on July 1.[20]

While the making of law proceeded, a parallel deal developed, providing an opportunity for personal financial gain. Racing speculators at work in the Chicago area knew of the legislation from conferences with Powell. They assured the Speaker that their plans for harness racing at Sportsman's Park, a thoroughbred racing venue, would provide great demand for horses bred by southern Illinois interests. With Powell's encouragement the Chicago people filed incorporation papers on May 4 for Chicago Downs. When it became clear that legislation would pass, investors formed a trust holding all shares of stock for the venture. The first meeting of Chicago Downs occurred on July 18.[21]

During the remaining weeks of summer the payoff took form. Heading the effort was a racing operative named Irwin (Big Sam) Wiedrick, who had connections to more than one Chicago area track.[22] He had worked behind the scenes with Powell and friends on the legislation as a promoter and investor in the Chicago Downs concept. In order to compensate those legislators who helped set the Chicago Downs table, Wiedrick offered stock to about forty selected individuals at ten cents a share.[23] At the top of the list, Powell purchased 16,900 shares in the name of his wife, Daisy. Fewer shares were offered to other participants. Clyde Lee purchased 1,000 shares. Others included Representative Reed F. Cutler, Republican dealmaker from Lewistown, 1,000 shares; Senator Fribley, 500; Anna Mae Harris, wife of Representative Lloyd (Curly) Harris, Democrat of Granite City, 100; Senator Roland V. Libonati, Democrat of Chicago, 200; Senator Everett Peters, Republican of St. Joseph and benefactor of the U of I, 1,000; wife of James Ryan, Chicago's leader in the House, 1,000; and Senator Frank Ryan, of Chicago, 2,000. Except for Powell, reasons for the precise number of shares offered were never made public. Naturally, when the deal became public all participants denied the purchases had anything to do with passage of the law. Lee said, "Best investment I ever made . . . If I'd have had any judgment I could have bought more stock. But I thought that a hundred dollars was all I could take a chance on."[24]

Participants soon learned the value of their shares. Chicago Downs issued a dividend of $1 a share almost as soon as the harness racing season began. Powell's wife received $16,900, all perfectly legal, and in Powell's case carefully listed on his income tax return for 1949. As Chicago Downs prospered, it was a gift that kept giving for Powell until his death in 1970. A close relationship with Wiedrick for the next twenty years also paid handsomely for Powell.

Critics of laws expanding horse racing and track betting claimed primarily that the beneficiaries were cronies and that serving them was wrong. A few argued that tracks encouraged gambling, attracted unsavory elements, and generally were a public nuisance. They also objected to legislation that lined the pockets of politicians and track owners, and they promoted bills to increase taxes on racing operations. There were not enough angry legislators to stop pro-racetrack momentum.

However, winning the legislative battles was not enough for track promoters. For the purpose of marketing, public discourse, and arguments during the consideration of legislation, supporters claimed that state revenues from racing benefited the general public through numerous specific state programs. Racing operations provided thousands of jobs and paid healthy dividends to investors other than insiders. Track revenues paid for security, financed facilities upkeep, and maintained public safety measures. From the standpoint of entertainment, increasing attendance numbers testified to customer interest. The total mutuel handle—the amount waged at all tracks—increased from $205,619,228 in 1946 to $344,712,055 in 1963.[25]

Proceeds from taxes on wagering, admission taxes, and license and application fees provided funds for programs that otherwise would have used general fund money or would not have been funded. For example, during the biennium 1963–64 track revenue sources amounted to $52,978,371. The state general fund received $4,876,234, or only 9.2 percent of the total.[26] Specific funds receiving the balance included retirement of bonds for bonuses paid to veterans of World War II and the Korean conflict, grants-in-aid to state and county fairs, racing purses and stakes for colts at county fairs and racetracks licensed by the state racing board, retirement of bonds for McCormick Place in Chicago, veterans rehabilitation funds, and money for harness racing purses at the Illinois State Fair.

Coincidentally, the rapid increase in racetrack income and revenues to the state occurred from 1946 to 1964 when Powell and associates held legislative leadership positions.

Cahokia Downs: A Political Blessing

John Stelle's fertile mind seemed at work no matter how many others projects were under way or being formulated. In the wake of the gubernatorial disaster of 1940, he and two well-connected political friends from St. Clair and Madison counties fashioned their dream of a thoroughbred racetrack built across the Mississippi River from St. Louis.[27] They imagined a track operation financed by investors from the ranks of business and politics across the state. The goals: entertainment, wealth, and patronage. The three agreed there would be no partisan political lines drawn for investors. Participants would be chosen for their ability to succeed in politics, regardless of party. It became the home place of one of the mightiest political coalitions of the 1950s and 1960s.

For Stelle, the idea stemmed from his association with county fairs, horse breeders, people with money, and, naturally, politics. He shared the idea with two political kingpins, Dan McGlynn, Republican fund-raiser (especially for Governor Dwight Green) and operative in the East St. Louis bipartisan government machine; and Schaefer O'Neill, a successful Alton lawyer and Democrat who served six terms in the state House from 1933 to 1943.[28] All three of the track dreamers were political contemporaries connected to various local and state maneuvers.

Stelle could not have picked two men more able to make things happen in the two counties that bordered the Mississippi River across from St. Louis. They knew the people who would be interested, they knew how to manipulate laws, and they knew how to keep a secret until it was time to go public. Aside from his connection with St. Clair County power brokers, McGlynn's key role was selection of a site for the track in St. Clair County. Paul Powell became part of the master plan, although his role was carefully concealed from the public. This was the storied beginning of Cahokia Downs racetrack in Alorton, just outside East St. Louis.

The racetrack connection with Daniel McGlynn of East St. Louis is a classic example of Stelle reaching beyond partisanship to an individual who fit the need and brought much to the table in terms of political experience and raising money. There may not have been any more effective operative on the ground for locating Cahokia Downs.

McGlynn, an attorney in East St. Louis, emerged from Republican domination of local and state politics in the 1920s. He did an apprenticeship in Republican precinct politics, discovering that running campaigns for others improved his political resume. Over more than thirty years of activism he never ran for public office. McGlynn's grassroots work helped elect Republican Frank Doyle mayor of East St. Louis in 1929.[29] Doyle appointed McGlynn the city's corporation counsel, a position he held during Republican and Democratic administrations until 1950, except for the period 1929–33, when he was named to the state commerce commission.[30] Always near the seat of power, McGlynn became Mr. Inside. To others, he was Mr. Republican in a Democratic-controlled environment.

At one time McGlynn said publicly, "I want to make it clear that I have always been a Republican, and always will be."[31] After retiring from politics in the late 1950s, he stated, "I have never voted a straight ticket in my life," adding that no slate of candidates was perfect.[32]

In the 1928 state election McGlynn helped round up Republican votes for Louis Emmerson, who won the battle for governor. His reward was a four-year term on the Illinois Commerce Commission that regulated utilities and transportation. He served until the election of Governor Horner in 1932. McGlynn's next opportunity to help a Republican candidate for governor occurred in the election of 1940. Republicans nominated Dwight Green, the prosecutor who helped send Al Capone to prison. Green needed a robust turnout downstate to overcome the Chicago machine's expected turnout. He also needed money for his campaign. McGlynn knew about political money, having raised it successfully for years, for Democrats and Republicans.[33]

McGlynn earned a place in Green's heart, or at least toward the top of his list of benefactors. Green also knew that McGlynn could help narrow the assumed Democratic margin in St. Clair County, although no one expected a Republican majority in that location. McGlynn figured Green would be a top-notch source of patronage if he won, and that incentive made the Irishman work hard for the Republican candidate. During his final campaign visit in East St. Louis in October 1940 Green concluded a meeting with precinct committeemen by saying, "I want everybody to know that Dan McGlynn is not only a leader in East St. Louis, but in downstate as well, and when I am elected governor he will sit beside me."[34] The closest McGlynn came to serving in a state position secured by Green was when the governor named the East St. Louisan to the state housing board in 1943.[35]

Green won election with a plurality of 256,945 votes or 52.93 percent of the total.[36] Amazingly, the Republican won by a slim margin in Cook County and rolled up victory margins in the suburban collar counties. St. Clair County provided 36,361 votes for Green, while his Democratic opponent Harry Hershey captured 50,632.[37] McGlynn did not provide a triumph in St. Clair, but he had gained sufficient stature with the new governor to be named recipient of the governor's patronage for the region. While the spoils went to the winner, it brought notoriety, as McGlynn learned during Green's eight-year tenure. The governor's patronage for St. Clair County involved more than 600 county residents on the state payroll.[38]

McGlynn's fund-raising relationship with Green continued in the governor's reelection campaigns of 1944 and 1948. The nagging presence of commercial gambling and related rackets throughout the state gained headlines during the 1948 state elections that ended with the election of Adlai E. Stevenson II as governor. He rode to victory on waves of articles by newspapers that documented widespread illegal gambling operations and corruption involving high-ranking Republicans. The most aggressive reporting appeared in issues of the *St. Louis Post-Dispatch* and included articles about the raising of campaign money with ties to questionable influences for incumbent governor Green. Articles by investigative reporter Theodore C. (Ted) Link in September 1948 exposed contributions to the Green campaign in 1944 and declared the same was occurring in 1948. The revelations about 1944 solicitations included fund-raising efforts by McGlynn.

Link wrote in one article, "The East Side [Illinois] fund for Gov. Green was raised under the direction of Dan McGlynn, East St. Louis lawyer and St. Clair County Republican boss. Gamblers who contributed told the *Post-Dispatch* they did so after learning that McGlynn wanted them to. There was no interference from authorities in St. Clair County."[39] Link claimed that "policy kings," meaning McGlynn and associates in Madison County, contributed $15,000 in Green's primary campaign and $25,000 for his general election fund. In the 1940s those were substantial numbers. Without the benefit of campaign disclosure laws, Link and other reporters depended on anonymous sources that included people with close ties to gamblers.

The victory of Stevenson ended McGlynn's long run as a statewide Republican operative, but he continued as a political force in St. Clair County. Regarding the Alorton racetrack subject, McGlynn's notoriety as a fund-raiser would not have concerned Stelle. In fact, McGlynn's access to the pocketbooks of politicians and businessmen assured his place in the formation of Cahokia Downs.

Stelle was no stranger to activism in behalf of pari-mutuel betting and horse racing. In 1945 he collaborated with Powell, then serving as Democratic assistant minority leader in the state House of Representatives, to pass the Illinois Harness Racing Act. Republican governor Dwight Green signed the bill and was applauded by the state organization of county fairs that supported Stelle and Powell in their legislative efforts. Green's participation underscored bipartisan flavor for horse racing.

Accomplishing the Cahokia Downs goal took years of work behind the scenes. The three founders intended to involve blue-chip political friends in a land trust that would provide initial funding for the venture. About a hundred people were contacted to invest $5,000 each, with portions allocated to shares in the trust and shares of common stock.[40] Prior to 1953 financing for the scheme was in place, and the track opened a year later with widespread publicity, the first thoroughbred racing venue outside the Chicago area. Political people across Illinois were "all in" the scheme up to their foreheads. Until his death in 1962, Stelle remained president of Cahokia Downs. He owned shares in other Illinois racetracks that paid greater returns, but Cahokia received more public attention, especially in southern Illinois, and formed the core of legislative support for many ventures. The ownership arrangement included several forms of potential income for investors:

1. *A land trust.* These investors owned the land beneath the racetrack. By Illinois law the names of owners remained confidential. These shares were preferred by investors and paid the most consistent dividends. Holders of trust shares remained unknown publicly until after 1970 when legal inquiries into the estate of Paul Powell required disclosure. But until then, investors remained anonymous. When revealed, trust shares totaled eighty-five, with most individuals holding a single share, except for a handful of insiders.

2. *Common stock in the operation of Cahokia Downs.* These shares, held widely throughout Illinois, paid small dividends because rent on the land paid from revenues went to land trust owners. Thus, the holders of common stock paid rent to themselves if they were owners of trust stock. Shareholders were known publicly. Original investors owned the bulk of shares before they were offered widely.

3. *Debentures and bonds.* When capital was required for racetrack operations and capital improvements, land trust investors loaned money for debentures and bonds. They received interest rates of 8 percent per year. Ten-year bonds also were issued for the original racetrack and paid 6 percent interest.

The world became aware of those involved, with total disclosure of shareholder interests only after the 1970 death of Powell, a holder of trust shares, common stock, and debentures, and a leader in political operations at the track. Because of federal and state tax investigations into Powell's estate, the state racing commission ruled that stock owners no longer could receive exemption from public scrutiny. That ruling and documents in Powell's papers revealed the extent of political involvement and the payoff for St. Clair and Madison counties in patronage. Newspapers pounced on the information and spread it across the state. The revelations were eye-openers.

The list of investors in all forms of securities leaned heavily toward politics and business.[41] Most had connections with Stelle, McGlynn, Powell, and O'Neill and provided impressive influence in the legislature, where racetrack bills frequently surfaced and were debated. The names of prominent investors included these:

- State representative Clyde Choate, who by 1954 was one of Powell's closest operatives in the legislature
- State representative Clyde Lee, southern Illinois Democratic leader and investor with Powell, Stelle, Choate, and others in Chicago area racetracks
- George Edward Day, who became manager of Cahokia Downs primarily on the strength of his role as former state purchasing agent in the administration of Governor Stelle (Among original shareholders he was one of the few drawing a salary. He owned about 13 percent of the common stock shares, second only to Stelle.)
- Jean Barrett of Chicago, wife of Edward J. Barrett, former secretary of state and close friend of Stelle, Powell, Choate, and others in southern Illinois politics
- State senator Everett Peters, strong supporter of the U of I who produced compromises with Powell that benefited SIU projects
- Mrs. Janice Lewis Marsh of Tuscola, daughter of Republican John S. Lewis, who served as Speaker of the House in the 1963 session
- U.S. representative Mel Price, longtime congressman from St. Clair County and friend of countless participants in Cahokia Downs
- Alvin Fields, mayor of East St. Louis from 1951 to 1971, vice chairman of the Democratic State Central Committee and leader of the strongest party political organization outside of Cook County

- Francis Fields, Alvin's brother who managed the family plumbing business (The Fields brothers benefited directly through installation and continuing maintenance of the racetrack's plumbing features.)
- John M. Karns Jr., Democratic state's attorney of St. Clair County and later a judge
- S. H. Kernan, former chief engineer of the politically driven East Side Levee District and political ally of Fields
- William W. Downey, aide to former governor William Stratton, and Patricia Downey

The opening of the track in Alorton, just outside East St. Louis, was a special political gift to Mayor Fields. With little more than a nod to those who dreamed of the track and made it happen, he was handed instant patronage in the form of jobs for people in St. Clair County. Because of the founders' political connections, Fields's reach to legislators who voted appropriations for cities was widened. State legislators and officials who bought stock and made frequent trips to the betting window were a who's who of leaders in both parties. Cahokia Downs was a political institution built and maintained by personal contributions and favors.

Alvin Fields was no overnight political wonder. The road to power and influence at the local and state levels required an apprenticeship of more than twenty years of labor in the backroom precincts of East St. Louis and St. Clair County. When he became mayor of the city in 1951, Fields had earned the title of "Survivor-in-Chief." He spent the next two decades consolidating his grasp of a tarnished ring. Fields took control of a city with a financial crisis so severe that it paralyzed municipal operations. The Cahokia Downs political blessing came at a propitious time, when Fields needed to consolidate forces after a bruising election campaign. Handing out jobs worked wonders.

Fields was proof that timing can be almost everything in politics and that successful comebacks go to those who slog through the political mud with head held just a little higher than the competition. Fortunately for him and his family he had a day job in the plumbing business that paid the bills while he dabbled in politics. In spite of all that had been crummy and criminal in the history of East St. Louis for decades, Fields escaped indictment, imprisonment, and attempts to remove him from office. After his election in 1951, efforts to change the picture of East St. Louis never got off the ground, because managing machine politics consumed most waking hours and reform would have spelled political disaster. If politics is local, then politicians are the ones who define "local." Fields was a prime product and practitioner of local politics.

By all accounts, Fields was always ambitious politically, but he also had shown initiative in shaping his working career. After graduation from East St. Louis High School he attended night school at Washington University in St. Louis while working as a plumber's apprentice. To improve his prospects, Fields attended a trade school to learn about blueprints and drafting, both important elements in a plumber's career. During that time he joined the East St. Louis Plumbers Union Local 360 and from 1927 to 1932 served as its business agent.[42] For two decades while other politicians came and went in East St. Louis, Fields hung around, in and out of office. In 1947 he was elected to the city council, which proved a stepping-stone to mayor in 1951.

At no point in Fields's twenty years as mayor did his administration overcome revenue shortages and escalating municipal debt. In large part that was the result of years of revenue shortages before Fields became mayor. Over the years businesses and industries that might have helped the city with tax revenues moved outside the city limits where they hoped to remain out of the clutches of a tax-hungry machine.

Without prospects for new streams of tax revenue, pressures mounted to cut city expenses. Fields and his administration refused to consider that alternative. The idea would have endangered the political machine's ability to hand out jobs and keep wages relatively high. This was just one of the dilemmas for a dominant machine whose primary role was to maintain the status quo. If the city administration could not come to grips with its problems, it was not likely to get help from people who made deals in the state legislature. Try at he might in pleas to governors and legislators, Fields was unable to get much attention or access to state funds.[43] When a state income tax materialized in 1969, any part of the revenues diverted to city coffers would have been too late.

During Fields's early years as mayor he got an earful from the dealmakers, even if they did not come to his aid. In 1954, the year Cahokia Downs opened, Fields received this letter from Paul Powell:

> The other night on my way home I stopped in Mt. Vernon and
> while reading the paper I saw where your city needs state aid
> and that you were trying to find ways to raise funds for your city.
> While reading this, I could not help but remember when your
> own State Representative [Al] Dixon voted "no" on House Bill
> 411 in the recent [1953] session which would have given you all
> the funds you need. It might be a good idea to find out now just
> where he will stand in the next session—merely a suggestion
> because you know where I will be for anything that you want.[44]

Powell sent along an entrance pass to all racetracks in the state.

The letter represents more antipathy toward Dixon by Powell than a fair statement of Dixon's support for Fields and East St. Louis. Through his years in the House from 1951 to 1963, and in the state Senate from 1963 to 1971, Dixon carried a load of legislation for Fields, including Cahokia Airport, payment of relocation expenses due to displacement for highway construction, "back-door referendums," and financial needs for the city.[45] As a result, Dixon could always count on support of the Fields machine at election time and when he needed help in obtaining leadership positions in the state Senate. While Powell did not count Dixon among his associates and Dixon did not consider himself friendly with Powell, they both counted on Fields for help.[46]

On another occasion, before Democrats chose House leadership for the 1955 session, Powell wrote in a letter to Fields that he heard longtime state representative from East St. Louis, Frank Holten, was seeking support from members and party officials. After explaining his approach to being chosen House leader, Powell said, "I believe that we are going to have some very controversial legislation in the coming session, and whoever is selected as the leader will have to be someone who can slug it out and who knows the ins and outs of legislative procedure. I am wondering if you would want to talk with Holten regarding this."[47] Powell was chosen minority leader.

The election of Fields, the forty-eight-year-old master plumber and veteran politician, pulled St. Clair and Madison counties into the statewide spotlight. He joined the Democratic State Central Committee by election in 1952, representing the Twenty-fourth Congressional District, made up mostly of St. Clair and Madison counties. He won reelection easily in 1954 and 1956.[48] At that point Richard Daley sat as chairman of the powerful committee that slated candidates for state offices. Out of respect for the Democratic voting strength of the region, Daley made Fields vice chairman. As Fields's relationship with Daley blossomed, rumors circulated that Fields might be slated for a state office, but he denied any interest.

In terms of power, being vice chairman did not mean much. Daley called the shots, although he went through the motions of listening to members of the committee. The benefits of being vice chairman included sharing some spotlight with Daley and being in line for state and national patronage. Fields could express his opinion about statewide candidates, but that was about the limit. His voice could be lifted on behalf of downstate and southern Illinois interests, but the impact was difficult to measure. Fields also needed all the connections he could muster among legislators to help East St. Louis. He appealed often to state legislators and governors for increased state aid to cities, with few substantial results. The only time southern Illinois legislators came to the city was to play the ponies at Cahokia Downs. From Fields's point of view, at least they were nearby.

Jobs at the track were spread among lower-level political appointees and government employees in the two counties, including workers for both political parties. The founders placed family members in jobs, also. Because of their bipartisan background, both parties benefited.

A look at the list of employees of the track, published in a 1962 newspaper series on Cahokia Downs, revealed the extent of patronage, which did not change much in numbers over the years.[49] Some of those with jobs were a grandson of a state representative, Fields's son-in-law, McGlynn's nephews, a state parole agent, president of the East St. Louis park board, a Madison County juvenile probation officer (former mayor of Venice), an administrative assistant of East St. Louis sewer district, a clerk for county jury commission, East St. Louis city comptroller, township assistant supervisors, an East St. Louis city clerk, and a former East St. Louis school board member and state license inspector. Most of the employees of the department concerned with wagering at the track were hired through the county political system. They included members of the Building Service Employees Union.

One of the largest shareholders in Cahokia Downs was Powell, at the time perhaps the state's most controversial and influential legislator. For obvious reasons, Stelle, and others involved, decided to keep Powell's name off the list of public ownership. Consequently, Stelle and Day held Powell's common stock shares in their names, while Powell paid the income taxes.[50] Newspaper reporters could never pinpoint Powell's racetrack total ownership at Cahokia Downs until after his death. While there is no public record of Stelle's income from his Cahokia investments, or that of Choate and Lee, Powell's income tax records were made public after his death in 1970, and information is available for speculation because he was among the largest shareholders.

Powell's tax returns provide a glimpse of the income claimed by one of the racetrack's biggest and most influential investors. Powell received income from two and five-eighths shares of the land trust, common stock shares dividends, and interest on debentures. From the outset of financial returns in 1954 until 1969, the year before Powell died, he declared income of $33,120, an annual average of $2,208.[51] Those were hardly astronomical returns when compared to Powell's income from other racetrack investments. Choate, with one land trust share, in 1963 held 250 common stock shares, a comparatively small number when compared to the founders. Lee held one and three-eighths shares in the land trust. Judging from Powell's numbers, no one got rich during the first fifteen years of operations, perhaps with the exception of Day.

Notwithstanding the modest returns, Powell squeezed the operation for every ounce of political leverage. When it came to wining and dining state politicians from near and far, Powell and Stelle were at the center of activity, working hand in hand with Day and Clyde Lee, who served primarily as Powell's right hand. Specifically, favors went to those who provided a quid pro quo when it came to voting on racetrack legislation. They received free passes to Cahokia Downs, their requests for horse stalls were honored, and they were invited as special guests to cocktail and dinner parties at the track. The favored politicians also became nominees for stock holdings.

Powell kept a record of votes on key legislation by those who had received favors.[52] In one case, Representative Charles W. Clabaugh of Champaign failed to vote with Powell on one issue and didn't vote on another. Powell wrote, "Send no additional passes." Representative Gale Williams from southern Illinois voted against Powell on two track bills, and Powell wrote, "Don't send any additional passes." On one occasion in 1963, after a major vote on track appropriations in the state Senate, he wrote about

Senator Dixon from Belleville, "This damn Senator Dixon from Belleville voted against us in the Senate. I gave him some passes to Cahokia, but I sure as hell will not give him any more."

By all outward indications, the Cahokia Downs operation during the years of Stelle's involvement as president rocked along without serious public controversy. And that may be a tribute to Stelle, who dealt personally with members of the board as well as longtime friends and associates. Any clashes were handled quietly.

Stelle's friends included J. Ralph Hutchison Sr., who grew up within twenty miles of Stelle in the McLeansboro-Harrisburg area. Although not a follower of horse racing or a member of racing interest groups, Hutchison was offered shares in the trust and 5,000 shares of common stock. He obtained 8 percent annual return on $20,000 in debenture notes and was named to the board of directors. Hutchison explained his insider opportunity: "I bought when Stelle was promoting the track and because it was a good investment."[53] When Hutchison wanted information about operations, he went directly to Stelle and did not bother with asking Day, the operations manager. Hutchison trusted his friend Stelle as a "shrewd, hard but fair businessman." Hutchison and Day did not form a friendship.

After Stelle's death, Day assumed greater control of Cahokia Downs, not to the liking of Hutchison, who said, "Day and I never did see eye-to-eye. He always resented me going over his head to Stelle to get information. My first real clash with Day occurred when I asked about the Cahokia Downs payroll. I wanted to know who was getting what salary. I went to the bookkeeper, and he held me off until he contacted Day."

Not long after Stelle's death, Day moved to reduce the board from fifteen members to eleven. One of those dropped from the board was Hutchison, who explained, "I was aware they wanted apple polishers and yes men as members. Also, I knew that after Stelle died I would have to fall in line or get out, and I got out." Hutchison said during his board membership, "I fought to keep the race track clean and free of all hoodlum connections. My constant inquiries along these lines were resented, and I knew it." Newspaper accounts of activities at Cahokia Downs frequently claimed that employees at the track included those with criminal records and histories as gang members. Although Day and others may have wanted Hutchison to sell his share of the operations, he did not. He stated in 1963, "This has proven to be a sound investment and I have no intention of selling."

Stelle's sons held shares in various racetrack operations, including Cahokia Downs, and inherited their father's extensive holdings. After Stelle's death, officials of Cahokia Downs, including those who were part of the early conversations, wrote to all shareholders about Stelle's interest in the formation of Cahokia Downs: "Cahokia was one of John Stelle's most important dreams. He loved the sport of thoroughbred racing from boyhood, and into Cahokia in the past nine years he poured his constant efforts and time, all contributed personally, with no expense or charge to the track. He sought in every way to keep the ownership and management of Cahokia on a high level."[54] His son John A. Stelle took over as president and served until 1978. He participated fully in concealing Powell's holdings, as had his father.

The favored investors in Cahokia Downs also benefited from ownership in other racetrack operations that began as part of the St. Clair County operation. Egyptian Trotting Association—obviously a reference to southern Illinois territory—was a harness racing venture that began at Cahokia Downs in 1957.[55] The plan was to keep racing in motion as much of the year as possible, offsetting fixed operational costs and providing further opportunities for profits and political gratuities. This was also seen as establishing a stronger track presence in downstate Illinois.

Stelle owned 12,590 shares of common stock, and debentures worth $5,000, in both cases more than any other investor. Powell, a strong booster of Egyptian, held 6,750 shares and $2,700 in debentures. According to a racetrack statement in 1962, Egyptian shareholders included political powers Mayor Fields (3,375 shares); McGlynn (5,862.5); Day (4,750); Clyde Lee (4,050); Clyde Choate (6,750); Carl H. Preihs, legislator and Powell's partner in ownership of a racehorse (6,750); U.S. representative Daniel Rostenkowski of Chicago, a powerful member of Congress (2,500); and state senator Everett Peters (2,700). All had holdings in debentures.[56]

The first years for Egyptian ended in revenue losses, and it became apparent that harness racing at Cahokia Downs had no future. With Clyde Lee's leadership, Egyptian relocated to Maywood Park in the Chicago area, where it almost overnight found favor and returned handsome profits for shareholders. Powell's federal tax returns provide one view of dividends and interest from which comparisons can be made for others. From 1961 through 1969, Powell received $67,411 from his Egyptian holdings, averaging $7,490 per year. The avalanche of profits, however, started in 1964.

Powell declared $8,437 in 1964, $11,837 in 1965, $3,375 in 1966, $16,875 in 1967, $18,225 in 1968, and $7,425 in 1969.[57] Assuming he held the same number of shares listed in 1961, one comparison is with Choate, whose number of shares was the same as Powell's. It is possible that both men either increased their holdings or sold shares. Nonetheless, participants in Egyptian reaped a harvest of profits outstripping amounts received from Cahokia Downs.

Newspaper reports indicated Stelle also owned 3,874 shares in Chicago's Fox Valley racetrack. Other investors receiving Fox Valley dividends included Powell, McGlynn, Day, and O'Neill. Political connections across the state and especially in southern Illinois paid off in the 1950s and 1960s when the legislature passed laws allowing racetracks to hold racing meetings for longer periods each year and to pay lower rates of tax on betting income. Powell and other investors in Cahokia pushed the legislation through and blunted attempts by a few legislators to increase taxes on horse racing.

Because Powell's tax returns were made public, there is a record of payments he received—and on which he paid taxes—for such vague reasons as "finder's fees" and "public relations."[58] Powell was under no obligation on his tax return to explain how much business he found or what public relations services he provided. In reality, they were payments for his help in building and maintaining horse racing in the 1950s and 1960s. Some payments were made while he served in the legislature, but he received substantial amounts after he was elected secretary of state in 1964. The assumption must be that no matter what position he held, Powell served and received. The payments were the finest examples of the chumminess that existed on the record and off, for which there is only presumption and rumor regarding friends of Powell.

Clyde Lee was eternally grateful to Powell for bringing him on board as the legislature constructed and passed laws enlarging horse racing in Illinois. Lee served strategically on committees in the House and in pushing legislation developed and guided by Powell. When Cahokia Downs opened, Lee was a beneficiary and served as an unpaid political associate. All of that must be viewed as helping a loyal associate. But when the Powell-Stelle-O'Neill group produced Egyptian Trotting, Lee's world changed. He followed Egyptian to the Chicago area, where it became a substantial financial success.[59] Lee ran the operation and worked closely with other racetrack interests in the region. Powell was already a major shareholder in Egyptian, so what could Lee do for him? The answer began in 1963 and lasted until 1969. Egyptian Trotting, presumably at the behest of Lee, paid Powell $3,000 a year for public relations.

However, Egyptian's payment was chump change when compared to the arrangement Powell had with track and political operative Irwin S. (Big Sam) Wiedrick. Powell, Stelle, Lee, and all the major players in horse racing were associated with Wiedrick beginning in the 1940s and continuing at least until Powell's death in 1970. Wiedrick, operating as a consultant for Chicago area tracks, helped set up the payoff scheme for legislators in 1949 who passed harness racing laws that helped create Chicago Downs racetrack and opened the door to increased track activity.[60] As a measure of thanks to the legislators, Wiedrick arranged for them to purchase stock in Chicago Downs for ten cents a share. Thanks to Wiedrick's generosity, Powell's tax returns reveal that he received $451,045 in Chicago Downs dividends before his death in 1970.[61]

The sweetheart part of the arrangement between Wiedrick and Powell was a series of payments under the heading of "finder's fee," or consultant's fee. Wiedrick agreed to split his consulting fees from Chicago tracks fifty-fifty with Powell for helping Wiedrick's business. The annual individual payments ranged from $7,500 to $20,000, and by Powell's death reached a total of $140,000. Powell said about the arrangement, "My dealings with Sam Wiedrick were completely legal, legitimate, honest and honorable, unless making money has been declared to be a crime."[62] By virtue of the dividends and fee splitting with Wiedrick, Powell received nearly $600,000. With this mountain of annual cash flow Powell was able to invest widely in small town banks and corporate stocks, increasing his net worth substantially. That is how he got by on a state government salary that never exceeded $30,000 a year. Few of his track cohorts did as well as Powell, but horse racing money flowed freely to many, thanks to the coalition of interests.

Paul Powell grew up in this Victorian house, referred to as the "Thomas Powell House" in Vienna. Courtesy of the Johnson County Genealogical and Historical Society.

John H. Stelle issued a proclamation on October 7, 1940, for a ten-day observance of mourning for Governor Henry Horner. Abraham Lincoln Presidential Library and Museum.

Governor John Stelle rides a mule presented by Sam Plant of Murphysboro, who allegedly stole a mule from Stelle during World War I in France. Plant is seen holding the mule. Abraham Lincoln Presidential Library and Museum.

Secretary of State Edward J. Barrett was a close political friend of southern Illinois legislators. Abraham Lincoln Presidential Library and Museum.

Staff Sergeant Clyde L. Choate, of Anna, Illinois, is awarded the Medal of Honor by President Harry S. Truman on August 23, 1945. National Archives (111-SC-210881).

Tank destroyer of the 601st Tank Destroyer Battalion is guided down the ramp on-shore at St. Tropez, France, August 1944. The tank destroyer is similar to one used in combat by Staff Sergeant Clyde L. Choate. Richard Heller, warfoto.com.

Democrat Paul Powell (left) and Republican governor William Stratton often found common ground on issues affecting downstate Illinois. Abraham Lincoln Presidential Library and Museum.

Representative Paul Powell (left), nearing the end of his legislative career in 1964, greets Southern Illinois University president Delyte Morris after a state budgetary commission subcommittee meeting in Edwardsville. Abraham Lincoln Presidential Library and Museum.

Alvin G. Fields, mayor of East St. Louis for twenty years, benefited politically from operations of Cahokia Downs racetrack. Abraham Lincoln Presidential Library and Museum.

Paul Powell (left) and Chicago mayor Richard J. Daley were cordial in public but had political battles in private. Abraham Lincoln Presidential Library and Museum.

Representative Clyde Choate (left) and Paul Powell received awards from the Illinois Quarter Horse Association. Abraham Lincoln Presidential Library and Museum.

4.
Glory Years for Downstate

The Illinois General Assembly sessions from 1953 to 1963 are historically significant for deals and results that favored downstate interests. The overwhelming political strength of Chicago and Cook County
developed after that decade.

Today's observers might find statements about the earlier days hard to
digest given the direction of contemporary legislative activities and executive leadership. This is even more extraordinary when studying the reasons
for results in the earlier years. Much of the progressive record in state government depended on bipartisan behavior and coalitions that cut across
geographic regions. Chicago Democrats needed downstate Democrats and
sometimes Republicans to pass their agendas. Downstate leaders fared better if they could peel off some Chicago votes to go with other factions. No
political party or faction could force its will on the rest of the state for long.

Another factor influencing outcomes in the 1950s and early 1960s was
the change in Chicago leadership. Richard J. Daley ascended to mayor of
Chicago in 1955. While his imprint was immediate, he took a few years to
grasp the controls after the reapportionment of the legislature that favored
Chicago and Cook County. During that time Republican governor William Stratton and Speaker Warren Wood and Democratic leaders such as
Paul Powell and Clyde Choate maintained important leverage. A critical
element in outcomes was Powell's election as Speaker of the House in
1959 and 1961, which provided a momentary counter to Chicago interests.

Powell, Stratton, and other realistic politicians could see the future, and they knew time was running out for downstate.

The Near-Miracle of SIU

In this period of dynamic change brought on by the roaring postwar economy and veterans and their families, pressure mounted rapidly on the state's higher education system and the sources of revenue. Illinois depended almost totally on sales taxes to support operations. Out of this mix of turmoil and opportunity came the unpredictable—and in some ways improbable—story of Southern Illinois University (SIU).

Miracles rarely happen in state politics. While SIU's rise from 1946 to 1961 now looks explosive and preordained, it took a huge effort, some luck, forceful advocates, and time. The building blocks of progress are easy to see in retrospect. The arrival of veterans after World War II and an improved economy provided a natural increase in student population, even though SIU remained a "teachers college." With a new president, Delyte Morris, and state government recognition in 1947 of the school as a "university," hard work still remained. For the state to provide sufficient funds for real and anticipated growth, SIU needed prestige, and that required an expanded curriculum to include professions such as engineering, medicine, dentistry, and law. An accelerated building program, featuring offices and student residences, would be necessary to accommodate an expanding school population. If accomplished, an impressive campus would lure even more students.

As the 1950s decade opened, the University of Illinois (U of I) sat atop the hill of state higher education as a formidable giant. Retention of that position depended on maintaining a tradition of distinction and excellence. Much of its prowess relied on the influence of its graduates working in state government and on loyalists scattered across the state who could be rallied to a cause at a moment's notice. Beneath the U of I in stature were all the other four-year state colleges: Southern, Eastern, Northern, Western, and Illinois State, originally designated as teachers colleges. SIU had begun to emerge from the pack with legislative recognition as a university and with a board of trustees devoted solely to the school. Those advancements provided the first view of a threat in Urbana-Champaign. However, the U of I stood firm for its prerogatives and did not intend to share. Increasingly, SIU partisans identified the U of I as an obstacle that had to be attacked head on.

SIU powerhouses applied pressure on critical pieces of growth strategy: budget increases, buildings, and curriculum. In terms of clout and energy, they had the bases covered. President Morris took the public route, testifying, making speeches, and issuing public statements. Powell, with Choate at his side, handled House proceedings, and Powell used his position on the legislative budgetary commission to confront U of I partisans.[1]

Joining Powell and Choate in Springfield was a recent graduate of the U of I College of Law named John S. Rendleman, who quickly became a valuable asset. Morris had appointed him SIU's acting legal counsel and lobbyist in 1951, a role that put Rendleman at Morris's side and in Powell's pocket for much of the university's heyday in Springfield. As Powell's personal lawyer and executor of his estate, Rendleman was a factor in Powell's life and death.[2] Senator Crisenberry, an essential resource, had a firm grip on issues in the state Senate. Running interference, whether as a member of the SIU trustees or as Powell's spear-carrier, was Dr. Leo Brown of Carbondale and a host of other volunteers. The common mission and coordinated efforts combined to elevate SIU in the statewide higher education picture.

As an indication of SIU growth after World War II, enrollment reveals a part of SIU's story, as it applied pressure for legislative action. The beginning student enrollment for the Carbondale campus totaled 2,734 in 1949 and by 1957 had reached 8,311 including students at centers in East St. Louis and Alton.[3] While the U of I enjoyed a larger increase in numbers over the same period, the rate of growth at SIU was greater. As all colleges and universities showed increases in enrollments, they projected even larger numbers for the future in hopes that those numbers would spur the legislature to provide increased funds. In the late 1950s, SIU officials claimed the 1970 enrollment would top 16,000 for the Carbondale campus.[4] Rarely did the General Assembly respond to hyped numbers or estimates that stretched out farther than a year or two. All schools had to fight tenaciously for every dollar each legislative session. The history of increases in enrollment, however, provided evidence that the trend was upward.

Another aspect of the picture was the battle for funds to meet the demands of students on hand. In that respect, increases in revenue were more dramatic because of the larger numbers and relentless pressure from all of higher education. Back in 1935—Paul Powell's first term in the House— when SIU was referred to as Southern Illinois Normal College, the school received a state appropriation of $663,900 to cover two years.[5]

The legislature met in the odd-numbered years to pass a state budget for the biennium. This was the budgeting method for the period in these comparisons. By 1949, Powell's first year as Speaker of the House, SIU received a two-year appropriation for general expenses that was ten times the 1935 number: $6,500,634.[6] The biennial appropriations for "ordinary and contingent expenses" through 1961 for SIU were:

1949	$6,500,634
1951	$7,092,400
1953	$9,794,003
1955	$14,677,426
1957	$22,902,139
1959	$32,142,000
1961	$42,285,690

These were the beginning appropriations, but there were additional amounts for capital expenditures to maintain and to expand the physical campus. Also, more funds were appropriated for "ordinary and contingent expenses" when expenditures outstripped budgets. Capital expenses were appropriated separately. In 1949 the legislature approved $7,100,000 for land acquisition, completion of a training school, and final work on the power plant.[7] During the 1951–52 biennium SIU needed an additional $520,000 to balance the general fund books, and it was provided by a special appropriation. At best, then, the original appropriations figures are useful only for comparative purposes, and in almost every biennium the total amount was greater. This system resulted in part from the approach to budgeting by school and state officials. The university offered a proposed budget for the biennium; the governor often reduced that amount in his proposed budget; and the legislature arrived at a number in between.

State representative James Holloway, a Democrat, was first elected to the state legislature in 1959 and thereafter served in the same southern Illinois district with Clyde Choate. In an oral history Holloway offered this practical description for the process of making up shortfalls in appropriations: "A few times we had to go back in for reappropriation because they were running out of money . . . I think at that time, during those years, budgets were a little less than what they figured because we were growing by leaps and bounds . . . They always estimated low and it looked better because when you went in before the Budgetary Commission the next year you could always refer back and say, 'Look, you know, there's no fat in this thing because we had to come back and ask for more money.'"[8]

Regardless of the vagaries of the appropriations process, the facts are clear: the funds available for SIU's operations increased significantly in the period under discussion. And the same was true for all higher education institutions. The tug-of-war behind the headlines often involved the two strongest personalities on the state budgetary commission, Senator Peters and Powell.[9] Legend has it that on a number of occasions Powell said he would not approve the U of I budget figure unless he received substantial increases for SIU. A primary keeper of the Powell stories was Dr. Brown, who served one term as an SIU trustee and lobbied energetically for a measure of parity with the U of I. He told this story: "The principal force to achieve this [separate board of trustees] was established by Paul Powell of Vienna, Illinois. I was present when he shook his fist in the face of the president of the University of Illinois Board of Trustees and the president of the university and stated, 'Goddammit I will not call your God damn [appropriations] bill unless Southern Illinois University at Carbondale gets its separate board of trustees and begins to get a piece of the pie.'"[10] The story varied a bit according to the audience listening. It would be a mistake, however, to presume that Powell always got his way or that U of I interests slinked away in defeat and humiliation.

Between SIU and the U of I there were many "showdowns," none more dramatic than fights over curriculum and degree demands by the "new kid on the block." As demonstrated, SIU added students, but an additional propellant for funding came from changes in curriculum. The administration under the leadership of Morris and the autonomous board of trustees proposed and authorized numerous changes and put funding requests in budgets presented to the legislature. These changes helped the image of SIU as a growing factor in higher education, but that was a small hill to climb compared to receiving permission to offer professional degrees.

Simply speaking, the U of I had the law on its side. In a law passed during the 1943 General Assembly, SIU was specifically prohibited from issuing professional degrees in "law, medicine, dentistry, pharmacy, engineering or agriculture."[11] The two universities entered the curriculum battlefield when Senator Crisenberry submitted a bill in the 1953 legislative session authorizing the school to provide bachelor degrees in agriculture and engineering. (He was a member of the state Senate when the 1943 law was passed.) Without a new law granting degree authority, SIU still offered instruction in agriculture and engineering for two years. At that point, majors either sought a different degree or transferred to another university.

Whether Crisenberry truly expected little trouble in getting passage, or wanted to poke the giant to see if it was awake, he didn't say. Crisenberry explained why he waited until early May to offer the Senate bill: "I purposely waited until our budget bill had gone through the Senate before introducing this bill because this bill does not require any more money. For that reason I didn't feel it was necessary to get the governor's approval for this bill. There should be no opposition since no addition to the faculty or the buildings and equipment is needed."[12] So much for wishful thinking. The giant was not asleep.

Within its authority granted by the General Assembly, the U of I controlled the issuing of degrees in agriculture and engineering, and its officials did not intend to allow SIU to change the 1943 law. At a hearing before the Senate Education Committee at the end of May 1953, the U of I came out in force to contest the assumptions of Crisenberry and SIU and to defend its authority to offer degrees in agriculture and engineering.[13] Morris led the SIU contingent and spoke to the need for professional degrees. Primarily, he stated an argument based on the "depressed economy" of the region and the need to have facilities close at hand for students with limited resources.

When testimony shifted to agriculture, Dean Robert R. Hudelson of the U of I College of Agriculture said, "The state can't afford to develop a complete college of agriculture beyond that at the land-grant university. An agriculture college at SIU is not needed or justified."[14] He added that an SIU college "would cost millions." Hudelson commented further about SIU youths not being able to afford going away from the area to college: "I earned my way through college, and I have watched hundreds of others do the same. A young man strongly anxious to get an education is not prevented from doing so because he would have to move away from home."

Professor W. G. Kammlade, director of agriculture extension at the U of I, said he "resented" the implication that the large university had no interest in southern Illinois. Of prospective students, he added, "All they need is desire and effort to get an education. What we need to do is to teach these people they have opportunities at the University of Illinois."

U of I officials also summarily dismissed the plea for a degree only in industrial engineering. Professor Norman A. Parker, head of the Department of Mechanical Engineering, said the U of I offered all degree choices in engineering and could take care of "double the number of students now enrolled." He offered to make room for all transfers from SIU. Senator Peters, the U of I's strongest advocate in the Senate, said the U of I did not neglect southern Illinois' educational needs. The Senate Education Committee rejected the bill by a vote of 10 to 3.[15] Whether that reflected an opinion about agriculture and engineering, or just one of the two, remained unclear.

Two years later in the 1955 session of the General Assembly, SIU forces decided to pursue agriculture and engineering in separate bills. Freed of the more controversial engineering proposal, the bill for degrees in agriculture passed, setting in motion a proposal for agriculture and greenhouse facilities on campus. Momentum for the project had begun in 1954 and received overwhelming support from the Jackson County Building and Construction Trades Council, representing various American Federation of Labor construction crafts union locals in the county, and Local 841 of the United Brotherhood of Carpenters and Joiners of America.[16] Also backing the building plan were the Illinois Agriculture Association, Southern Illinois Horticultural Society, and Prairie Farms Creamery of Carbondale. When approved in 1955, the proposed building was to contain twenty-six classrooms and a 500-seat auditorium. The projected total cost was $2.6 million, with completion scheduled for the spring of 1957.

At a cornerstone-laying ceremony in June 1956, Governor Stratton stated, "It is important to realize that developing the agriculture program here at Southern Illinois University is of vital interest to all the people of the state."[17] Morris noted in his comments that the ceremony marked the fourth successive year in which the governor had laid the cornerstone for a new building. Already on schedule for dedication in 1957 were six dormitories.

When the legislature began its biennial session in 1957, the engineering proposal remained in limbo with no signs of weakening by U of I officials and supporters. SIU had worked every nook and cranny of the state Senate for support beginning in 1953, and appeared little closer to victory. Crisenberry submitted a new bill as the session opened, setting the stage for a series of hearings by the education committee. Meanwhile, two subjects related to the future of higher education and SIU gathered momentum. One involved establishing an oversight state board of education that would referee disputes among universities over degree programs. Also, in the Metro-East area across the Mississippi River from St. Louis talk escalated about an increased SIU presence. In the dynamic period of the 1950s, no single subject, such as an engineering program, could dominate discussions for long.

Bills were introduced in 1951 and 1953 to establish what some called a "super board" that would have broad powers to control programs and budgets for higher education. University and college officials reacted negatively to the idea, and the bills did not progress. The issue of coordination among the schools, ignited every session by controversies between the U of I and SIU, would not go away. Prompted by Governor Stratton, who knew better than anyone the relentless pressures on state revenues, the legislature in 1955 established a bipartisan higher education commission made up of nine members with no ties to any of the state colleges or universities. The commission's report in 1957 recommended an advisory board consisting of one member representing each of the boards for SIU, the U of I, and teachers colleges. Community colleges and private institutions also had representation. The two large universities supported the concept but kept a watchful eye on further recommendations.[18]

The SIU board in 1949 had authorized a "residence center" in Belleville to provide area schoolteachers and administrators with continuing education opportunities. This decision had generated demand for course offerings to serve students from St. Clair and Madison counties. A special representative from SIU, Harold W. See, organized the Southwestern Illinois Council for Higher Education (SWICHE) to coordinate interests and activists in the region. See and SWICHE convinced President Morris of the increased demand for higher education in the heavily populated area, and studies for more specifics began.[19] During 1957 SIU opened additional residence centers in Alton and in East St. Louis, with expanded course offerings. These efforts produced a groundswell of support for a second SIU campus.

In anticipation of a further fight for an engineering school during the 1957 session, SIU had received a supportive report in December from Professor Ovid W. Eshbach, former dean of Northwestern University's

Technological Institute. The university hired Eshbach to conduct a six-month impact study for an engineering degree in time for the 1957 session.[20] Eshbach would be a primary witness for SIU at the hearings. The bill went to the Senate Education Committee on January 14. In support of the bill, SIU stated that the lack of an engineering program was hurting efforts to attract industry to southern Illinois. To counter arguments that a second engineering school would be too costly, SIU said only thirteen new faculty members would be added in the first five years, to complement the existing faculty for the two-year program.[21] Facilities for the school would be built for $4,500,000, the university said.

At the first committee hearing on May 1, engineering dean William L. Everitt presented the U of I case against expansion. He said a single engineering program at the U of I could do a better job of educating undergraduate and graduate students, adding that outstanding teachers were in short supply. Appearing for SIU were Morris and SIU board chairman John P. Wham. Eshbach offered his conclusions that a second engineering school would increase total engineering enrollment in Illinois: "The program contemplated at Southern is not a big one, and does not include graduate work in engineering. But with the national shortage of engineers, four-year graduates in that field can easily take their places in good positions in industry."[22] He also leveled a shot at the U of I, claiming that the school's opposition was "the selfish promotion of their own prestige." Committee members deadlocked 8 to 8 at the hearing's conclusion. At a second session of the committee on May 8 the committee vote remained 8 to 8.[23] No one wanted to give ground.

Throughout the session the two sides lobbied hard. U of I loyalists swamped legislators with calls and letters. While it appeared to be an organized effort, U of I president David D. Henry denied any campaign. He said, "There is no pattern of opposition. Where there have been differences of opinion each case has been regarded on its merits without any general overtones."[24] SIU partisans weren't buying it. Crisenberry claimed, "I feel the University of Illinois would like to see all higher education controlled on one campus."[25] Meanwhile, SIU asked downstate labor leaders to call on Governor Stratton, and the regional promotional organization, Southern Illinois Inc., prepared materials and appeared at the hearings.

A third Senate committee vote on June 5 decided the matter for the 1957 biennium. Members voted down the proposal 9 to 5. Some members of the committee acknowledged that they caved in to pressure from U of I sympathizers.[26] At least one said it was the toughest vote he had made, and while he supported SIU's request, he could not ignore lobbying by the opponents.

An indication of the incendiary feelings on both sides was a letter made public after the vote from a leading Rosiclare, Illinois, industrialist, Jacob Blecheisen, who accused President Henry of "standing in the way of the educational and economic improvement of the southern Illinois area . . . If it be true that your university stands in the ranks of the opposition—then I say it reflects adversely upon you and the University of Illinois."[27] Splitting hairs later, state representative Holloway of southern Illinois, stated, "I wouldn't necessarily say they [U of I] were in opposition to the other state schools such as Southern Illinois University but more in competition with them. They all vied for appropriations in competition with one another. So from that standpoint, yes, there would be opposition to the expansion of Southern Illinois University."[28]

Beyond the struggles of the two universities over curriculum, financial pressures produced cooperative momentum for a statewide bond issue to expand facilities. SIU wanted increased capital funds to meet future enrollment expectations. Also, interest in a second campus to serve the Metro-East area had led SIU trustees to explore land options in Madison and St. Clair counties in the spring of 1958.

Meanwhile in Chicago, Mayor Daley applied pressure for a downtown campus of the U of I. The estimated cost of locating a campus in Chicago was staggering. It also was still a dream, for Daley did not have a specific site and had not won approval of the U of I Board of Trustees.[29]

If financed out of the state's general fund, there would be no leftover funds available to run the state. The answer: a 1958 statewide bond issue vote. The Edwardsville campus of SIU and the Chicago campus of the U of I headed the list. But in the spirit of spreading the benefits around to assure a positive vote, funds would have gone to the Carbondale campus of SIU, the Urbana-Champaign campus of the U of I, and all teachers colleges. To broaden interest in the vote, bonds also were proposed for welfare department capital needs. The total amount: $248 million.

A simple majority of those voting on the issue was not sufficient for approval because of a peculiar provision in the 1870 Illinois Constitution that regulated approval by a majority of persons voting for members of the Illinois General Assembly. For example, if five million people voted in the election and 4,675,000 voted for legislators, then 2,337,501 yes votes on the bond issue would be required for passage. As bond issue promoters explained to citizens, a vote not cast on the bond issue was actually a "no" vote.[30]

The bond proposal failed at the ballot box. It received 1,460,701 yes votes, a simple majority, but not enough to meet the constitutional standard. The highest legislative vote totaled 3,209,908 votes, which meant the bond issue needed 1,604,955 yes votes to pass. Supporters had no choice but to go back to the drawing board for the 1960 election.

The legislature began by separating the two bond proposals so that each would stand on its own in the election. Higher education would receive $195 million and welfare facilities $150 million. The total exceeded the 1958 bond issue by $105 million.[31] By the standards of today, those numbers look modest, but in 1960 they were massive. The same universities would receive funds, with emphasis on SIU at Edwardsville and the Chicago campus of the U of I.

In a well-orchestrated public relations campaign, daily newspapers near the universities ran countless articles and editorials promoting approval. More than 200 students carried torches for 750 miles from southern to northern Illinois. Speeches by presidents Henry and Morris cited statistics to show current facilities could not handle the expected onslaught of enrollments. The leaders' speeches stoked fears that students would be turned away.[32] Governor Stratton, seeking a third term, and his Democratic opponent, Otto Kerner, backed the proposal. Stratton had appointed a "Committee of 100" to work for the issue, saying, "We will be set back at least a generation . . . if we don't get it."

On election day voters approved both bond issues.[33] Only 12 of 102 counties provided constitutional majorities for the higher education proposal: Cook, Will, McHenry, McDonough, Champaign, Marion, Madison, Macoupin, DuPage, Kane, Lake, and LaSalle. Notably missing were St. Clair, near the SIU-Edwardsville location, and Jackson, home of SIU, which gave simple majorities but failed the constitutional test.[34] Large majorities in Cook and Madison provided the margin of victory. Behind the scenes the big winners were those who had pushed for General Assembly backing. As will be shown, the campaign had the effect of bringing Paul Powell and Everett Peters together. It appeared everyone could claim victory.

Legislation setting the bond issue vote did not include amounts to be divided among the beneficiaries, but an agreement of school officials and legislators was confirmed in 1961 with plans to appropriate the money. SIU was to receive $53,200,000, with $25,000,000 designated for launching the Edwardsville campus.[35] The U of I was the big winner with $98,500,000 allotted to the Chicago plan and the Urbana-Champaign campus combined. Governor Kerner signed appropriations bills passed by the legislature for those amounts in July 1961. As funds were appropriated, SIU announced plans for six major buildings to be constructed at the Carbondale campus.[36]

Although universities and legislators cooperated on the extensive non-partisan 1960 bond campaign, no progress was made in the 1959 legislative session on the matter of an engineering degree at SIU. One reason was the political effort required to launch the bond issue campaign. Another was the uproar created at the beginning of the 1959 session when Paul Powell, Governor Stratton, and Republican House members engineered a deal for Speaker of the House. For the first time since 1948, Democrats elected a majority of members to the House, 91 to 86. Mayor Daley automatically controlled the votes of fifty-four members from Chicago and Cook County. They endorsed Joseph L. De La Cour of Chicago for Speaker. Powell announced his own candidacy for Speaker. He reached agreement for support of thirty-two downstate Democrats at a separate caucus of invited members, which caused a serious split in the party. It simply was not acceptable to party leaders for a "rump" caucus to be held.[37]

A southern Illinois rookie House member, James Holloway, later explained the importance of a downstate vote for Powell.[38] Shortly after arriving in Springfield before his first session in 1959, a House member close to Powell said to Holloway, "Powell wants to see you." Holloway followed the command and met Powell in his headquarters at the St. Nicholas Hotel. When Powell and Holloway were alone, the veteran said, according to Holloway, "I want to ask you to bolt the Democratic caucus tonight. Instead, I want you to meet with me and the other downstate Democrats at a place on the southwest side of Springfield, out on the Old Jacksonville Road. I'm asking you to vote for me for speaker of the House come tomorrow morning." Holloway said he would think about it. He consulted with James Ronan, a Democratic Party official, and was told: "I want you to vote for Powell for speaker tomorrow morning. You happen to be the only new downstate Democrat and more in particular right in his own backyard. If you don't support his candidacy for speaker, he'll cut your head off and you'll bleed to death . . . You know you outran Clyde Choate in the general election and you can just bet they're [Choate's friends] going to throw the kitchen sink at you in the next election. There's no use making any more problems or trouble for yourself than you're already going to have." Holloway voted for Powell. Holloway said he always called Powell "Mister."

With Democrats deadlocked, Powell worked the backroom to get support of all but a few Republican House members. They planned to vote on the first ballot for Warren L. Wood, who had been Speaker for the sessions beginning in 1951. On the second ballot, Republicans agreed to vote for Powell. That script was followed almost to the letter with Powell elected Speaker 116 to 59.[39]

Critical Links between Powell and Stratton

The relationship between Powell and Stratton created a critical bargaining link during the governor's two terms and led to the passage of significant state policy. Powell seemed eager to work with Stratton after a four-year testy relationship with Governor Adlai E. Stevenson. Before election as governor in 1952, Stratton had performed in state and federal offices as a conservative who was willing to work with Democrats, which appealed to Powell. Their cooperation on major legislation appeared in some cases to be unification against Chicago interests, but both men knew when and how to work with northeastern Illinois Democrats, especially after the election of Daley as mayor. The other major factor in reaching agreements was that Republicans held a majority in the House and Senate in the sessions of 1951, 1953, 1955, and 1957. Powell needed help working across the partisan aisle.

One of Stratton's first priorities as governor was to redistrict the state House and Senate to balance districts according to population. According to the 1950 census, Chicago's population of 3,620,962 accounted for 42 percent of the state's total. Together with Cook County, the percentage was 52.[40] That figure did not include the suburbs outside Cook County. Chicago's growth had been increasing significantly for decades, while downstate numbers decreased.

Regardless of the trend, Illinois had not altered its legislative district plan for fifty years. That had perpetuated downstate strength in the General

Assembly in spite of population shifts. While the Illinois Constitution called for periodic redistricting, legislatures ignored that provision and courts chose not to interfere. Stratton was determined to change the picture. He submitted a resolution to the General Assembly during the 1953 session that called for fifty-nine House districts, an increase of seven, and fifty-eight Senate districts, an increase of six.[41] The increases would have involved districts in the Chicago influence zone. Stratton's resolution called for a statewide vote in 1954, and if approved the changes would occur during the 1955 General Assembly session. The governor believed that by increasing the total number of districts he could provide Cook County a bigger piece of the action without reducing the districts downstate. His plan would have left the Senate controlled by downstate interests regardless of the increase in districts.

Unsure of giving any ground to Chicago and Cook County, key downstate politicians of both parties balked, bringing a near stalemate on the Stratton resolution in the House. Powell, then minority leader, was among the earliest to object and attempt to stop the movement toward a vote. Stratton compromised enough for Powell to back off and allow the House to approve the resolution. While the governor's plan for redistricting the House was untouched, he agreed not to make any changes in the Senate district layout. Also, by adding to House districts in northeast Illinois, it virtually assured that incumbent representatives downstate would be protected.

That's when the real fight began. Stratton had put together an impressive pro–constitutional amendment task force to convince voters. Richard J. Daley, then preparing his race for mayor and serving as Cook County Democratic chairman, pledged precinct support for the amendment. Stratton went on the state campaign trail to add his voice to the discussion. As the campaign progressed, Powell became the primary voice of opposition. He claimed Stratton "was selfishly trying to use the remap to make political hay in Chicago."[42] Dredging up longtime fears by downstaters of Chicago dominating public affairs, Powell listed potential shifts of power to the big city: "Schools in sparsely settled areas in Illinois will be closed, a state property tax will be reinstituted, the University of Illinois and the state capital will both be moved to Chicago, and a state sales tax would be cut to benefit Chicago and Cook County residents."[43]

Not for the first time—nor for the last—Representative Alan J. Dixon, Democrat of Belleville, bucked the rhetorical winds of southern Illinois legislative leaders regarding the 1954 proposal to reapportion the General Assembly. While many of the voices around Dixon, primarily Powell and friends, claimed that approval of reapportionment would give Cook County control of the House and Senate, Dixon argued, "I voted for the resolution [to put the issue on the ballot] and I am supporting the proposal amendment now. The opponents of this resolution cannot honestly claim, as unfortunately some are doing, that this proposed amendment will give Cook County control of the legislature. I hear this repeatedly from the lips of some of the most intelligent, well-informed, downstate legislators. The honest fact of the matter, as every legislator knows, is that the balance of power will still be quite safely tucked away in the back pocket of downstate legislators."[44]

Dixon cited the ballot proposal as "an honorable compromise, as is almost any legislation in Illinois, or the nation, that is highly controversial in character. There is nothing shameful about honest compromise." Dixon offered the audience three reasons for his support of reapportionment:

1. The amendment still leaves control of both houses in the Illinois legislature in the hands of the so-called downstate-thinking legislators.
2. This amendment is an honorable compromise, which, while completely satisfying almost no one, embodies most of the elementary principles of fair play.
3. This amendment will reapportion a great modern midwestern state after over fifty years of inaction and lethargy, and more perfectly attune it to the times.

Dixon's choice may have been easier because the amendment would have little or no impact on St. Clair or Madison counties, the center of downstate's strongest Democratic political machine.

Powell's smooth-talking oratory failed to convince voters. The amendment passed 2 to 1 downstate and 11 to 1 in Cook County.[45] In his chapter on Illinois reapportionment in *Redistricting: An Exercise in Prophesy*, Professor Paul M. Green, a keen observer of state government, concluded, "Despite five decades of fears and apprehensions, the political ramifications of the 1955 reapportionment were not earthshaking."[46] He quoted Sam Gove, another expert on state political affairs: "A post session analysis of the 1956 election concluded that reapportionment had brought about no profound changes."[47]

The Powell-Stratton clash might have seriously damaged relationships between the two men had the principals not been Powell and Stratton. They were consummate dealmakers with a quick reading of legislative votes and mostly rhetorical loyalty to political parties. Both intended to be on the scene for a number of years, and they could see the need for future coalitions.

During the redistricting fight they worked with Republican Speaker Warren Wood and Representative Reed Cutler, Republican dealmaker from Lewistown in Fulton County, to create a Department of Personnel that was approved in 1955.[48] The proposal upset many legislators who feared it would have a negative influence on patronage. However, Powell, who never turned down an opportunity to spread patronage, won over many reluctant colleagues and led House Democrats in support of the idea. There would come a time when Powell received payment in full.

Not everyone in Illinois politics agreed with the coalition of interests led by Stratton and Powell. This became evident in 1959 when the governor proposed an increase of a half cent in the state sales tax. In an attempt to sway legislators, Stratton agreed to use proceeds for school districts. House Chicago Democrats, led by majority leader William Clark—Powell was Speaker—opposed the increase. All but a handful of Republicans backed the governor. In an unusual move during lengthy debate of the idea, Powell stepped out of the Speaker's chair and onto the floor and gave a rousing speech in support of the increase, basing his advocacy on the need for school funding and to deny any "deal" with Stratton.[49] Of course, Stratton and Republicans had made it possible for Powell to be chosen Speaker in the first place. He swayed enough downstate votes to pass the proposal and raise the tax. Downstate Democrats voting against him included Paul Simon, Alan Dixon, Clyde Choate, Clyde Lee, and James Holloway, all from the southern half of Illinois and many who helped Powell with other deals.[50]

Powell had used up most of his clout in the Speaker election and on the tax increase for something as controversial as SIU curriculum. Any agreement on an engineering degree for SIU, even if it passed the state Senate—an unlikely prospect given past votes—would be difficult to craft given present emotions. Failure of an agreement in the 1959 session marked the fourth consecutive session at which U of I interests prevailed.

SIU did not fare well on financial fronts either, probably reflecting agreements reached for the 1960 bond issue election. Having received more than $22 million from the state for general fund operations in the 1957 biennium, Morris presented the General Assembly with a request for $47.8 million in 1959. Stratton's budget reduced that amount to $27.1 million. Morris was irate. He stated, "The operating budget figure as released in the press is inadequate for correction of excessive stringencies in the current year . . . We cannot afford to sacrifice the large gains we have made in quality."[51] He asked Stratton for a meeting.

Meanwhile, at ground level in the legislature, Clyde Choate, with Powell's blessing, worked the halls to get twenty sponsors of two SIU appropriations bills. While those individuals represented mostly southern Illinois constituencies, notably two of the number were Representative William G. Clark of Chicago, House majority leader and Daley's floor captain, and Representative De La Cour, who lost the Speaker race to Powell. A general fund amount for SIU of $32.2 million, a figure midway between those advocated by Morris and Stratton, was passed and approved by the governor. Morris had requested $62 million for capital improvements, including construction of new buildings. Choate and his cohorts put a halt to that dream by agreeing to $7.1 million.[52] This obviously reflected hope that SIU would receive a large portion of bond issue funds. It also meant that in the 1959 biennium there would be no money for new buildings at SIU.

Powell's position as Speaker also meant that he would be heard by a mixture of audiences when he spoke to issues outside the legislature. As candidates lined up, or were lined up by others, for the 1960 state elections, Powell led cheers for some of his favorites. Knowing that Mayor Daley and the Democratic State Central Committee would present the party's slate for executive offices, Powell inserted his associate Clyde Choate for secretary of state. Republican Charles Carpentier had held that position since 1953. Choate, then serving as party whip in the House, did not suggest that he wanted an executive position. Hoping for someone as a candidate for governor who had close ties to downstate interests, Powell recommended his longtime friend Edward J. Barrett, who had been elected Chicago city clerk. Powell knew Daley would not greet these two suggestions with enthusiasm, and he was right. Neither person was slated.

Deal making reached a fever pitch in advance of the 1961 General Assembly session. Setting the stage was the contest for Speaker of the House. In spite of a Democratic victory for Otto Kerner as governor, reelection of Senator Paul Douglas, and a razor blade–thin plurality for presidential candidate John F. Kennedy, Republicans controlled the General Assembly. Historically strong in the Senate, the GOP held a 31 to 27 margin, and in the House the Republicans outnumbered Democrats 89 to 88.[53] The House picture begged for some kind of deal, and who but Paul Powell started to work. "All I need is 89 votes," he said bluntly. Control of the speakership rested in the hands of nominal Republicans from Chicago, all of whom worked for the Metropolitan Sanitary District. Referred to in the press and by many in the General Assembly as the "West Side Bloc," the handful of House members mostly voted with Republicans unless Mayor Daley needed their votes. That was the deal in 1961. One of Chicago's West Side Bloc Republicans voted for Powell, and for the first time in Illinois history a member of the minority party was elected Speaker.[54] For the third and last time Powell held all the cards in the House.

With that deal settled, Powell, Choate, and friends moved to settle the long-sought permission for SIU to offer an engineering degree. Identical bills were introduced in the Senate and House early in the session. Through maneuvers never fully disclosed, Senator Peters dropped his opposition to the proposal. Rumors hinted that Peters had some special-interest bills that Powell helped pass in the House. Democratic senators, with help from some Republicans, built momentum for passage. Senator William L. Grindle, from Herrin, later said he talked directly to Daley and asked for and received a promise of all the mayor's "votes."[55] By the first week in March the deal was done and virtually delivered. The Senate Education Committee, previously the roadblock to passage, approved the plan 11 to 0. Powell, with Choate taking the lead, moved the bill on a fast track without consideration by the House Education Committee.[56] A full floor vote by the House required two-thirds approval and that was granted, 107 to 35. A week later, the full House approved it 109 to 3. The Senate followed. Governor Kerner signed the bill in April.[57]

The turnaround by Peters raised an eyebrow or two, and he did nothing to clarify matters. After voting for the proposal Peters said his mind was changed because in the last two years engineering enrollment had increased enough to indicate that the state needed more engineering education. Perhaps influencing his decision was approval during the session for distribution of funds to build the U of I campus in Chicago, along with sizable revenues for the Urbana-Champaign campus. Additionally, Peters said he was seeking support for his bill to set up the fifteen-member higher education coordinating board. Not surprisingly, the bill was approved.[58] As originally approved in 1961, the Illinois Board of Higher Education had three responsibilities: 1) prepare a master plan for all public universities and junior colleges; 2) approve or disapprove establishment of all new colleges, schools, institutes, departments, or research programs; and 3) analyze university budgets and submit recommendations to the governor and General Assembly. The U of I and SIU initially had the advantage of two members—one from each campus—while all others had only one.

As might be expected, everyone with any connection to SIU inside the legislature and out took credit for the breakthrough. They knew the wall had crumbled and that it was only a matter of time before SIU would offer degrees in medicine, dentistry, and law. While SIU officials remained cautious until passage by the General Assembly, plans were under way to begin offering courses leading to an engineering degree as soon as 1962. Southern Illinois, Inc., held a celebration at which Morris was cited for his leadership.[59] In remarks, Morris said that when he came to SIU, he believed three things had to be done: improve the area's educational system, improve its agriculture, and bring about industrial development. He added, "The university's School of Agriculture is a continuing answer to the second area problem. The university now has a chance to contribute more in ways directly bearing on the third problem."

On the political side, everyone concerned with the engineering outcome knew who should have shared the applause with Morris. And Powell knew it, too. Typical of the political self-congratulations, Senator Grindle took a bow but added, "Of course, understand, I had Paul Powell's help on the thing and all his weight behind, to do that."[60]

Paul Simon: A Puzzle for Dealers

Paul Simon, who served in Illinois elective offices for forty years, had multiple opportunities to join coalitions in behalf of southern Illinois. He represented Madison County in the state House and Senate from 1955 to 1969, and he was a U.S. congressman from the state's southernmost district from 1975 to 1985.

Through all those years, and others when he represented the entire state, Simon had a reputation for opposing many of the political interests that worked to bring state funds and facilities to the region. Even when in Congress he was criticized for not bringing enough federal pork to his district.[61]

What was it with Simon?

First of all, Simon did work for aid projects in his state and federal districts. For example, he supported sending state dollars to East St. Louis when the city was nearly bankrupt. However, when compared to other Democrats who served the same areas, he was noticeably absent. Those who worked with him as staff members and were close friends acknowledged that his definition of service leaned more toward social issues and subjects of larger scope such as ethics legislation rather than pork. For example, his good friend Alan Dixon, who served simultaneously with Simon in state and federal public offices, was considered more attentive to state issues when both served in the U.S. Senate, while Simon operated on a global scale and wrote books accordingly.[62] Those circumstances accounted for a part of the answer to the Simon question. But, there were other reasons of a much more personal and philosophical nature.

Regarding political power groups of state government, Powell and Simon were at opposite ends. One of the most powerful groups consisted of Powell, Clyde Choate, and friends, including Republicans—Chicago mayor Daley and his circle was the other. A third small group of independent liberals, including Simon and occasionally Dixon, objected to Powell's legislative agenda and Daley's party dominance. Simon fought tirelessly against Powell's favoritism for horse racing and bills that he pushed for friends and political associates.[63] He believed unseen payoffs were behind many of those proposals. Without many victories to count, Simon and friends did little more than complain and vent their frustrations. In that state government environment, Simon and Powell could not find common ground for more than a few minutes at a time.

Powell and Simon came as close to being sworn enemies as could be found in southern Illinois. There were few pauses in the constant warfare. Simon said the two did become friendly on the campaign trail in 1968 when both were seeking statewide election. However, that failed to repair the breach. After Powell's death, Simon talked positively about Powell's support of SIU and social legislation, but he drew the line on any further compliments.[64] Regarding SIU, Simon questioned Powell's motives, claiming that he was inspired mostly by political gain. Politics for Powell was a means to all ends, and Simon disagreed.

Generally speaking, Simon believed Powell was crooked and corrupt, although he admitted being unable to prove anything. His public position about Powell's dealings left little to the imagination. In 1964, *Harper's Magazine* published Simon's article about alleged corruption in the Illinois legislature.[65] Much of what he wrote was aimed at Powell, although not by name. The accusations cost him dearly with legislative colleagues and failed to initiate legislation. Later, in a magazine article, Simon wrote, "My relationship with Powell was an up and down one. When he had bills that clearly smelled of bribery I would oppose him, and he would get lividly angry."[66]

Even with Powell no longer available to kick around, Simon's lack of respect appeared in one of his favorite stories. As Simon told it, he and Chicago mayor Richard J. Daley stood together before Powell's open casket at the 1970 funeral. Simon remembered, "There I am talking to Daley, who said, 'You know I believe if you're honest then the people below you are going to be honest.' He said Powell took money and everybody took money. I thought Powell would rise up at that moment."[67]

Some of Simon's personal positions on public issues puzzled those who labored for southern Illinois benefits, including Powell. When higher education interests across the state promoted a massive bond issue in 1958 and again in 1960 that included funds for the beginning of SIU's Edwardsville campus, Simon opposed the measure.[68] The Edwardsville campus was proposed for a site only a few miles from Simon's home in Troy. During his term as lieutenant governor, Simon tried to derail Governor Richard Ogilvie's huge bond plan for highway infrastructure. Representative Clyde Choate, then a party leader in the House, supported the Ogilvie plan because it meant improved highways in the southern half of Illinois.

Simon's occasional incursions into Powell-Choate territory kept the relationship at a boil. In the wake of the 1955 change in the territory of legislative districts, Democratic Party leaders targeted a few regions where additional members might be elected. Democrats had not controlled the House since 1949. That effort brought Simon into the backyard of Powell and Choate.

The House district in which Choate served usually elected two Republicans and one Democrat—Choate. The new alignment for Choate's district after 1955 included the counties of Monroe, Randolph, Jackson,

Union, Pulaski, and Alexander, a substantial acreage that party leaders thought might elect two Democrats. In advance of the 1958 elections Paul Simon and Alan Dixon, both members of the House, began conversations with James Holloway, from Randolph County in the northern part of the House district, about running in the primary election. Their presumed intention was to elect two Democrats. Holloway said in an oral history, "I knew that the odds were probably slim that I would be nominated let alone elected. However, because of the urging and insistence of Paul Simon and Al Dixon, I decided to make the effort to see if we could nominate two Democrats and elect two in the general election."[69]

To Choate and Powell this looked like an invasion to challenge Choate rather than an attempt to acquire a second Democrat from the district. The decision to put two Democrats on the ticket was the responsibility of the district's representative committee, and that happened by a narrow vote margin. In the general election voters would have a choice between two Republicans and two Democrats for three seats. The committee's decision put Choate in an unfamiliar general election contest. His seat had been almost an automatic winner. As Holloway said later, "I am sure it would have put him [Choate] a little out of sorts to have to go through the lengthy process."[70] In all likelihood, Choate was furious, and he knew who set it up: Simon and Dixon.

Holloway, who had the least name recognition, took the most votes in the general election. A Republican incumbent finished second, and Choate barely defeated the other Republican candidate for third. Holloway later understated Choate's reaction, saying, "I'm quite sure Clyde was very surprised that he ran third." The whole business was another roadblock in relations between Simon/Dixon and Powell/Choate. However, Democrats won the House in the 1958 election, and Powell was chosen Speaker with a vote from Holloway.

Behind the scenes, Simon actively sought people to run against Powell for the legislature. Futile as that was, given Powell's hold on the House seat in Johnson County, Simon nevertheless pursued potential opponents and encouraged them. There is evidence that Powell returned the favor in backing Simon's opponents in Madison County. On more than one occasion Simon helped editors at the *Southern Illinoisan* newspaper in Carbondale confront Powell at preelection interviews by sending a long list of suggested questions regarding presumed unethical behavior.[71]

The quarrels between Powell and Simon ranged over a lengthy list of political encounters. During his years in the legislature Simon searched for prospective statewide candidates—often for governor—noted for their independence of the Chicago machine and the state central committee. One who fit his definition was Stephen A. Mitchell, a close ally of Adlai E. Stevenson II and a former national party chairman who had not held public office in Illinois. Simon promoted Mitchell for the 1960 Democratic nomination as governor. Powell had a history of arguments over party issues with Mitchell, and the Stevenson connection didn't help. At the mention of a possible Mitchell candidacy with Simon backing, Powell went on the attack. During a party meeting he called Mitchell a "phony" and a "cry-baby." He offered to run for governor if Mitchell were the only other candidate. Powell said, "There's nothing I'd rather do than debate issues all over the state against that cry-baby who is trying to be a candidate for governor."[72] Simon maintained support of Mitchell until Mayor Daley chose Otto Kerner to run for governor.

Simon's opinion of Powell as the evil presence in Illinois politics did not endear him to those who worked side by side with the Vienna politician. However, Simon considered Powell's friends equally guilty of seeking favors and using the legislature to further their business affairs. Choate, too, had tired of Simon's accusations of corruption and greed. In the aftermath of Simon's article in *Harper's* and efforts to pass ethics legislation, he said attempts to legislate morality would not clean up what little corruption existed. He stated that some corrupt activities could be expected even if officials warned against it. In an oblique reference to Simon, Choate added, "Frequently the charges turn out to have been erroneous ones from disappointed and frustrated individuals."[73]

Tensions between Choate and Simon flared behind the scenes as well. When Simon's name came before the Democratic State Central Committee in 1968 as Daley's candidate for lieutenant governor, Choate, a member of the committee, said, "But, mayor, he might become governor." To which Daley is alleged to have said, "It's Simon."[74]

It was no surprise in 1974, when Simon announced for the Democratic nomination as congressman in the southernmost district, that Choate and other state party officials from the region worked for another candidate. Joe Browning, Simon's primary opponent, came from a Franklin County family and was a personality on a West Frankfort radio station. Although a political neophyte, Browning had name recognition and local ties. After Simon won the primary, Choate did not endorse him in the general election.[75]

There were a number of answers to the question about Simon. Obviously, he did not want his legacy of public service to include even the slightest hint that he cooperated with politicians whose ethics were questionable and whose choice of priority issues left him cold. However, Simon's protestations and efforts to corral corruption did little to deter Powell and his associates.

Last Hurrah for Legislator Powell

Sitting in the Speaker's chair for the last time in his political career in 1961, Powell wanted to leave a legacy that extended beyond southern Illinois. He knew the issues that would gain most of the Democratic votes, and he felt sure he could bargain for enough Republicans to enact his agenda. He also anticipated that newly elected governor Kerner would be receptive. With Powell's blessing, Choate introduced a bill creating a commission on services for children and their families and explained the bill at an appropriations hearing. The bill stated that a commission would study and investigate "all aspects of the care, treatment and assistance services for children and their families conducted or dealt with by each governmental unit or branch within the state."[76] An appropriation of $45,000 for commission work was included. It called for a report to the governor in two years. The bill whizzed through the General Assembly with few objections.

Another more controversial bill introduced by Choate, Powell, and partner Clyde Lee proposed creating a Board of Economic Development, a council of economic advisers, and the Office of Executive Director of the board. They needed all the Democrats and a smattering of Republicans to get the measure through the House and Senate. For example, the House Industrial Affairs Committee approved it by a 7 to 5 vote. By the end of the session it was on the governor's desk for signing.[77]

When Powell sat as House minority leader in the 1963 session, he played a major role in creating a Department of Children and Family Services, based on findings from the 1961 study. House Bill 236, introduced by Choate, carried Powell's name as a sponsor. At a hearing of the House Committee on Public Aid, Health, Welfare and Safety, in February, Choate spoke for the bill and the committee approved it 27 to 0. By early April the House and Senate had agreed, and Kerner signed it.[78] With these key bills, and many others, Powell left the House to serve as secretary of state in 1965, leaving Clyde Choate to carry on as champion of downstate and southern Illinois interests and keeper of the bipartisan flame that in truth was barely flickering.

Hindsight being what it is, many of those who served in the General Assembly during Powell's time developed more than a slight distaste for his leadership. If pushed, they grudgingly acknowledged his talents and skill in running the chamber or being one of its power brokers when not leading. But when it came to assessing his motivations, they let fly at the man. Those most vocal in condemning Powell's personal agenda had felt the sting of his disdain, had their personal bills killed, and were named to meaningless committees. He was not kind to those who viewed him as evil. They occasionally voted with him out of their own interests, when they deemed no principle was at risk. They also criticized Chicago leadership, or did so when it served their purposes. They declined to join the Republicans, and probably would not have been welcome if not accompanied by Powell, Choate, and friends. Their unfavorable treatment of Powell's legacy focused on a dark side, but few of them viewed his work in a larger context.

Abner Mikva, Democrat from suburban Chicago, gave Powell his due:

> [He] had an incredible instinct for the legislative process, with no legal training and little education. He could stand before the House and receive a bill he never had seen before, scan it quickly and decide who would support it and who wouldn't and who it would benefit or not benefit. I was in awe, literally, that he understood as much as he did about the legislative process. In addition he was a great orator; he could get the House a-hollerin' whenever he wanted. All that talent was going to waste as far as I was concerned. I tried to emulate his idea of building coalitions and compromising. I was inclined to stand on principle too much, and it never got me much . . . There was nobody so crooked or so talented.[79]

Paul Simon, Democrat from Troy, clashed openly and behind closed doors with Powell for much of his six years in the House, and occasionally after. As a congressman from 1975 to 1985, he worked some of the same southern Illinois precincts as Powell did before he left the legislature in 1965. They shared an interest in SIU. Simon said, "There was no question he was powerful; he was gutsy; he had courage. He was corrupt, and he had some areas where he did good things: Southern Illinois University, minimum wage. He had the philosophy of helping people, a benevolent side to him . . . It was clear he was championing the SIU cause—who knows the motivation. Among other things it was great political cover for him in terms he could go back to the people in Johnson County and say he was a champion of the university. And at that point it helped the region economically."[80]

Few had harsher words about Powell than Anthony Scariano, Democrat from northern Illinois. About Powell and SIU, Scariano said, "Whatever he did for Southern Illinois University was only because . . . he helped to build it with appropriations. And [Everett] Peters helped to build the University of Illinois with appropriations. But they got a quid pro quo. It wasn't that they were interested in higher education. How many more jobs does this give you in my area? How many more favors can I do for people in my area?"[81]

Alan Dixon, during Powell's time a House Democrat from Belleville, wrote in measured terms about Powell in his book *The Gentleman from Illinois* but left no doubt about the relationship:

> He was a rogue, but he also was a strong leader of House Democrats and a man of considerable, if sometimes rough-hewn, charm. I never was part of the diverse group of legislators, Republicans as well as Democrats, who were extremely loyal to him. I was among those not to be trusted, and he made this clear to me to my face. Yet, in spite of my support of legislative reforms and association with like-minded young Democrats who refused to go along with Powell's questionable schemes, he was good to his word in regard to his input on issues of importance to me. I, too, recognized his skills in legislative maneuvering were second to none.[82]

And there were many who sang his praises, none more than his friend and legislative sidekick Clyde Choate. In an interview with Richard Icen of Lindsay-Schaub newspapers, Choate said, "Powell and I were friends. We lived within 20 miles of each other and our voting records on most things were quite similar because we had the same interests in our districts." Choate knew more and said less about Powell than any other person. He called him "the most unforgettable man ever to walk these halls."[83]

5.
Clyde Choate's Leadership Legacy

Taking on the Income-Tax Challenge

When Paul Powell took over as secretary of state in 1965, he stepped away from a position of legislative authority, especially when it involved direct teamwork with Clyde Choate. The Anna representative had served loyally, and importantly, as Powell's floor leader, vote counter, and muscle—when needed. Finally, he was the House's top Democrat. However, even with the change, Powell remained influential in policy making. He was no more than a telephone call away from Choate. It was not as if Powell had retired and moved to Florida.

Choate inherited Powell's downstate legislative followers, although there may have been a few who left the fold. Clyde Lee would soon move to Chicago, where he managed racetrack business. Others, such as Senator Crisenberry, who held hands with Powell on many issues, had retired. His replacement in the Senate was John G. Gilbert from Jackson County, who served from 1961 to 1973, much of that time on the education committee.[1] His ties to Southern Illinois University (SIU) dated to his father, John P. Gilbert, who graduated from the college when it was Southern Illinois Normal College and served more than a decade as head of the school's Department of Biology and Agriculture.

The reign of Powell as Speaker ended with the 1961–62 session. Representative John W. Lewis Jr., a Republican from Clark County in east central Illinois, followed Powell in the post. At least Powell was assured that during his last two years in the House the Speaker was from down-state. After one session, the speakership shifted to Chicago, bringing with it a dramatic change in policy and power. Chicago mayor Daley had tried to put his man in the Speaker position since his election in 1955. Powell had thwarted the mayor's ambition, while allowing Chicago influence to grow in the House.

Other serious shifts in power were on the horizon. For years the regional political battle focused on the tug-of-war between Chicago and downstate. The 1960 census revealed that Chicago and Cook County population had fallen by 70,558 since 1950.[2] Also, the city's percentage of state population dropped 7 percent to 35. Downstate figures, especially in southern Illinois, declined as well. The big gainers were the suburbs and collar counties of northeast Illinois, bringing into play a third major element in the political picture, especially as it related to reapportionment of the General Assembly.

Even with Powell in the House during the 1963 session, questions naturally arose about Choate. Could he inherit Powell's role as lord of the House? Or even some of it? Were downstate's interests doomed to a second (or third) cousin status? What coalitions could be formed that would build and maintain influence in the legislature? A measure of Choate's influence after Powell was his membership on the legislative budgetary commission. He had served with Powell on that powerful body. Strength of leadership, when it came to Powell and Choate, was always about money.

As the last decade of Clyde Choate's career in the House unfolded, most of those questions received answers, some more quickly than others. However, before much could be determined, state government settled into the matter of legislative reapportionment as dictated by the Illinois Constitution. The principal players in the drama were the House and Senate, both controlled by Republicans, and the governorship, in the hands of Democrat Otto Kerner. Of course, Daley would play a key role.

The fallout for downstate regions was of earthquake proportions. After holding off Chicago and Cook County power grabs for decades, downstate politicians had become the losers in reapportionment wars with Chicago and the suburbs. Their numbers were reduced, and the leadership role filled by Powell and Choate was lessened. If downstate Democrats and Republicans wanted something significant from the legislature, they had to beg or borrow. Strategically speaking, Choate and his small knot of votes would be increasingly on the defensive, using the remaining strength to water down the worst of proposals from Chicago and Springfield while maintaining SIU's flow of appropriations. Choate would become pretty much a defensive player.

Facing a constitutional deadline of June 30, 1963, the Republican-led legislature passed a reapportionment bill and sent it to Kerner. He vetoed the bill, saying he found that the districts created by the bill were "wanting in that degree of proportionality and fairness that I believe our Constitution intended."[3] Primarily, he objected because the bill did not deal fully with suburban issues. That meant in political terms that it did not deal with suburban issues to satisfy Daley. He wanted Cook County districts to cross county lines in the suburban areas controlled by Republicans. Almost immediately, various Republicans mounted legal challenges to Kerner's veto, but none of them altered the outcome. The constitution called for Kerner to appoint a bipartisan ten-person commission to settle the issue, which he did. However, he did not appoint any members of the legislature and that angered Democrats and Republicans. Facing a December 31 deadline, the commission could not agree.[4] Kerner then called for an at-large election for House members in 1964.

Each party nominated 118 candidates to the 177-member House. The Democratic Party captured 118 seats, and the Republicans, 59. That became known as the infamous "bedsheet ballot," with so many names that it could hardly be handled by an individual in a voting booth or when votes were counted. Boosted by the landslide election of Lyndon B. Johnson for president over Republican Barry Goldwater, Democrats won the bedsheet vote and automatically held two-thirds of House membership for the 1965 General Assembly session.[5] John Touhy of Chicago became Speaker. The Senate was not involved in the reapportionment mess, so Republicans maintained control.

The chaos created by attempts at reapportionment continued into the 1965 session. Meanwhile the U.S. Supreme Court had issued its "one-man, one-vote" decision, *Reynolds v. Sims* (June 16, 1964), which declared that all legislatures must be reapportioned by population. That directly impacted the state Senate and determined how the House would be apportioned. No longer could Illinois apportion by geography only. The net result was to shift control of the legislature to the Chicago suburbs and city. Again facing a deadline to pass legislation by June 30, 1965, legislators continued their wrangling, and no decision was reached.[6]

After the legislative session Kerner appointed another commission to reapportion the House that included East St. Louis mayor Alvin Fields as a member. Meanwhile, a Senate remap agreement was reached in August by a special five-judge panel and Democrats and Republicans. By late November, Democratic and Republican commission members approved the House remap. Another bedsheet ballot was avoided in 1966. As one historian observed, downstate had become a "junior partner" in the running of the Illinois legislature.

Often the voice of compromise, especially when the Democratic Party appeared to be a winner, Fields expressed his approval of the House plan, stating the obvious: "I believe it was very close. Much will depend on which party has the most attractive candidates."[7] None of the revised districts in St. Clair and Madison counties, another arm of Daley's army, appeared to be in danger of a Republican invasion. Complimenting the commission's work, Fields added, "This is strictly a compromise, a matter of give and take and it is impossible to take care of all representatives. There were just too many." Mostly, Fields was relieved that another bedsheet ballot was avoided.

Fellow downstate Democrats were not as conciliatory, claiming the final map to be a sellout of the party in southern Illinois. Their retained lease on life was that cumulative voting remained in place. This new realignment in the political arena with three divisions of the state—downstate, suburbs, and city—became most obvious in the 1969 session with a Republican Speaker and governor.

For years, a number of Illinois elected officials and others concerned with the state's revenue challenge favored enacting an income tax. For as long as anyone could remember the primary source of state funds had come from a steadily rising sales tax. Those opposed to increasing the sales tax believed it weighed too heavily on the poor and low-wage earners. Even more aggressive than those preferring an income tax were those totally opposed to it. They prevailed session after session, even as the state's budget threatened to grow beyond available funds. Governors beginning with William Stratton and including Otto Kerner could see the straitjacket of state finances, as did some key legislators, but the time did not seem right until late in the 1960s. During the 1968 gubernatorial election campaign neither Governor Samuel Shapiro—who moved up from lieutenant governor when Kerner received a judicial appointment—nor

Republican challenger Richard B. Ogilvie made an issue of an income tax. Kerner had rarely mentioned such a tax.

After Ogilvie's election, matters soon developed in Springfield that put an income tax on the new governor's agenda. Pushing the tax idea from the House was the new Speaker, Ralph Tyler Smith of Alton. Republican majority leader W. Russell Arrington controlled the Senate with an iron hand. While Smith supported an income tax from the outset, Arrington had to be convinced of the need by Ogilvie. The first inkling of a tax change came during Ogilvie's message to a joint session of the General Assembly in February 1969—a traditional formality. He spoke generally about the need for more revenue to finance programs he intended to propose and to keep the state's head above deficit waters. At a joint session to hear his budget proposals on April 1, Ogilvie gave specifics of his plan and called for approval.[8]

When initially proposed, Ogilvie's plan called for a flat 4 percent tax on businesses and a 4 percent tax on individuals. The idea looked dead on arrival when introduced by Arrington as Senate Bill 1150. Although Republicans controlled both the state Senate and House, there were not enough willing party votes to pass a tax plan—in either chamber. There were even fewer supporters among Democrats. Most members of the General Assembly did not want it on their record as having voted for an income tax. At that time the minority leader of Democrats in the House was John Touhy from Chicago, a close associate of Mayor Richard J. Daley. The No. 2 Democrat in House leadership was Clyde Choate, who eventually assumed the role of provocateur. As the battle unfolded in the last two months of the session, observers realized this was more than another legislative issue game. The players were deadly serious about influencing the outcome and making it a matter of principle.

Ogilvie's chief driver for the tax was Senator Arrington. Even he could not muster enough votes for passage as the debate began. When the proposal meandered through preliminary steps in the Senate, members raised critical issues. One was Ogilvie's desire for businesses and individuals to pay the same percentage. Ogilvie and Arrington absolutely refused to consider any different split, and especially a smaller number for individuals. Ogilvie and supporters argued that the 1870 state constitution prohibited a split percentage.[9] However, the split would be a nonissue if there were not enough votes to pass anything. That led to the other question: where would the votes come from for passage?

Actually, no one doubted that an income tax would be adopted. The deal would be done when Ogilvie and Daley pounded out an agreement between them. The votes would come after they decided how to split the windfall. Ogilvie knew from his time as a public official in Cook County how to deal with the mayor.

The leadership picture in both chambers lined up in support of some kind of income tax in spite of the rank-and-file hesitation. Arrington was in harness after Ogilvie supplied adequate pressure, and the minority leader in the Senate, Thomas McGloon, a product of the Chicago Democratic machine, could be counted on.[10] He was reared on Chicago's West Side and graduated from DePaul University Law School. A tested veteran of World War II in the Pacific, McGloon served as an assistant public defender and assistant Cook County state's attorney before his election to the Senate in 1958. McGloon did show some hesitancy on the tax issue, but insiders knew he would do what Mayor Daley wanted. In the House, Speaker Smith of Alton did the governor's bidding on almost any issue. His labors for an income tax paid off for Smith in September 1969 when Ogilvie appointed him to fill the U.S. Senate seat vacated by the death of Everett Dirksen.[11] Minority leader Touhy might have been on the hot seat with a House divided on the tax issue. Still, he worked for whatever Daley wanted.

That left Choate, House minority whip, as the chief troublemaker. Deep down he might not have wanted an income tax, but Choate knew the votes would be there for something. He disagreed with the Ogilvie approach and marshaled his downstate forces to broker an outcome favorable to his political beliefs, whether they jibed with Daley's or not. Early in the 1969 General Assembly session Choate had introduced his own income tax scheme, House Bills 126 and 127, calling for a 5 percent corporation levy and 2 percent on individuals, setting his marker for the duration.[12] The bill for a 2 percent individual tax was read for a first time in the House and tabled. The bill for 5 percent on corporations was read a first and second time but was tabled and never made it to a third reading. Republican and Chicago leadership in the House would never have allowed those bills to survive as long as Ogilvie was running the show.

The lineup of leaders, including Daley and Ogilvie, left the door open for someone to take the political position as spokesman for the individual taxpayer. Ogilvie wanted an income tax that would generate the money to spend on a long list of public initiatives. McGloon and Touhy, as Daley's warriors, angled for a chunk of the tax to finance the mayor's spending agenda.[13] The Republicans went along with Ogilvie because he was governor. That left Choate to assume the role as protector of the "little guy." Choate had proved during his twenty-two years in the legislature that he understood how to count votes. In the case of an income tax, the magic number of downstate House votes needed was around thirty to influence the outcome. This was no small-time intramural contest. A state income tax would be the single most important revenue source in the state's history and an increased burden for individuals and corporations, regardless of percentages.

As the tax issue moved into June—the legislative session was to end on June 30—Ogilvie had accumulated significant support outside the General Assembly for an income tax. The groups included the Illinois Chamber of Commerce, the Illinois Education Association, the American Federation of Labor and Congress of Industrial Organizations (AFL-CIO), and the Illinois Agricultural Association.[14] Each of those organizations had significant lobbying influence with legislators, although they could not guarantee that those who voted for an income tax would be protected from a later voter revolt. Republican legislative leaders, especially Arrington, concluded that the governor's 4/4 plan did not have sufficient support to pass. After consulting with Ogilvie, Arrington took the issue to the Senate Revenue Committee, asking for approval of a 3/3 scheme. The committee approved the measure and sent it to the full Senate with a "do pass" recommendation.

The "deal" for a tax between Daley and Ogilvie—primarily for Daley's votes in the legislature—became public by mid-June. In effect, Ogilvie had agreed that one-twelfth of the new revenue would go to Illinois cities. Quietly, he also had agreed to expand bonding power for Chicago and Cook County and to a larger amount of sales tax money for Chicago use. He pledged to increase school aid levels.[15] Other tax increases were scattered among bills still before the legislature, most of which added something to the Chicago coffers.

Until that moment the opposition of Choate had been mostly out of public view. But a presumed deal between the two leaders brought him up swinging, after speaking with his mentor Secretary of State Powell. Choate began by saying, "Two people in this state are not going to sit down and make an agreement that is supposed to be binding on this legislature and the people of this state. The mayor and the governor are trying to double-cross the people."[16] He didn't stop there. Choate drafted a statement announcing his resignation as Democratic whip. If issued, this would have been a slap in the face of Daley and House leadership. He was supported in a statement by fellow downstate Democrat James Holloway, who said, "I don't like it. Maybe half the people live in Cook County, but there is a helluva a lot to the rest of Illinois."[17] The uprising caused Daley to claim he never made a deal. And Choate did not resign.

Choate then rallied his closest supporters and launched a filibuster on the House floor that lasted two hours. He ended the delaying tactic with an announcement that Cook County Democrats had lined up with the downstate revolt. Choate added, "We don't care what the rate is, but we want corporations taxed on a 2-to-1 ratio that is twice as much as individuals."[18] Touhy and the Cook County contingent did not attend a caucus of the downstate Democrats. However, he met with Choate to make the unity announcement. House Republicans had ninety-three members and Democrats eighty-one. Any measure needed eighty-nine votes to pass. Press reports said Choate's filibuster also had the support of downstate and suburban Republicans who refused to vote for a tax that meant bonuses for Chicago inner-city schools. In the Senate Arrington decided not to call for a floor vote, causing Senator Alan Dixon of Belleville to say, "Everybody says they will go along 'if' . . . Everybody has their price. It's a real can of spaghetti."[19]

With the Ogilvie 3/3 plan in trouble, House and Senate Democrats proposed a state income tax of 4 percent on corporations and 2 percent on individuals, as an alternative. This would have met Choate's declaration for a 2-to-1 differential. The presumption was that Democratic leadership, McGloon and Touhy, would have not joined the bandwagon without a nod from Daley. Touhy said, "Our caucus is absolutely bound and determined that there will be an income tax differential." He added that House Republicans told him "if they had to vote for an income tax it would be easier to vote for one with a differential."[20] Republican leaders refused to budge. Speaker Smith stated, "We cannot risk complete financial chaos by passing something almost certainly unconstitutional."

Ogilvie turned on his tough public face to respond: "Our proposal calls for a 3 per cent tax with the same rate applicable to individuals and corporations. I shall not recede from that position." He said further, "I want to make it crystal clear if the events which began yesterday [when Democrats made the 4/2 proposal] are permitted to continue there will be no income tax."[21] He referred to Democratic motives as "a soak-the-rich charade." A day later Arrington called the Democratic proposal "neither responsible nor accurate," and "political doubletalk."[22] He said there would be no compromise. He assailed the 2 percent level for individuals as inadequate to provide needed services and school aid. The rhetorical battle continued with McGloon saying the 2 percent level was sound financially and would yield enough money to operate the state. Eight days remained before adjournment.

Ogilvie turned up the shrill-meter, accusing Democrats of any number of deeds detrimental to the state's needs. Newspaper reporters called it the governor's "last-ditch plea." It turned out that way. A day later, leadership of both parties agreed on a split of 4 percent for corporations and 2.5 percent for individuals. Two days remained before adjournment.

It wasn't easy. First, Ogilvie insisted that Republican leaders make one more approach to Democrats for the votes to pass the 3/3 proposal. No deal, the Democrats said.[23] The Republicans did not have enough votes to pass the tax bill. Ogilvie, knowing he had to make a deal, called the party leaders to the capitol, where he put them in two separate rooms. He began the shuffle approach designed to get approval. First, they had to agree on the package, not just the split but also the side issues that would guarantee enough votes and approval of the mayor. That included setting aside one-twelfth of tax revenue to be rebated to local governments, for block grants to aid school districts, or for other purposes. After reaching agreement, the issue became whether Senate Democrats would provide the votes needed to pass that chamber. With further involvement of Ogilvie in person-to-person negotiations, Arrington announced he had enough votes.[24] Voting against the plan, along with three other Democratic senators, was Dixon from Belleville, who had announced his opposition early in the session.

When the House took the issue, Choate tried once more to lower the individual number from 4 or 3 percent to 2 percent. He said that would be enough revenue for the state and anything more would be "a considerable over-soaking" of taxpayers. He and other downstate Democrats fought the Ogilvie compromise to the end, denying the governor forty-eight votes, including Choate's. The official count showed the bill for 4/2.5 passed the House 91 to 73.[26] However, the final vote was not an accurate reflection of the division. Once Mayor Daley could see he had enough votes, certain members from Chicago were sheltered from having to vote for the tax. Secretary of State Powell, who made the most of downstate votes during his time in the House, said it was "too bad" the sales tax could not have been cut to balance the ledger somewhat.[27]

In a manner of speaking, Choate deserved credit for keeping enough votes in his pocket to reject Ogilvie's original plan of 4/4, and his first compromise to 3/3. He may not have endeared himself to Chicago Democrats, but they got what they wanted anyway. The income tax, regardless of its benefits to the state coffers and to Ogilvie's plans for spending, cost Republicans dearly at election time. It may have been the deciding factor in Ogilvie's loss to Daniel Walker.

The Unruly 1972 Convention

Until the Democratic National Convention of 1972 the standard approach for selecting Illinois delegates gave control to Mayor Daley. For example, in 1968 all but a handful of the 118 delegates were chosen either directly or indirectly by the mayor and his allies. Technically, two delegates were chosen by direct election from each of twenty-four congressional districts. Considering the districts under control of the Chicago machine and influenced by the Democratic organization in St. Clair and Madison counties, most of those elected were regular Democrats, willing to go along with direction from the mayor. A large number of regular officeholders and party officials were chosen by the Democratic State Central Committee.

Opposition to this method of selection was almost nonexistent. When the Illinois Democratic Party held its convention in Springfield during June 1968, one of the few delegates present who opposed Daley's leadership was Dick Mudge Jr., a former state's attorney from Edwardsville. He had won an upset election for convention delegate from St. Clair and Madison counties in spite of the political machine of East St. Louis mayor Alvin Fields. A major business item on the convention agenda was routine approval of sixty-eight at-large delegates chosen by the state central committee. After a voice vote to approve the group of regulars, Mudge sought recognition to call for the vote to be overruled and for appointment of twenty "peace" delegates. Mudge's candidacy had energized antiwar activists in his district. Daley initially silenced Mudge but later gave the dissident an opportunity to address the state delegates.[28] Mudge's motion did not receive a second. That was the extent of objections to the standard Democratic delegation selection system.

When time came to vote for the party nominee at the national convention in Chicago, eventual nominee Hubert Humphrey received 112 of the 118, at the instruction of Daley. Mudge voted for antiwar candidate Senator Eugene McCarthy.[29] Riots in Chicago's streets, a strong antiwar sentiment among delegates, and pictures of Daley shaking his fist at convention speakers he disapproved of, all seemed to have no impact on the mayor's control of votes. But the memories of Chicago in 1968 ushered in changes for future party conventions.[30]

After the national presidential election, which Richard M. Nixon won, and the loss of the Illinois governorship to Republican Richard B. Ogilvie, the anger level rose among Democrats in the state and across the nation who blamed the ruins on the rule by big-city bosses. This led to the party drastically revising its rules for choosing national convention delegates.[31] Leading the movement was a commission of the Democratic National Committee headed by South Dakota senator George McGovern, who had received modest mention for president among delegates in 1968.

New rules declared that delegates had to be "in reasonable relationship" to proportions of minority groups, women, and young people in the state. Also, no more than 10 percent of delegates could be named by the state Democratic committee. Rules called for "timely selection" of delegates by publicizing meetings at which delegates were chosen and for public notification of delegates' preferences. In other words, the new convention regulations demolished the system used in Illinois by party kingpins and limited the authority of Daley and his friends who had trooped to the conventions mostly to have a good time and vote as they were told. It came as no surprise that Mayor Daley did not believe the rules applied to him and Chicago.

With altered convention delegate rules in the background, new and familiar leadership faces showed up when it came time to choose 170 Illinois delegates for the 1972 Democratic National Convention in Miami Beach. Across downstate, but not in Chicago, McGovern delegates contested successfully in congressional district primary elections, initially winning fourteen delegates. The leader of the McGovern delegates was James M. (Jim) Wall, a soft-spoken United Methodist minister and candidate for congress from DuPage County. Wall later became editor and publisher of the *Christian Century* magazine.[32] Also outside Chicago was a movement in behalf of Edmund Muskie, promoted by U.S. senator Adlai E. Stevenson III. Both Stevenson and Wall were delegates. A handful of those elected outside Chicago were uncommitted.

In Chicago, Daley controlled the election of fifty-nine delegates in the primary and guided the choices of the state central committee. Unaccustomed to being told what to do, the mayor ignored guidelines of the national committee, and Illinois delegate selection did not conform to the rules.

As if the delegation was not already on the edge of a division of interests, two well-known independent political figures in Chicago filed a formal challenge to Daley's selection process with the national committee. They were William Singer, a maverick alderman from the North Side of Chicago who won his city council seat at age twenty-nine in 1969, and the Reverend Jesse Jackson Sr., who was appointed in 1966 by Dr. Martin Luther King Jr. as the Chicago leader of Operation Breadbasket. By 1972 Jackson had organized People United to Save Humanity (PUSH). Singer, whose ambition was to defeat Daley for mayor in 1975, became an official delegate to the convention, but Jackson was not.[33] They developed a list of delegates that complied with the convention rules. The challenge did not affect delegates appointed by the central committee such as former Speaker John Touhy, who many remember as a dapper man almost always wearing a suit and tie even during the hottest, most humid moments of the July convention.[34]

Clyde Choate, elected as a "regular party delegate," steered clear of the Chicago fracas and concerned himself with legislative matters as minority leader in the state House. His fondest hope was to have a strong national candidate that would give Democrats a state House majority. Missing from the delegation was the party's candidate for governor, Daniel Walker, who had defeated Lieutenant Governor Paul Simon in the March primary election. He chose to remain in Illinois and campaign against the incumbent governor Richard Ogilvie.[35] Walker also did not want to be beholden to Mayor Daley in any fashion for an appointment as delegate.

Behind the scenes political operatives tried various initiatives to change the shape of the delegation. Senator Stevenson was especially active.[36] He worked unsuccessfully to depose Daley as chairman of the delegation and take control as favorite son. Before the convention, Stevenson and Wall met in Washington to discuss strategies. The senator, supporting his Senate colleague Edmund Muskie, wanted Wall to support his favorite son campaign. Wall said later, "I declined since for me McGovern was on target with my ideology. I also liked him personally and felt he would make an excellent president."[37]

Wall walked a delicate line amid the mixture of Illinois party leadership. He did not want to upset Stevenson because Muskie delegates might commit to McGovern as the Maine senator's campaign diminished. At the same time, Wall was careful not to alienate Daley, whose support McGovern would need in a McGovern race against President Nixon. Wall managed the situation well while keeping the confidence of his unconventional delegates who had a single purpose at the convention, with little interest in the Chicago skirmish. The assortment of feminists and antiwar activists were outsiders in the Illinois party, totally committed in ideology to McGovern.[38] It might be said that, culturally speaking, McGovern people were on a different planet by choice.

As convention week approached, an uncomfortable stalemate existed. The Chicago situation would not be resolved until the first convention session. Daley's delegates anticipated having to leave their hotel rooms by Tuesday. Singer's delegates rubbed their hands together in anticipation of a vote Monday by convention delegates that would make them official. Everyone watched to see what Daley would do next, and what the national committee's decision would be.

The press, politicians, and just plain observers looked for Daley. Was he in Miami Beach? Had anyone seen him? Would he show up at a delegation caucus on Sunday? Michael Howlett, state auditor, en route to a Sunday morning golf game, told a reporter, "He's here."[39] But where? "He's here," Howlett repeated, and then left for his game. There was a curiosity about the whereabouts of Jesse Jackson as well, but there was never any doubt. When the TV lights burned through the weekend, Jesse was everywhere, although he did not have a vote to cast. He never ran for delegate. He came along for the ride and what publicity he might squeeze out of being there.

Although rumor of defections settled over the delegates on Sunday, the numbers of commitments had not changed much. In order to keep people in place, Stevenson spent hours talking to Muskie delegates before holding a brief press conference in the evening. McGovern delegates also held a caucus Sunday, mostly to discuss how they would vote Monday on seating Chicago delegates.

The Illinois delegation required a chairman to conduct business and prepare for the convention opening on Monday. As vice chair appointed by Daley, but without an approving vote by delegates, Choate assumed the role as acting chairman.[40] On Sunday he met with Muskie, McGovern, and downstate uncommitted delegates to make sure no attempt would be made to unseat him as temporary leader at the caucus until the convention vote on Monday. Unsure whether he could trust Choate because of his standing with regular Democrats, Singer preferred a different acting or permanent chair, but even if his group were seated on Monday, he did not have enough votes to reject Choate.

Choate maintained communication with Daley's office and political officials in Chicago by leaning for advice on Touhy, acting chairman of the state central committee. Before time neared for the caucus meeting ahead of the convention vote Monday, Choate and Touhy agreed that the session should be open to all delegates and alternates whether they were challenged or unchallenged. At the door of the caucus room, Choate announced, "All delegates and alternates should come into the room and then it will be open to all others who want to attend."[41] If there were any folks looking for a public argument, Choate disarmed the situation quickly. He was in charge of a brief and businesslike meeting that kept the waters calm. There was a parade of state elected officials and candidates for office who spoke of party unity and avoided any direct mention of the factions. Nothing had happened, and that is the way Choate wanted it.

Monday night at the convention was credentials showdown time for two state delegations: Illinois and California. In the California primary on June 6, McGovern defeated Hubert Humphrey in a winner-take-all battle for 271 delegate votes. The number was critical to McGovern's chance to win the nomination. The convention credentials committee ruled by a vote of 72 to 66 on June 29 that McGovern could receive only 120 of the delegates because of a violation of convention rules. A challenge to the committee vote was lodged in the federal court system, which ended with the U.S. Supreme Court avoiding involvement. Members argued that courts should not be involved in political matters. That put it back in the lap of the Democratic National Committee and its chairman Larry O'Brien (also the convention chair). He called for a vote of delegates on Monday night. McGovern received enough delegate votes to assure nomination.[42]

The credential challenge to Chicago's fifty-nine elected delegates was on the convention agenda after the California vote. A last-minute proposal for compromise surfaced from Wall and McGovern interests. They called for each Daley and Singer delegate to receive a half vote. Both delegate groups turned down the compromise idea. Choate agreed with the party regulars believing it was disrespectful of the party leadership.[43]

On the convention floor before the vote Choate announced his opposition to the compromise and called for the vote. About 3:30 A.M. Tuesday delegates voted to seat the Singer group, as almost everyone had expected. Singer delegates celebrated on the convention floor. Choate had guided the delegation through the first session without incident and convinced all parties he could be trusted.

At a delegation caucus on Tuesday the first order of business was to name a permanent chairman. Singer praised Choate's work and called for his election. He said, "We all respect the way you handled your duties fairly and with wisdom." After approval, Choate responded, "I'm pledging to you that we shall leave Florida with a unified party and a party dedicated to victory in November."[44] Joining Choate with a unity statement was Auditor Michael Howlett, an at-large delegate. Wall received an invitation from Choate to serve as vice chair of the delegation, but according to the new party rules, to meet the required gender formula, if an elected chair is male, a woman had to be elected as vice chair. To meet this requirement, Choate added Anna R. Langford from the Singer delegation as vice chair.[45]

After settling the Chicago delegation issue, Muskie dropped out of the race and released his delegates. Many of them in Illinois switched to McGovern. As the convention progressed to the moment of voting for the nomination, Wall assumed a significant role in the McGovern strategy and plans for victory. Being a practical man, Choate respected the arrangement.

An episode during the voting illustrated Wall's rank. Gary Hart, McGovern's convention and campaign manager and later a senator from Colorado, contacted Wall about a key role for Illinois in the roll-call vote. When Illinois was called for its vote, Choate was to say, "Illinois passes." Choate followed the orders as passed along from Wall. As the counting got close enough that the Illinois vote would clinch the nomination, Hart gave the signal for Choate to announce the state's numbers.[46] It placed

Illinois at the climax of McGovern's nomination, with Choate shouting the delegation vote that put McGovern over the top, with Wall standing nearby. Choate cast his own vote for Henry "Scoop" Jackson, U.S. senator from Washington State.

On the surface it appeared the Illinois delegation ran smoothly to the convention's end, and for the most part it did. Choate knew that McGovern would receive the bulk of votes and that Wall was McGovern's man. Everyone knew, as well, that Singer's ambition was publicity that would lead him to victory in a campaign for mayor of Chicago, a goal Singer never achieved. Wall summarized relationships among delegates and leaders this way: "It was a rebellious crowd, all outsiders."[47]

Years later, Wall looked with approval at Choate's performance as chair of the delegation. He said, "Choate and I worked well together because we needed to get our work done. None of my people disliked him, except for those few who disliked anyone who was a 'regular.'" In retrospect, Wall considered the question, why Choate? They seemed to get along in spite of their political differences. Wall offered, "Choate came from a southern Illinois culture. I came from a southern Georgia culture. I don't know Clyde's religion but I suspect we were not far apart. That could have helped me relate to him."[48] Choate's handling of the riotous situation in the Illinois delegation gained him respect across the state. Wall retained a leadership role in the 1972 McGovern general election campaign. In 1976 Wall was chosen by Jimmy Carter to chair Carter's Illinois campaigns in both the primary and general elections. Wall was then elected, with President Carter's backing, to serve from 1977 to 1981 as one of six Illinois members of the Democratic National Committee, replacing Chicago "regular" alderman Edward Vrdolyak.

Choate's performance, tension filled as it was, did nothing to damage his relationship with Daley and the Chicago regular crowd. They would have reasons enough to influence Choate's dream of becoming Speaker of the House, but not for three more years.

6.
The Fight for Speaker—and Beyond

"Well, Clyde Is Clyde"

If Clyde Choate were to have penned a memoir of his time in the legislature, there is little doubt that under the heading "Your Biggest Challenge" would be "The Fight for Speaker of the House." Choate's goal in the Illinois House of Representatives was to be the top dog. He didn't plan to exceed the record of his mentor Paul Powell in number of times as Speaker: three. But one time would be vindication for more than three decades of service, most of them in some top role in Democratic Party leadership.

No doubt Choate had been thinking of a time when the speakership was within grasp. Regardless, others, including the press, had it on the political speculation agenda for years. It was a moot point as long as Republicans controlled the House of Representatives, and that party was in the driver's seat for most of the years from 1961 until 1975.[1] In the 1972 elections when Daniel Walker defeated Richard Ogilvie for governor, Democrats were just a single vote shy of controlling the House. That opened the door to thoughts about the election of 1974 and whether Democrats might take the House.

Although Walker publicly expressed no interest in the choice of a Speaker, few believed that would be the case when the subject arose. He spoke philosophically about the importance of the executive, which he was, and he believed that politicians, scholars, and the press placed too much emphasis on how a governor's program fared in the legislature.[2]

Showing a smattering of disdain, he turned matters of the legislature over to his deputy Victor DeGrazia, who hired a young but experienced Democratic staff member to work the General Assembly for Walker. Ironically, Douglas Kane had worked on the campaign staff of Paul Simon in the 1972 primary against Walker. After that he served on staff for Democrats in the House, where he became a close adviser and loyalist to Choate. His maneuvering among opposing Democratic forces appeared not to harm his political future. Kane served in the Illinois House from 1975 to 1983.[3] In the year he worked for the Walker administration, Kane discovered that most Democrats and some Republicans in the General Assembly had no use for the new governor. This meant many of Walker's proposals were dead on arrival and was a harbinger of nasty relationships between legislators and Walker during his four years in office.

Choate ranked as one whom the governor did not trust. During the 1972 campaign, Walker cited Choate as an example of leaders who ran the legislature for their own personal benefit. He also criticized politicians who had connections to racetracks, although he did not specifically mention Choate. However, on a campaign appearance in Carbondale with Choate present, Walker ignored remarks prepared for him criticizing racetrack stockholders. Instead, he warmly endorsed Choate as a kind of champion of the common folk.[4] In most campaigns over the years personal criticisms made during a campaign for governor rarely hung in the air long after the election. With Walker, it was different, and presumably that reflected Choate's attitude, too.

The early stories—those appearing in newspapers prior to the 1972 election—about a potential Choate candidacy for Speaker carefully spoke highly of his legislative work without bringing up any negatives. Representative Gerald Shea, Daley's manager in the House and assistant minority leader, said, "He did a capable, outstanding job for the party in his four years as whip under John Touhy. Part of his ability is being able to sit down and work out compromises."[5] Shea then mentioned Choate's work in shaping a road bond issue during the Ogilvie administration and his work as a sponsor of bills to raise levels of workers' compensation. An unidentified Chicago Democrat stated, "I would rather talk to Clyde Choate than I would to some 'holier than thou' character. What I mean is that he speaks plainly and when he tells you something you can depend upon it." Democrat representative Leland Rayson of Tinley Park, added, "Strangely enough I find

Clyde Choate quite amenable to work with. He's a pragmatist. He won't treat you like dust. He may be full of games and double talk or he may level with you. You can depend upon him."[6] Republicans were less enthusiastic about working with Choate but offered no public backstabs.

Even if unable to pry a criticism from legislative colleagues, commentators and reporters offered some on their own. These criticisms fell into two categories that partly overlapped. One was Choate's longtime association with Paul Powell and the tactics Powell used to get his way. Powell had died in 1970 and no longer could enforce longstanding alliances and trade-offs. Officials were slow to condemn him, but any lingering bad memories carried over to Choate. Answering those innuendoes and charges later in the Speaker contest, Choate used familiar words in claiming Powell as a close friend who had voted with him on many subjects of importance to downstate.

The other matter hanging over Choate had a connection with Powell. After Powell's death, disclosures of his racetrack stock holdings and payments for "public relations" painted a picture of inside deals, even if legal. Choate's racetrack stock naturally created rumbles among those who disapproved. Persons who also benefited from Powell's track connections kept quiet. Regarding his stock, Choate declared, "I think the courts have said that was all right as an investment. I never hid it from anyone. There were all those investigations right after Powell died, and if I had done anything illegal I'm sure I would have been indicted."[7] That is about the extent of any public comments Choate made regarding their personal relationship and horse racing. In 1998, when interviewed for a biography of Powell, Choate politely refused to answer questions with anything more than a generalization.[8]

If and when Democrats again controlled the House, three individuals would influence the choice of Speaker: Mayor Daley, Governor Walker, and Choate. Among them they controlled the votes of Democratic House members. In Walker's first two years as governor his negative attitude toward any matters of interest to Daley and Chicago meant that agreement between the two leaders on a Speaker would be unlikely. As matters developed, Choate could see his hope for Speaker depended on a working relationship with the mayor and independent downstate Democrats. That reality became clearer soon after Walker took office as governor.

Difficulties between Walker and the legislature arose early in 1973. The legislature approved a bill granting emergency aid to the Chicago

Transit Authority and other mass transit systems, which Walker vetoed.[9] He wanted any amount paid from the state treasury to Chicago matched by funds from the City of Chicago and Cook County. Daley and his followers immediately termed this an attack on the mayor, reminiscent of Walker's anti-Daley rhetoric during the election campaign. The House and Senate prepared to override the veto, which required a majority in each chamber of 60 percent or more. Word favoring the override went out to downstate legislators through former East St. Louis mayor Alvin Fields, an ally of Daley who had served many years on the Democratic State Central Committee as vice chairman. Fields had no reason to help Walker. During the governor's campaign Walker designated Francis Touchette, a political adversary of Fields, for East St. Louis area patronage. Also working to put together a coalition for override in the House was Choate and the Republican Speaker W. Robert Blair. The override succeeded. The number of vetoes during Walker's four years in office—468—underscores his difficulty with the legislature. The General Assembly overrode Walker only eight times, one of which was the Chicago transit issue.[10]

With Republicans holding a one-vote margin in the House in 1973—on any given day neither party would have all of its members in the chamber— a close working arrangement between Speaker Blair and Choate, the minority leader, became necessary if any legislation were to pass the House. Publicly, the two argued about public policy and politics. Choate once accused Blair of "Hitler-like tactics" and acting as a "super-judge."[11] But when it came to legislation, they were chums, or at least chummy. Partisan colleagues of Blair did not like the bipartisan efforts, calling the Speaker "Clyde Blair." In the 1971 session, before Walker's election, the two leaders had agreed on a massive transportation bond issue, a capital development bond issue, and a reasonably tough ethics plan. A *Chicago Daily News* writer wrote, "Blair and Choate are totally political and completely non-ideological. It is impossible to imagine either of them getting worked up over an issue like abortion or capital punishment . . . Both readily and publicly admit that they prepare legislation through backroom political deals."[12]

Choate shocked his colleagues and most anyone familiar with state government when on December 5, 1973, he announced plans to retire, citing poor health and a desire to spend time with his family. Almost everyone had an opinion about the decision and its cause, but Choate added no fuel to the fire, except to say it was "the most difficult decision of my life." Rumors included one that Choate would be indicted over involvement with Powell and the estate.

Supporters throughout the fifty-ninth legislative district rallied and started a petition drive in hopes of convincing Choate to reverse his direction. Leo Brown, Choate's doctor and a former trustee of Southern Illinois University (SIU), encouraged them. "He has no serious disease that can incapacitate him," Brown said. "What he is suffering from is severe physical and emotional exhaustion from long hours in smoke-filled rooms, irregular eating and sleeping habits and helping to run the multimillion dollar business that is the State of Illinois."[13] He added that Choate needed two months of "complete separation" from his work. "He ought to go fishing," Brown added. The petitions with hundreds of signatures were presented to Choate.

Two weeks later, Choate reversed field and said he would not retire. The change of mind occurred on the last day to file for reelection in 1974. His only explanation: "When I said I was retiring, I was 100 per cent serious. But now after making my decision it's hit me square in the face that I won't be in the General Assembly after November of next year."[14] He said his health had improved.

During Choate's hiatus David Vaught, twenty-six, a graduate of West Point, had filed to run for the legislature from Choate's district. Incidentally, he was Walker's son-in-law.[15] Vaught had been given a job by the Walker administration to promote tourism in southern Illinois. Back in November when word first circulated that Vaught might be interested in running for the House, Choate was sufficiently upset to call DeGrazia. After that, Vaught's sister was fired from her job in the Department of Mental Health. No connection with Choate was proven. Needless to say, Choate buried Vaught in the race. Walker had been quoted as saying, "I'll never forgive that man for what he did to my son-in-law." Choate's comment: "What'd he expect me to do? Let the kid beat me?"[16] Inevitably, this episode shaped the background to the Speaker fight.

As talk about the November 1974 election warmed up, newspaper reporters had plenty of time and motivation to explore Choate's chance at becoming Speaker, if a sufficient number of Democrats were elected in November. In the lull of Springfield activity, a reporter for the *Decatur Herald and Review* visited with Choate and his wife at their home in Anna. The House minority leader, dressed in shorts and a sport shirt, sat with the reporter at a table under a shade tree. He sipped iced tea and talked about his life and politics, when not interrupted by friends who dropped by to pay respects. This was Choate's bailiwick, his home office and territory.[17] About the visitors he said, "Today's been kind of quiet but you should have been here this morning. What you have to realize about politics down here is that, first of all, we're all friends. Now a lot of the people who were here this morning needed jobs."

Choate had much to say about the difference between political life in Union County and the metropolitan Chicago area. He stated,

> You go to Chicago and you see an elected official up there eating lunch in a restaurant and the people who come up to him and chat for a while are other elected officials. I go to a restaurant around here like the Purple Crackle [a supper club near Cape Girardeau, Missouri, with a gambling room "out back"] or the Holiday Inn with Donna [wife] or Kim [daughter] and it's not always the elected officials who come around. A lot of them are just plain John W. Public [sic]. And they'll say, "Hi, Clyde" or "Hi, Donna" and "How are you." It's a lot more personal."

About becoming Speaker, Choate unlimbered his tongue carefully: "Certainly, it would be a real honor. It would place me in a position of being able to do something for the people of the area. But as for having a burning desire to be speaker of the house, I think I would have to take a back seat to some of the other members. Before anyone can consider themselves a candidate for speaker they've got to be elected to the House. And then we've got to elect a Democratic majority in the House."

Toward the end of the interview, he reminisced about Clyde Choate in the third person: "I don't believe there's an iota of change in Clyde Choate since the time when my daddy was on the WPA back in the Depression in the 30s. I don't think there's a difference between Clyde Choate now and the time he was elected to office. And there won't be any change between now and the time they bury Clyde Choate."

Choate was reelected for the fourteenth time as a member of the House in November 1974. Democrats took control of the state House by a comfortable margin of 101 to 76. A Speaker would be chosen at the beginning of the General Assembly session in 1975. The postelection clamor began with Choate the favorite, and the target.

Behind the scenes, Choate worked the network to Mayor Daley with what the press called "love letters."[18] They were sent through John Touhy and Gerald Shea, both close associates of the mayor, seeking support in the Speaker contest. Naturally, no one would confirm the letters or whether any promises had resulted from them. Meanwhile, agents of Walker whispered that Choate's contacts with Daley were made without talking to the governor. Choate could count. Daley controlled 40 to 45 votes in the House, and at the most Walker controlled a dozen. Another problem for the governor: he had no candidate for Speaker. In an interview Walker increasingly dodged questions about support for Choate. Instead, he said a Speaker should be reasonably well liked by colleagues, have the ability to get large numbers of votes on important issues, be honorable in dealing with other branches of government, and have wide experience in legislative matters. He added that several members of the House met those expectations.[19] That was not exactly a statement of rousing support for Choate.

Long after the soldiers of various constituencies had left the battlefield and reflected on their legacies, the intensity failed to be reflected in recollections. Choate remembered those days this way:

> I was an extremely close personal as well as political friend of Mayor [Richard J.] Daley and the family as well as many Democratic leaders in the County of Cook. Mayor Daley on several occasions tried to get me to run for higher office, such as lieutenant governor, treasurer, etc. Mayor Daley, contrary to popular belief was one of the most strictly honest and family-minded people that I have ever met in my life, bar none. Major Daley and the Chicago organization, for example, helped me so strongly and provided votes to help me pass much of the legislation creating funding for SIU to make it the worldwide known school it is today.[20]

Choate was well aware that Chicago votes could mean life or death for downstate legislators. And, during Choate's time there were many instances when the mayor needed Choate's help, too. As time to select a Speaker approached, it looked like an opportunity for Choate to collect on those times when he had helped Daley.

Critics talked about Choate being of the "old school" of legislative leader, an obvious reference to Powell and others who strong-armed members to pass public policy for personal gain. Also, talk picked up about Choate's ownership of racetrack stock and stock ownership in banks in Springfield and Franklin Park. Other targets included Choate's real estate developments in southern Illinois and the racetrack stock, purchased at bargain-basement prices, that had earned handsome dividends over the years.[21] When asked about the charges, Choate, stated, "I have no comments regarding their accusations. It's up to the membership of the House to decide. They know what I've done in the past. They know what I hope to do in the future. They know about my programs."

During the first week of January Choate issued a public statement declaring his candidacy for Speaker. It contained references to his record and personal background as might be expected. He mentioned actions he would take as Speaker and the opportunity facing the Democratic Party:

> I already have made suggestions for streamlining and improving rules and procedures of the House designed to make its work more effective, fair and to better serve the people of Illinois. In fact, I proposed these detailed rules only two days after the November 5 election and asked for suggestions and comments from not only members but all other interested persons. For the first time in 38 years Democrats control both houses and have a Democratic governor on the second floor. We have a marvelous opportunity to demonstrate that we are the responsible party in this state when we are given an opportunity. We should not be so concerned today, tomorrow, or for the next two years with political infighting as we should be concerned about creating a service for people—particularly jobs for the unemployed as unemployment rates increase everyday.[22]

As the vote for Speaker approached, the Walker administration's anti-Choate campaign quickened. In spite of the governor's "no involvement" declaration he endorsed Representative Gerald Bradley of Bloomington for the job.[23] Bradley gained little traction, but that encouraged at least another five wannabes to enter the field, some devoted simply to preventing Choate from getting the job. Rolland Tipsword of Taylorville and William Redmond from suburban Bensenville fell into that category. Most of the open anti-Choate feeling among Democrats represented central to northern Illinois districts. Choate responded to the Walker initiatives: "As I've said in the past, I've felt I've done more than an adequate job for the administration under some adverse and trying circumstances."[24] He did not need to go into details.

Helped along by a whispering campaign from the governor's office, opponents of Choate picked up on his presumed involvement in a legislative scheme to make it possible for him to renew a real estate license without having to take an examination. Choate's license had lapsed for more than five years. Under that law Choate would have to take a new test to qualify for renewal. A new law passed with his blessing extended renewal to seven years without examination.[25] The number of House voters influenced by that rumble was impossible to determine.

Editorial pages picked up on any number of issues to claim Choate undeserving of the speakership. The *Chicago Tribune* stated, "The last thing Illinois—or the Democratic party—needs is another speaker in the mold of the late Paul Powell. Mr. Choate, a Powell protégé, is another of those politicians who 'can smell the meat a-cookin.' Freshman Democrats should consider carefully, before voting for speaker, whether they want honest, efficient leadership or more politics as usual."[26]

Occasionally, a newspaper editor took a look at Walker's role in the unfolding drama. The *Decatur Herald and Review* said, after noting anonymous comments supporting Bradley, "The governor has legitimate grounds in his own mind to oppose Rep. Choate's candidacy. Yet it hardly does his administration credit to campaign through the back alley, whispering innuendoes to all who care to listen."[27]

Two days before the House vote an article in the *Metro-East Journal* reported that Walker's agents had pressured Democratic chairmen in St. Clair and Madison counties to insist that representatives vote for Bradley. If not, the agents said, the counties would lose patronage jobs. Some state employees already had received notices of being fired. An unnamed aid to Choate responded, "It started out on the basis that the governor wanted people to come out anti-Choate and when that didn't happen they wanted to go with Bradley and then started firing people because other House members wouldn't fall in line behind Bradley."[28]

Walker escalated his campaign a day before the House vote by flying from Springfield to Chicago for a face-to-face meeting with Mayor Daley.[29] His purpose was to convince the mayor to turn his back on Choate. After the conference, attended just by the two men, Walker said in a statement, "I pointed out to the mayor that the recent election showed that the people of Illinois want reform, not return to the old way of doing business. I emphasized that the leaders of the Democratic Party should be above reproach. I listed the names of candidates other than Clyde Choate who have announced their candidacies for speaker and said that all of them would make outstanding speakers." The mayor, speaking to the press as he hurried back to work, added, "We discussed the leadership of the legislature. He talked to me about Choate. I told him that members of the legislature should decide who the leaders are . . . No one should interfere."[30] To carry the silliness further, Daley denied wielding influence for Choate.

With each statement, the process of choosing a Speaker moved ahead. The night before the vote Democratic members caucused to see who had votes for next day's balloting. Opponents of Choate hoped to stop the candidate from getting a first-ballot victory.

The caucus vote carried disappointing news for Choate. His opponents stopped him cold for a first-ballot victory. He received 59 of the necessary 89 votes, all but about 20 from Mayor Daley's army. The rest, a disappointing number, came from Choate's supposed strength downstate.[31] A first reading gave Governor Walker credit for slicing off what many thought would put Choate over the top. Independent members from near Chicago abandoned Choate en masse. Others receiving votes were William Redmond, 13; Gerald Bradley, 11; Rolland Tipsword, 7; Harold Washington of Chicago, 4; John Matijevich of Chicago, 2. Everyone claimed victory, no matter the truth of the vote that became official on Wednesday, January 8. Walker's spokesman sounded pleased; Choate predicted that the election would go beyond one ballot but that he would pick up support as the day went on. "I don't think it will be as lengthy a process as a lot of people are predicting," he said.[32] Almost immediately Choate's opponents worried that House Republicans might throw votes into the fray. Choate cooled that speculation, saying, "I have never asked a single solitary Republican about voting for me." Republicans vocally took to the sidelines and said they would let the Democrats elect the Speaker.

With an occasional recess during Wednesday, House members voted, with the numbers changing little. Choate vowed, "I'm prepared to go as long as it takes to settle this matter."[33] Thursday votes stayed the same in spite of talks, threats, and maneuvers. By the end of the day twenty-eight ballots had taken place. Many of those from downstate who did not vote for Choate disclaimed any movement inspired by Walker, saying they voted for others as a protest against "old-style" leadership. Among the twenty-two freshmen Democrats who were elected in 1972, many grew bitter at being expected to go along with whatever deals were cut by their leaders. If they had revenge in mind, it appeared to be happening in 1975.

The first major shift in the stalemate occurred on Friday, January 10, when Daley true believers abandoned Choate and swung their 42 votes in support of Redmond, giving him 79 of the needed 89 for election.[34] The signal to change came from Gerald Shea, the floor spokesman for the mayor. Realizing Choate could not get more than 61 votes, Daley had abandoned his candidate. Choate's support had shrunk to 16, with little prospect of more, after thirty-eight ballots. Visibly worn and frustrated, he observed, "I find it funny that I started in the majority and the minority was wagging the tale of the majority. Now I find myself in one of the splinter groups and in the minority that is still wagging the tail of the majority." Redmond seemed puzzled why he couldn't get the support of loyalists to Choate.

The weekend brought no clarity to the situation. The vote remained unchanged on Monday. Choate left the House floor on Tuesday to be with his wife, who had undergone exploratory surgery in St. Louis. Before leaving, he gave a fiery speech, vowing to fight on in his effort to block the election of Redmond. Choate said those voting for him were free to vote as they wished, but no one indicated a change. Choate said, "They are taking this position on principle. They are voting their consciences. And if all of you are not doing the same, then shame on you."[35] Shortly after Choate left, Democrats voted for the seventy-seventh time without electing a Speaker.

Nothing much changed in Springfield as the deadlock continued through a second weekend. An occasional newspaper story hinted that Republicans might cross over and elect Redmond, but GOP leaders kept their caucus out of the Democratic fight. When two Republicans from Redmond's district voted for their neighbor, they received catcalls from many others in the caucus. Newspaper editorialists continued to call for Choate's supporters to cease being loyal and finish the fight, but those comments had no influence with the sixteen. As the standoff neared two weeks, and ninety ballots, fourteen Democrats met for hours seeking a compromise.[36] Choate's men, refusing to vote for Redmond, mentioned Tipsword from Taylorville and Representative Horace L. Calvo from Granite City as acceptable choices. Redmond rejected the offering. To further confuse the issue, Choate backers demanded that party leadership be thrown out. The attempted compromise failed. Meanwhile, on the last vote Redmond received 89, Choate 16, and a handful went to others.[37]

Ninety-three. Thirteen.

Those were the magic numbers that put William Redmond, a sixty-five-year-old Democrat representative in the Speaker's chair. It took ninety-three ballots over thirteen days. In the end, Redmond needed and received 7 Republican votes.[38] As all of these were from the Chicago area, everyone surmised that Mayor Daley realized Choate could not win and applied sufficient pressure for Redmond to get the needed 89 votes.

In the final tally, Choate, who a little more than two weeks earlier had been the favorite to become Speaker, received 15 votes—referred to jokingly by his colleagues as the "embattled fifteen." He was in St. Louis with his wife during the last vote. The votes for Choate told a tale beyond the winner. Eight of his votes came from members in Little Egypt districts, the others from central and northern Illinois.[39]

The message was clear: the end of an era was at hand. The southern half of Illinois no longer could pull a sufficient number of party votes to keep a hold on House leadership. Historically speaking, downstate interests had resisted the growth in numbers and power of the northeastern part of Illinois since 1945, when Powell first held a leadership position. One extraordinary aspect of that period was the combined thirty-year tenure of Powell and Choate. General Assembly reapportionment in 1955, 1965, and 1971 eroded their strength by enlarging the number of districts in the suburban counties outside Cook. Along the way, Mayor Daley became a relentless force to be reckoned with. The reign of Powell and Choate ended as did their brand of wheeling and dealing, building coalitions across partisan boundaries, and rewarding their supporters. In reality, the change meant mostly that deals and rewards would continue to be handed out, just not by southern Illinoisans.

Two days after Redmond became Speaker Choate returned to Springfield from St. Louis for a press conference. He kept up a familiar banter, often part of his public face, and appeared to have accepted the outcome, no matter how disappointing. He was hurt but did not show it. He told reporters, "I intend to retain a positive position in this legislature. At no time will I be an obstructionist."[40] With that he moved out of his large office in the capitol building and across the street where rank-and-file members had much smaller workspaces. Observers were reminded of Governor Walker's description of Choate after an earlier contest: "Well, Clyde is Clyde."

Choate and the Sinking Congressional Remap

Mythology was always part of the mix in assessing Clyde Choate's impact on Illinois public policy. During his time it enhanced his reputation and earned him countless newspaper headlines. Actually, the crafty Choate worked his legislative "miracles" with a mixture of clout and public relations. One such illustration occurred after his disappointing loss in the run for Speaker of the House in 1975 and during his last session before retirement.

For the first time since his earliest years in the General Assembly, Choate had been stripped of his station. The loss for Speaker not only cost him in terms of reputation and prestige, but he also lost an impressive office in the capitol building. He had no close connection to the Speaker, William Redmond, and seemed by many to be out of the mainstream. However, a factor that principal players forgot during the session of 1977 was Choate's skill at stopping or altering a presumed outcome that he disliked. That skill had always been one of his major assets.

Choate commanded a small band of sixteen or seventeen Democratic votes from downstate that stayed with him in the Speaker's contest and therefore could still influence the balance of power and the outcome on a given issue if the vote were close. Also, in those days personalities could still shake the House chamber, although that time was coming to an end. Over his twenty-eight years in the House, Choate's personal strength resulted in large part from past favors, old allegiances, and ties made by being a party leader.

A proposal before the legislature in 1977 was Senate Bill 1250, which called for a dramatic change in the congressional district landscape. The specific language stated, "Reapportionment: 24 Congressional Districts, redistricts state, repeals old act."[41]

Under the geographic boundaries at the time, Chicago mayor Daley had political control of seven of the twenty-four districts. The reapportion plan would have increased that number to nine by relocating two districts from downstate. The power grab by Daley was real. Control of more congressional seats spread his reach in delegates to the Democratic National Convention and therefore in the selection of Democratic candidates for president.

As might be expected, the plan divided the legislature, with members from Cook County, Chicago, and some parts of the suburbs generally supportive. Republicans in the House objected. After the Senate approved the bill, the showdown moved to the House, where Daley needed eighty-nine votes to win. He did not have that many under his direct control. In doubt were those members influenced by Governor Walker and Choate.[42]

Newspaper columnists added one other issue to Daley's motivation: getting even with U.S. representative Abner J. Mikva, a renegade Democrat elected from city and suburban districts. Daley resented Mikva for not supporting his reelection bid in 1971.[43] That should not have surprised the mayor. Mikva always maintained an independent streak dating to his years in the state legislature when he often opposed the Chicago machine's interests, and those of Powell and Choate. Moving Mikva's district to the mayor's influence zone would seriously impact Mikva's future.

As the issue percolated toward the end of May, a month ahead of adjournment, Governor Walker entered the picture in opposition to Daley's plan. Any members who followed the advice of Walker were likely to stand opposed unless the remap appeared to favor their local situation. Speculation about the vote indicated the possibility that Daley could receive as many as fifteen Republican votes from those serving suburban districts. That left only Choate and his compatriots who could influence the outcome. As the bill neared floor consideration, Choate remained noncommittal. He had said he did not like the idea when the bill was introduced but had not seen the most recent version. Choate let the drama build.

Columnists could see either side of the issue from Choate's viewpoint. By voting with the mayor he would revive the partnership that served both men's purposes in the past. He would be viewed as the man who passed the redistricting plan, proving that he was not "dead" in the House. The other side Choate would consider had the strong element of revenge. Daley's abandonment in the Speaker's race must still have irked Choate, although he had plenty of experience with disappointments over almost thirty years of highs and lows.

The bill proceeded through the House and passed on two readings.[44] A third and final reading remained before the final floor vote. This is where mythology enters the picture. As the moment of truth neared in the House, Choate presumably sat in a Springfield restaurant manipulating it all. One account stated, "This really was his hour of revenge because Old Man Daley really wanted the redistricting proposal badly. Choate was able to orchestrate the opposition from a phone booth and beat them."[45] Phone booth? (Perhaps, like Clark Kent as Superman.) The fact remains that the proposal did not go past the second reading, and died, when it became obvious that a floor vote would fail.

Although he finished his legislative service with the 1977 session, he had earlier announced his intentions to retire. He later explained, "I went to the '77 legislative season and we were on the floor of the house to take our oath of office and I got recognition from the acting Speaker, which was Secretary of State Mike Howlett, and gave my swan song, gave my retirement speech and walked off the floor of the house before I was sworn into office for the two years I had been elected to . . . Nobody can say that I retired because I couldn't win." He told House members, "I have enjoyed every single second I've spent in the General Assembly, I love ya. I will be back with you."[46] He was fifty-six years old.

Often when legislators of long and distinguished service retired, the chamber passed a resolution of praise and thanks. During the 1977 legislative session the House did its duty for Choate. In part, the resolution stated,

> Whereas, the traits of leadership and determination which served him well on the battlefields of France and the beachhead at Anzio have been apparent in his service in this House, during which he has served 4 terms as Minority Whip, 2 terms as Minority Leader, 2 terms as Majority Whip and one term as Majority Leader; and Whereas, In addition to his long and illustrious career as a legislator, Clyde Choate has been actively involved in the Democratic Party, for which he was chosen as Chairman of the Illinois delegation to the 1972 Democratic Convention, and is a valuable member of the American Legion, Disabled American Veterans, Military Order of the Purple Heart, Elks and Moose; Resolved, that we commend the Honorable Clyde L. Choate for his enviable accomplishments as a citizen, soldier and Representative; that we extend our best wishes for success in all his future endeavors.[47]

Thanks from SIU: A Job as Lobbyist

Choate's retirement from the General Assembly did not mean retirement from dealings with state government. Before the formal public retirement, he had signed on with officials at SIU to be a lobbyist for the university. Unquestionably, the decision reflected his close relationship with many in the General Assembly, but it also reflected that Choate had been in the forefront of battles to help build a major university with two campuses. In terms of wages paid for services rendered, it was small change for Choate's contribution to SIU's coffers over the decades.

At a news conference to announce his new job, Choate said, "I think I can be of just as much benefit to the continued growth of Southern Illinois in my new position as I would have been by staying in the legislature."[48] He reported to a vice president of SIU and began with the title of Director of University Relations. That was changed in 1995 to Director of External Affairs. He rarely appeared at an office on the SIU campus but commented for a newspaper reporter on his duties. He said it was a full-time job that included everything from representing the university in the legislature to helping students and faculty with problems they might have. He said the job did allow him time to slow down and enjoy his family.

Employee records at SIU provide some information regarding payments for his services but no details nor specific reports on his services and results.[49] In the first four years as lobbyist, beginning in the school year 1977–78 through 1980–81, SIU paid Choate $23,500, $25,984, $29,092, and $32,020. Records for the next five years were not available. Choate continued as lobbyist from 1986–87 to 1993–94, during which time his annual pay increased from $44,826 to $57,225. In 1994–95 he went on emeritus status and was paid $29,340 for each of three consecutive years. He continued as emeritus from 1998 until 2001, being paid a few hundred dollars each year. Choate died in 2002 at age eighty-one.

Whatever legacy Choate produced in the legislature or in work for SIU, he will always have supporters and critics. He will always be associated with downstate and southern Illinois friends and associates, as he should be. However, he crossed the philosophical aisle enough with Chicago interests to have made at least one close friend, Ted Lechowicz, who entered the state House in the 1969–70 session of the General Assembly. They became fast friends, as described by Lechowicz in a "Tribute to Clyde

Choate" he wrote for the fiftieth anniversary of the end of World War II. As a testimonial, it speaks to the collegial style of Choate. The tribute appeared in a special section published by the Anna *Gazette-Democrat* on June 15, 1995. In part, here is what Lechowicz wrote:

> As a young legislator just arriving in Springfield, I was green and unwise in the ways of our government. I was lucky as a person could be to meet Clyde and hit it off with him. He was my mentor and my friend. We shared quarters during all the remaining years of his legislative career. He taught me the importance of establishing a relationship with downstate Democratic colleagues and with those from across the aisle. As a legislative leader he taught me to work collegially, something that carries me in good stead to this day in a different legislative forum, the Cook County Board of Commissioners.[50]

7.
Good Times in Small Places

Rural area politics differs little from urban politics in its manifesta-
tions. In applications it usually follows similar patterns. Secret or
quiet meeting places. Public backslapping and demonstrations of affection
or affectation. They are ever so, whether in the 1950s or 2010s, Chicago
or Vienna.

When Little Egypt political plotting required a safe-room location, many
traveled to just east of the Mississippi River and Cape Girardeau, Missouri.[1]
They went to the Purple Crackle, a nightclub by some standards, a roadhouse
by others, which opened in 1939. Owner Clyde (Bud) Pearce Jr. explained
the origin: "The club didn't have a very extravagant beginning. It opened with
a bottle in a box and a crap game. And the name—Purple Crackle—was a
mistake. My father had named the club the Purple Grackle, after the bird,
but I guess the crack of the dice led everyone to call it Crackle, and the name
stuck." It drew first-class entertainment: Benny Goodman, Duke Ellington,
Woody Herman, all played at the Crackle, according to written accounts.

In the friendly and protected confines Illinoisans knew secrets were
kept while plans were made for public policy efforts in Springfield, Illinois.
The food was special, leaning toward big, thick steaks. In small buildings
out back, high-stakes poker was favored. Female companionship may have
been available upon request.

The testimonial dinner ranked high as an excuse to honor politicians
who brought a measure of fame and recognition, along with jobs, for local

consumption. Usually, the program ignored any setbacks or failures along the way, except in a humorous vein. The outpouring of accolades carried the night. Such was the celebration on June 8, 1946, when John H. Stelle "returned" to McLeansboro after successfully drafting and selling the GI Bill of Rights and serving a year as national commander of the American Legion, ending in late 1945.

As one local historian wrote, the event was "a gigantic homecoming for Hamilton County's gigantic man: John Stelle Day."[2] Top state officials showed up—no one dared to miss it because everyone attending was watching everyone else. In this case the delegation was headed by Governor Dwight Green, Governor Ralph Gates of Indiana, Secretary of State Edward J. Barrett, Illinois Legion Department commander Omer J. Macklin, and an assortment of local and regional friends and well-wishers.

A huge parade preceded the festivities featuring eight bands and drum and bugle corps and Illinois State Police marching as a group, leading everyone to the fairgrounds. Three radio stations covered the event. After receiving praise heaped by others, Stelle stepped forward to acknowledge the warmth and express his appreciation, with emphasis on patriotism and how everyone must guard and protect the nation.[3] The party continued on into the evening with entertainment and a spectacular fireworks display. Six years earlier Stelle's name had generated widespread animus as he swept through ninety-nine days as governor, but he had recovered nicely, thanks to the American Legion and loyal friends.

Not far from McLeansboro, in Vienna fifteen years later, on March 24, 1961, a crowd estimated at more than a thousand packed the high school gymnasium to honor hometown and Johnson County hero Paul Taylor Powell.[4] Less than three months earlier he had been elected Speaker of the Illinois House of Representatives for the third and last time. Powell was at the peak of prowess and power in state government. In recognition of his statewide influence, the big-name guest list included Lieutenant Governor Samuel Shapiro, Senator Everett Peters of St. Joseph, House minority whip Clyde Choate, Southern Illinois University (SIU) president Delyte Morris, state representative C. L. McCormick, and a host of state legislators, school officials, and state officeholders. Members of regional fair boards filled many seats to watch a presentation fashioned after the television program *This Is Your Life*. Longtime friend James M. (Stud) Walker was master of ceremonies. He and Choate had planned the affair. Preceding Powell's response, performers entertained guests with instrumental music, vocal solos, string bands, and tap dancing.

After accepting the "keys to the city," Powell spoke of his boyhood days, friends, revered mother, father, wife, and brother to the assembled crowd. He called the celebration "the greatest honor that has ever come to me."[5] Powell expressed regrets that his wife, Daisy, was unable to share the honors with him, saying that she was ill in a Chicago hospital. Virtually everyone in the audience had to hold back a snicker.

There were many such events to pay respects for political achievements and expressions of government expenditures for local causes. Local newspapers needed no excuses to praise citizens for various achievements. An example of a newspaper memorial occurred on June 15, 1995, in a special section of the Anna *Gazette-Democrat* newspaper.[6] In commemoration of the end of World War II fifty years earlier, much of the section was devoted to local and national military hero Clyde Lee Choate.

Also appearing was a reprint of an article from the *Philadelphia Inquirer* of April 26, 1986, titled "Members of Renowned World War II 601st Tank Destroyer Battalion Reunite." Choate was featured in the article stating, "It's amazing. Most of these fellows I haven't seen since the war, but I'm having no trouble recognizing faces and remembering faces."[7] The section carried an account of Choate's combat actions on October 26, 1944, which were acknowledged with the Medal of Honor. Reflecting on his service in the state House, another article stated, "War and Politics: Anna's Clyde Choate earned a Medal of Honor and then became one of the state's top political leaders." Another article reprinted from the June 8, 1975, *Chicago Sun-Times* carried the headline "'Gentleman from Union' Battles Partisan Politics of Redistricting." It spoke to the reputation Choate had for influencing legislation with a powerful speech or behind-the-scenes deal.[8]

These special occasions usually emphasized bipartisanship, illustrated by the appearance of Governor Green, a Republican, at the affair for Stelle, a Democrat. Other activities, minus the ballyhoo, underscored the friendships of Choate, Powell, and state representative C. L. McCormick. They shared close relationships with small-town celebrations and those who ran them. Holiday events drew politicians of all stripes. Behind the partisan rhetoric and applause by respective members of a political party, the friendships prospered.

Mike McCormick, son of C. L. McCormick, described those feelings in an oral history during which he talked at length about his father's political career in the state House. C. L. was a Republican in one of the few Republican-leaning counties of southern Illinois. He, Powell, and Choate served much the same constituency. The son described a journey in which he rode along with the adults:

> But I must tell you, my impression hearing my dad talk . . . My dad was always friends with Clyde; my dad was always friends with Paul Powell . . . There would be a Labor Day parade in Massac County, which was in Clyde and my dad's district, in Metropolis. I'd usually go along with my dad. Clyde was from Anna. He'd run by Vienna and he would pick us up. Of course, I would sit in the backseat. Dad and Clyde would talk all the way to Metropolis. Dad would go get on the Republican float, Clyde would get on the Democratic float, we'd all go out and have lunch afterwards and go home.[9]

WHILE WE LEARNED MUCH ABOUT the early lives and political careers of our three prime subjects, there is something also to be remembered from their deaths. Such it is with those who live large. Their deaths often mirror their time with us, or provide questions about their actions while living.

Paul Powell's unexpected death in October 1970 might have shocked those who did not know he was in failing health. But the news of death was a minor rumble compared to the crescendo of revelations as the aftermath of his death unfolded. Literally for years, newspapers, television stations, and radio networks poured over his income tax returns and probed the mysteries of the more than $800,000 in cash he left behind. Rumors—some were true, but most were not—proved little, but added to rampant speculation about the man's deeds, good and not so good.

Until Powell's estate was settled about nine years after his death, hardly a day went by without some tidbit getting press treatment. It may have been the most documented death of an Illinois public figure since Abraham Lincoln. Paul Taylor Powell claimed countless headlines during his thirty-five years of public service, but even he would have marveled at the trail he left behind.

Many a public figure that sees life ebbing tries to clear the air—or adds to the confusion—with a book he or she hopes will set some records straight and leave readers with a glowing report. In the case of John Henry Stelle that would have been a sensational story had he wanted that much detail on the record. Instead, as he lingered short of death on July 5, 1962, in a St. Louis hospital, Stelle decided to make final statements about former governor Horner and various tormentors, including Chicago newspaperman Milburn (Pete) Akers. He did not ask forgiveness.

One of those gathered at Stelle's bedside was Thomas B. Littlewood, who later would write the most complete biography of Horner. Naturally, that included much about Stelle's time as lieutenant governor. Apparently, Stelle wanted to clarify his thoughts about Horner. As quoted by Littlewood, Stelle regarded Horner as "one of the finest, grandest persons you ever knew," adding that his quarrels were with "those guys around him who could steal a hot stove in July." Further, Stelle called Horner "the best governor Illinois ever had." That might have surprised the Illinois political world. After fifty years in politics, he claimed he could still "get things done" in Springfield or Chicago.

One of the "thieves" Stelle saw around Horner was Akers. In a lengthy column on July 8, 1962, the *Chicago Sun-Times* editor reviewed Stelle's political and personal lives from the viewpoint of an antagonist. However, at one point Akers admitted, "Throughout the years Stelle, largely as a consequence of his own belligerence, was frequently charged with many things, charged conversationally, that is. A lot of the things laid at his door were false."

As Stelle's life faded, he uttered words that stand today as a summary of his political life: "I worked for my friends."

Clyde Choate remained active on behalf of SIU almost until the day he died, October 5, 2001. Blind and frail and requiring in-home health care, Choate relied on his wife, two daughters, and friends for comfort. Nevertheless, when SIU needed something from folks in Springfield, he still knew how to make contact. Perhaps nearly everyone in town knew where he was at any one time during the day, although in failing health. He was by far the most recognizable person in Anna.

As might be expected, obituaries and recollections featured his service in World War II and the Medal of Honor he received. Secondly, they recalled his many years of service to SIU. His thirty years in the House of Representatives received high marks for achievement. One longtime legislative colleague observed, "Southern Illinois University never had a better guardian angel than Clyde Choate." He made no final statements that attracted headlines.

The two hundred people filling pews at the First Evangelical Presbyterian Church ended the funeral service by singing "You Are My Sunshine." After five soldiers raised their rifles and fired twenty-one shots in the air, a solitary soldier stood near the burial grounds and played taps. *Dignity* is the word that comes to mind to describe the passing of Clyde Lee Choate.

Conclusions

The search for answers to questions about Illinois state legislative activism during the three decades after World War II is a journey of many twists and turns. Such would be the case for any similar period of modern state political history. Each has a different signature. In part, that explains the fascination with unraveling state government's trends, and it makes predictions about the future almost impossible.

The period 1947 to 1977 is a product of postwar resurgence in population and education, new faces in the General Assembly representing war veterans who wished to escape memories of a depression and a war, and opportunities to create a state government committed to economic growth. It helped to have political party leadership committed to big ideas and willing to cut the necessary deals. And don't forget the role of power, deceit, and greed. In other words, timing is everything, especially in politics, and money is usually the driver.

However, nothing remained the same for long. During the thirty years attitudes changed dramatically as the nation fought more wars—in Korea and Vietnam—and reformers triumphed briefly over old-school politicians late in the period. Pressures on state finances produced an income tax in what turned out to be a blessing and a curse. Regardless, legislative activism prevailed with a bipartisan flavor and rewarded practitioners who knew how to forge coalitions and balance the benefits across the state. Inevitably, the faces of leadership changed, reflecting the reality of aging and fresh attitudes.

What gave the period a certain uniqueness was a continuity of leadership and a regional political landscape that rewarded trade-offs and balance. Enter Paul Powell, John Stelle, Clyde Choate, and friends who represented a continuum through the decades and gave an advantage to downstate interests long after population trends had favored northeastern Illinois. The political world around them was in constant change, but the players managed to maintain control by adjusting tactics and applying the time-tested backroom methods that usually worked. And to the winners went the spoils: local projects, patronage, and insider money opportunities.

This is not intended to ignore other leaders who found their own versions of playground strategies. The names are familiar: William Stratton, Richard J. Daley, W. Russell Arrington, Richard Ogilvie, and Daniel Walker. Strong and forceful men all, and well-publicized agents and spokesmen of change. (Only Daley had a length of tenure that matched the downstaters.) Remarkably, the principal characters represented in this story prospered with and in spite of opposing forces. Details of specific projects such as the rise of Southern Illinois University and higher education generally, prosperity connected to horse racing, growth of social welfare programs, and greater taxation of businesses and citizens are not especially pretty. In fact, their progress to realization gives us an uncensored picture of the often messy and expensive sides of politics. Greater disclosure of governmental processes and higher levels of ethics had few advocates from 1947 to 1977.

HOW SHOULD ILLINOIS HISTORY TREAT the dealmakers and their deals? For some of those deeply involved, such as Powell, there is not much more for us to learn about their accomplishments and the trail of special favors they left. We know as much or more about Powell as we do about most others who provided political leadership in his lifetime. While it is not enough to say, "Politics is a messy business," neither does it serve a useful purpose to condemn the dealmakers as total miscreants unworthy of praise. Looking across the spectrum of modern Illinois political history the achievers rarely were puritans.

If one purpose of historical exploration is to uncover what happened and provide some context for understanding, then we need to know as much as can be discovered about the participants, from cradle to grave.

The hope is that we will measure the highs and lows en route to an assessment. If that effort is clouded by labeling all actions as destructive or all motives as blessed, exploration has failed its purpose.

In the literature of Illinois politics we know quite a bit about Powell. From the standpoint of John Stelle's involvement in state politics of the 1930s, much has been written and little of it casts a positive light. We know much less about Clyde Choate's political legacy, except as related in accounts about his associations with others such as Powell, Senate leader W. Russell Arrington, and various governors.

From the attention on Stelle and Choate in this book, we see more of the total picture because they were exceptional leaders and coalition builders. Stelle's work on the GI Bill of Rights alone guarantees him a place of honor in Illinois history. In combination with his long-standing support of the state's veterans, Stelle's political impact is substantial. The concentration on Choate reveals him as much more than someone who warmed a seat in the House for thirty years. He was an accomplished achiever.

Much good resulted from the deals made by these individuals, working in a less than perfect environment. We cannot, however, ignore their tactics, motives, and personal conduct as part of a complete picture.

Notes
Bibliography
Index

Notes

1. Common Ground in Small Towns

1. Chris Vlahoplus, United Press International, 20–22 May 1961, as appeared in the *East St. Louis Journal*. Louisa H. Bowen University Archives and Special Collections, Southern Illinois University–Edwardsville (hereinafter cited as Bowen Archives). See also "Speaker Powell's Typical Day Starts with Talks Night Before," Associated Press, 7 June 1961. Bowen Archives.

2. Powell family roots are deep in eighteenth-century southern Illinois history, although details are scant. Sources include *Johnson County, Illinois, History and Families* (Paducah: Turner, 1990); George Washington Smith, *A History of Southern Illinois, a Narrative Account of Its Historical Papers, Its People and Its Principal Interests* (Chicago: Lewis, 1912), vol. 1, 492; John H. Keiser, *Building for the Centuries: Illinois 1862–1898* (Urbana: University of Illinois Press, 1977); John W. Allen, *Legends and Lore of Southern Illinois* (Carbondale: Southern Illinois University Press, 1963); and Howard, *Illinois: A History of the Prairie State*.

3. Gary Hacker, from many interviews with the author over the years, tells of finances for operation of the Thomas Powell home and keeping it open to the public as wished by Paul Powell. It opened in 1979.

4. A few Powell personal items remained in the house, but the bulk of Powell's papers is kept at the Abraham Lincoln Presidential Library, Springfield, IL (hereinafter cited as ALPL). The state library received Powell's papers as a gift from John Rendleman, executor of Powell's estate.

5. Gary Hacker, interview with author and personal tour of house, 21 Feb. 1998.

6. Royce Hundley, interview with author, 21 Feb. 1998.

7. Mike McCormick, personal interview, 8 July 2010, with Mark DePue, director of the ALPL oral history program. The interview provides the recollections of his father's time in Vienna. C. L. McCormick earned the title "Great Entertainer" during his legislative years for his gift of storytelling.

8. McCormick interview.

9. Hacker, interview with author, cited an oral history tape made by Herbert Hook with Levi Locke of Vienna. Reports of the accident are mostly from oral recollections.

10. Hundley interview.

11. Michael Sneed, "Inside the Shoe Box Scandal," *Chicago Magazine*, Oct. 1978, 247.

12. "Johnson County Honors Speaker Paul Powell," *Vienna Times*, 24 Mar. 1961; James Walker, interview with author 21 Feb. 1998, and tape recording of Powell's dinner speech.

13. Hundley interview.

14. Hartley, *Paul Powell of Illinois*, 17–22; "Paul Powell, Secretary of State, Biography 1965," Paul Powell Papers (hereinafter cited as PP Papers); Richard H. Icen, "Paul Powell Story: Cumulative Voting Kept Him Going," *Metro-East Journal*, 26 Jan. 1971. Bowen Archives.

15. Sneed, "Inside the Shoe Box Scandal."

16. Hundley interview.

17. "Johnson County Honors Speaker Paul Powell."

18. Walker interview.

19. Ibid.

20. "A Final Round of Applause for Powell," *Chicago Tribune*, 16 July 1978. A similar version was told by Paul O'Neal in *Chicago Magazine*, Oct. 1978.

21. Walker interview, also tape recording of Powell dinner.

22. Paul Powell, inheritance tax return (amended), filed 3 June 1976, Illinois State Circuit Court, Johnson County.

23. Paul Powell, Last Will and Testament. Also, Sneed, "Inside the Shoe Box Scandal"; Hartley, *Paul Powell of Illinois*, 180.

24. Leo Brown, Vienna physician and friend of Powell, in interview with author, Feb. 1998.

25. Robert W. Sink, "Choate Unscathed by Stock Scandal," *Decatur Herald and Review*, 16 Apr. 1972.

26. Illinois Deaths and Stillbirths Index, 1916–1947, James I. Choate, birth date 28 Apr. 1876, Anna, Union County, Illinois, Ancestry.com, provided by ALPL.

27. *100 Years of Progress: The Centennial History of Anna, Illinois*, Anna Centennial Committee (Cape Girardeau: Missourian Printing and Stationery Co., 1954), 8. Obtained online from the library of the University of Illinois, Urbana-Champaign.

28. *100 Years of Progress*, 12.

29. Ibid., 13.

30. Ibid., 16.

31. Ibid., 17.

32. Ibid., 25–26.

33. Ibid., 23.

34. Twelfth Census of the United States, 1900, Anna, Union County, Illinois, roll 346, Anestry.com, ALPL.

35. Thirteenth Census of the United States, 1910, Anna Ward 1, Union County, Illinois, National Archives, roll T624_329, p. 4A, Ancestry.com, ALPL.

36. "East St. Louis Journal Biography," signed by Clyde L. Choate, 25 Oct. 1960. Bowen Archives; also, letter to author, 12 Nov. 2013, from Gwen Podeschi, reference librarian, ALPL.

37. World War I draft registration card, Franklin County, Illinois, Local Board, 12 Sept. 1918, registration roll 1613400, Ancestry.com, ALPL. See also Sink, "Choate Unscathed."

38. Hartley and Kenney, *Death Underground*, 4–12.

39. Fourteenth Census of the United States, 1920, West Frankfort, Franklin County, Illinois, National Archives, roll T625_364, Ancestry.com, ALPL.

40. "East St. Louis Journal Biography."

41. Angle, *Bloody Williamson*, 73.

42. Nameoki, Illinois, city directory, Ancestry.com, City Directories 1821–1989, ALPL.

43. Illinois Deaths and Stillbirths Index, 1916–1947, Ancestry.com, ALPL. Also, letter to author from Gwen Podeschi, ALPL.

44. Sixteenth Census of the United States, Anna, Union County, Illinois, National Archives, roll T627_896, p. 12B, Ancestry.com. ALPL.

45. Lockard, . . . *and even the stump is gone*, 1.

46. Robert W. Sink, "Life Was Not Easy on the Farm," *Decatur Herald and Review*, 16 Apr. 1972.

47. Sink, "Choate Unscathed."

48. Robert W. Sink, "He Bought Goat and Rabbit with His First Month's Pay," *Decatur Herald and Review*, 16 Apr. 1972.

49. Sink, "Life Was Not Easy on the Farm."

50. Ibid.

51. Sink, "He Bought Goat and Rabbit." Also, Robert W. Sink, "Military Record Set Up First Election," *Metro-East Journal*, 16 Apr. 1972. Bowen Archives; "Retire? Not Clyde Choate," Anna *Gazette-Democrat*, 11 Oct. 2001, 4.

52. Army of the United States, Honorable Discharge, 26 May 1945, enlisted record and report of separation, National Archives Personnel Records Center, St. Louis, MO (hereinafter cited as NARA).

53. Yeide, *Tank Killers*, 8.

54. Honorable discharge papers, NARA.

55. Harry S. Truman, Presidential Appointments—the President's Day, August 23, 1945, 10 A.M. in East Room of the White House. "The President will present twenty-eight Congressional Medals of Honor." Email to author, 22 Oct. 2013, from David Clark, archivist, Harry S. Truman Library.

56. Yeide, *Tank Killers*, 13.

57. Taggart, *History of the Third Infantry Division*, 566.

58. "Members of Renowned World War II 601st Tank Destroyer Battalion Reunite," Anna *Gazette-Democrat*, 15 June 1995, special section. Reprinted from *Philadelphia Inquirer*, 26 Apr. 1986.

59. Josowitz, "An Informal History of the 601st," 5.

60. Ibid., 6.

61. Ibid., 8.

62. Ibid., 10.

63. Atkinson, *An Army at Dawn*, 390.

64. Ibid., 441; see also Yeide, *Tank Killers*, 66.

65. Josowitz, "Informal History of the 601st," 12–13; Taggart, *History of Third Infantry Division*, 434.

66. Josowitz, "Informal History of the 601st," 21; Taggart, *History of Third Infantry Division*, 97–98.

67. Honorable discharge papers, NARA. Also, "Retire? Not Clyde Choate."

68. "Retire? Not Clyde Choate," 4.

69. Yeide, *Tank Killers*, 93.

70. Ibid., 97.

71. Taggart, *History of Third Infantry Division*, 566.

72. Honorable discharge papers, NARA. Also, Taggart, *History of Third Infantry Division*, 408.

73. Josowitz, "Informal History of the 601st," 24.

74. Ibid., 29.

75. A variety of sources used in this narrative reached the same conclusion that Operation Dragoon turned out to be one of the most successful operations fought by the United States in Western Europe.

76. Atkinson, *The Guns at Last Light*, 219.

77. Information taken from daily weather reports for October 1944 in Unit Journals of 601st TD Battalion, photocopies from NARA.

78. Unit Journal, 601st Battalion, 13 Oct. 1944, message received at 08:35 hours, NARA photocopies. Confusion exists regarding the precise date of the action involving Clyde Choate. The Medal of Honor citation states the date as 25 Oct. 1944. Josowitz, "Informal History of the 601st," gives no date. Presumably, the Unit Journal and Operations Report were in error.

79. Operations Report, 601st Tank Destroyer Battalion, 13 Oct. 1944. The Operations Report issued daily provided information about the actions of all companies in the battalion. This information was provided under "Results of Operations" for Company C, NARA photocopy.

80. Unit Journal, 13 Oct. 1944, 18:15 hours, NARA photocopy.

81. Taggart, *History of Third Infantry Division*, 253–54.

82. Josowitz, "Informal History of the 601st," 36. No details of the battle were included.

83. Taggart, *History of Third Infantry Division*, 225; Josowitz, "Informal History of the 601st," 38.

84. Presidential Unit Citation, Third Infantry Division, Executive Order 9396, according to Taggart, *History of Third Infantry Division*, 322. The citation included all attached units, including the 601st. "Members of the Battalion who fought in the Colmar Pocket are entitled to wear both the French Fourragere and the Presidential Citation," Josowitz, "Informal History of the 601st," 40.

85. Honorable discharge, Clyde L. Choate.

86. Army of the United States, Final Payment Roll, 26 May 1945, enlisted record and report of separation for Clyde L. Choate, NARA. Upon separation at Ft. Sheridan, Choate received pay for March, April, and May 1945 of $778.58. He may have saved other funds, for which there is no record.

87. Sink, "He Bought Goat and Rabbit."

88. Clyde Choate, interview with Taylor Pensoneau, 17 Dec. 1994. Information provided by Pensoneau, 10 Feb. 2014.

89. "War and Politics," Anna *Gazette-Democrat*, special section, 15 June 1995.

90. Harry S. Truman Library and Museum, 2 July 1945, copy provided by David Clark, archivist.

91. "War and Politics."

92. Ibid.

93. "Retire? Not Clyde Choate." Also, Sink, "He Bought Goat and Rabbit."

94. Alan J. Dixon, telephone interview with author, 10 Nov. 2012. Choate told Taylor Pensoneau in 17 Dec. 1974 interview that Paul Powell "wasn't even a factor in my first campaign."

95. "Retire? Not Clyde Choate."

96. Hartley, *Battleground 1948: Truman, Stevenson, Douglas, and the Most Surprising Election in Illinois History* (Carbondale: Southern Illinois University Press, 2013), 17.

97. Sink, "Choate Unscathed." Also, *Illinois Blue Book*, 1945–46, 282–83.

98. "Retire? Not Clyde Choate."

99. Sink, "Choate Unscathed."

100. *Illinois Blue Book*, 1945–46.

101. "War and Politics."

102. Sink, "Choate Unscathed."

103. "War and Politics."

104. "Retire? Not Clyde Choate."

105. Malinda Munsell, "A History of Hamilton County," 101. Ms. Munsell worked as a special education teacher and served on the McLeansboro City Council.

106. Buck, *Illinois in 1818*, 119–20; Reynolds, *The Pioneer History of Illinois*, 86.

107. Buck, *Illinois in 1818*, 70.

108. Munsell, "A History of Hamilton County," 101.

109. Ibid., 101.

110. Ibid., 101.

111. Ibid., 101.

112. Howard, *Mostly Good and Competent Men*, 263–64; Littlewood, *Horner of Illinois*, 74, 75.

113. Smith, *History of Illinois and Her People*.

114. McLeansboro Township, 1905 plat map, copy obtained from McCoy Memorial Public Library, McLeansboro, IL.

115. Smith, *Illinois in 1818*, 800; Munsell, "A History of Hamilton County," 101.

116. Howard, *Mostly Good and Competent Men*.

117. Kevin McCann, "Kitty League 101," *The Bull Pen Kitty League Newsletter*, June–July 2005; Munsell, "A History of Hamilton County," 102.

118. Munsell, "A History of Hamilton County," 102.

119. Hamilton County Clerk's office, map showing approval of John H. Stelle's Addition in the city of McLeansboro, 12 June 1915.

120. August Heckscher, *Woodrow Wilson: A Biography* (New York: Scribner's Sons, 1991), 433–41; Littlewood, *Soldiers Back Home*, 23; Smith, *Illinois in 1818*, 129.

121. Littlewood, *Soldiers Back Home*, 6.

122. Ibid., 23.

123. Ibid., 24.

124. Munsell, "A History of Hamilton County," 109. The author provides details of Stelle's American Legion organizational activities.

125. Ibid., 103.

126. Littlewood, *Horner of Illinois*, 76. According to the author both companies had failed by 1931.

127. Smith, *Illinois in 1818*, 129.

128. Littlewood, *Horner of Illinois*, 45.

129. Munsell, "A History of Hamilton County," 103.

130. Littlewood, *Horner of Illinois*, 60–61.

131. "Edward Barrett, Longtime Democrat Power, Dies," *Chicago Tribune*, 8 Apr. 1977.

132. Littlewood, *Horner of Illinois*, 244.

133. Clayton, *The Illinois Fact Book*, 141. From 1930 to 1953 Barrett served as state treasurer, auditor, and secretary of state. He later won election as Cook County clerk.

134. Illinois State Archives, vote totals provided to the author by John Reinhardt, supervisor, operations division.

135. Littlewood, *Soldiers Back Home*, 122.

136. State Archives, vote totals.

137. Ibid.

138. Biles, *Big City Boss*, 53.

139. Littlewood, *Horner of Illinois*, 178.

140. Littlewood, *Soldiers Back Home*, 140.

141. Littlewood, *Horner of Illinois*, 187.

142. Ibid., 218–19. Also, "Lieut. Governor Attacks Makers of Party Ticket," *East St. Louis Journal*, 18 Feb. 1940. Bowen Archives.

143. "Be Loyal or Quit Is Stelle's Edict," *Springfield State Journal*, 11 Oct. 1940, 1; "Resignations Collected for Stelle's Purge," *Chicago Times*, 10 Oct. 1940, 7; "Stelle Purge May Top 200 Off Payroll," *Chicago Times*, 8 Oct. 1940, 24.

144. Milburn P. (Pete) Akers served as Horner's publicity man, 1937–40. He held several top editor positions for the *Chicago Sun* and *Chicago Sun-Times*. He wrote political columns and editorials with a progressive Democrat slant. He retired from the *Sun-Times* in 1965.

145. "Edward Day Named State Purchasing Agent for Stelle," *Illinois State Journal*, 20 Oct. 1940, 4.

146. Littlewood, *Horner of Illinois*, 233; also, Russell Stelle, John Stelle's son, interview with author, 21 Apr. 2010.

147. Howard, *Memoir*. Howard, who worked as a newspaper reporter in Springfield after 1940, said, "I'm not sure that Stelle got a square deal from Horner people after Horner died."

148. Russell Stelle, interview.

149. Ibid.; also, Littlewood, *Horner of Illinois*, 244.

150. Russell Stelle, interview.

151. Ibid.

152. Ibid.

153. Linda Messmer, "Arketex Plant a Family Affair," *Brazil Times*, 31 Aug. 2004. Also, "Former Southenders to Reunite," 30 Aug. 2004, provided by Melissa Hicks, Brazil, IN, Public Library.

154. Kenny Turney, associated with the Clay County, Indiana, historical society, interview with author, 24 Nov. 2012. He doubted the 3,000 figure and said it was more like 1,000.

155. Federal income tax returns, PP Papers. After the death of Powell in 1970, the Internal Revenue Service and Federal Bureau of Investigation requested and received Powell's federal tax returns.

156. Russell Stelle, interview with author, 19 May 2010.

157. Illinois State Geological Survey, spreadsheet of John Stelle wells, provided by Bryan G. Huff, petroleum geologist, 27 Nov. 2012. Date for L & N site, 10 Sept. 1940.

158. Russell Stelle, interview with author, 22 Apr. 2010.

159. Illinois State Geological Survey spreadsheet.

160. Ibid., site date 25 Nov. 1947.

161. Ibid.

162. "Saline Oil Development Newest Stelle Enterprise," *McLeansboro Times-Leader*, 20 Oct. 1955, centennial edition.

163. "Ralph W. Choisser, Prominent Attorney, Dies," *Eldorado Daily Journal*, 24 Mar. 1975, 1.

164. "Cecil Sullivan Dies at Age 76," *Eldorado Journal*, 17 Nov. 1981, 1.

165. Littlewood, *Soldiers Back Home*, 152.

166. Munsell, "A History of Hamilton County," 110.

167. David Camelon, "How the First GI Bill Was Written," *American Legion Magazine*, January and February, 1969. Camelon originally wrote the articles for a 1949 issue of the magazine. The 1969 version was edited for the Legion's 50th anniversary. Camelon was one of three reporters assigned to cover efforts of the Legion in 1943 and 1944 by newspaper publisher Hearst, who also paid expenses in Washington for many working in behalf of the Legion. Camelon wrote at length about Stelle's leadership of the committee.

168. Camelon, 53, Part 1.

169. Camelon, 25, Part 2.

170. U.S. Department of Veterans Affairs, "History Born of Controversy: The GI Bill of Rights," http://www.va.gov/opa/publications/celebrate/gi-bill. pdf, 10 Feb. 2010.

171. The Education Commission of the States, "John H. Stelle," James Bryant Conant Award, 2004. The citation identifies Stelle as "Father of the GI Bill." Also, Munsell, "A History of Hamilton County," 111; Melvin Price, member of Congress, Illinois, *Congressional Record,* "Mr. Speaker, John Stelle of Illinois, more than any other man in the United States can be recognized as the Father of the GI Bill of Rights."

172. United Press, 23 Nov. 1945, as published by the *East St. Louis Journal.*

2. Southern Illinois Power Brokers

1. Paul Powell, "State Rep. Paul Powell Reports on Record in Legislature," *Southern Illinoisan,* 27 Oct. 1958. This account appeared as an op-ed article in Lindsay-Schaub newspapers. An editor's note stated, "Before the primary election, this newspaper attacked the record of State Rep. Paul Powell. At the invitation of the Southern Illinoisan, Rep. Powell has prepared the following report on his record as a legislator." PP Papers. This was just one example of Powell responding to criticism over the years. He also solicited reports from the Illinois Legislative Council to support his record of legislative activism.

2. "The Danger in Paul Powell," *St. Louis Post-Dispatch,* 11 Dec. 1948. Among other criticisms of Powell, the paper stated, "He has managed to serve 14 years at Springfield without identifying himself in the public mind with progressive or forward-looking causes or measures. He is essentially a patronage politician. He sees state government almost entirely in terms of making the precinct committeeman happy."

3. Paul Powell, "State Rep. Paul Powell Reports."

4. Hartley, *Paul Powell of Illinois,* 13.

5. Ibid., 14.

6. Clayton, *The Illinois Fact Book,* 194, "Political Complexion of the Illinois General Assembly, 1880–1968." Republicans controlled the House and Senate for the sessions of 1951, 1953, 1955, and 1957. Also, "Legislative Membership," Legislative Council memorandum to Rep. Paul Powell, 10 Mar. 1954, PP Papers.

7. Marion R. Lynes, "Powell Calls Gov. Stratton Tough to Beat," *St. Louis Globe-Democrat,* 22 Nov. 1959. Bowen Archives.

8. Scariano, *Memoir.*

9. Paul Simon, conversation with author, taped, 20 Feb. 1998. Simon said, "There was no question he was powerful; he was gutsy; he had courage. He was corrupt, and he had some areas where he did good things: Southern Illinois University, minimum wage."

10. Abner Mikva, telephone interview with author, 27 Dec. 1997; and letter to author, 18 Dec. 1997.

11. Robert D. Reid, "Powell's Philosophy: Making Money Hadn't Been 'Declared a Crime,'" *Metro-East Journal*, 30 Dec. 1970, 3. Bowen Archives.

12. Clyde Lee, *Memoir*, vol. 1, copy from Norris L. Brookens Library. Lee's family background and early life in Mount Vernon as recited in biographical information and the preface in the oral history. He discussed growing up on pp. 1–30.

13. Clyde Lee, "Jefferson County, IL, Obituaries," http://www.rootsweb. ancestry.com/iljeffer/obits/lee_clydeobit. Also, Lee, *Memoir*, says reelected consecutively: 1948, 1950, 1952, 1954, 1956, 1958, 1960, 1962, 1964.

14. Lee, *Memoir*, 125.

15. Ibid., 138.

16. Ibid., 189.

17. Hartley, *Paul Powell*, 25; also, Illinois Racing Board to author, 27 July 1996.

18. Howard, *Mostly Good and Competent Men*, 264.

19. *Chicago Sun*, "Democrats Put Faith on Vets," 4 Jan. 1998. Downstate candidates slated were Sherwood Dixon, of Dixon, for lieutenant governor; Ivan Elliott, Carmi, for attorney general; Benjamin Cooper, East St. Louis, for auditor; and Fred Harrison, Herrin, for treasurer.

20. Russell Stelle, interview, 21 Apr. 2010.

21. John Stelle, press release, 4 Nov. 1949, Scott Lucas Collection, box 144, ALPL.

22. Howard, *Mostly Good and Competent Men*, 263.

23. "Area's Hope for Dem Nomination Slim," *East St. Louis Journal*, 29 July 1952. Bowen Archives.

24. "Chicago Can Control Demo Governor Race," *East St. Louis Journal*, 11 Aug. 1952. Bowen Archives.

25. "Fields Says Last Ballot Unanimous," *East St. Louis Journal*, 13 Aug. 1952. Bowen Archives.

26. Russell Stelle, interview, 18 May 2010.

27. Clayton, *Illinois Fact Book*, 302–09.

28. Warren Wood Scrapbooks, 1934–1958, introduction, ALPL.

29. Ibid.

30. Clayton, *Illinois Fact Book*, 194.

31. Kenney, *A Political Passage*, 97.

32. Dixon, *The Gentleman from Illinois*, 65.

33. Dixon, interview with author, 10 Nov. 2010.

34. Gene Callahan, interview with Mark DePue, 6 July 2011, for ALPL oral history program.

35. Illinois House of Representatives, news release, 7 Jan. 1977, announced Choate's retirement from the House and new job as director of external affairs for SIU.

36. George W. Dunne, Chicago, memoir, Illinois General Assembly Oral History Program, 1983, 89. Dunne served in the House from 1955 to 1963.

3. Groundwork for the Future

1. "School Bills Sponsored by Rep. Paul Powell, 1935–1963," Illinois Legislative Council, 2 Oct. 1964. Powell's bill to establish Southern Illinois Normal as a university was filed in the 1943 session of the General Assembly, but failed to pass.

2. "Industrialists Applaud Engineering Bill," *Southern Illinoisan*, 3 May 1961. PP Papers. Morris told an audience he had three objectives when he became president in 1948: "improve the area's education system, improve its agriculture, and bring about industrial development."

3. Dr. Leo Brown, interview with author, 7 Feb. 1998, and 22 Feb. 1998. Brown took credit for recruiting Morris to SIU. He was appointed to the first SIU Board of Trustees and served as chairman. After a dispute with Gov. Adlai E. Stevenson, Brown was not reappointed to a second term. He worked closely with legislative members on a number of public policies favoring SIU.

4. "Crisenberry Thinks 2-Year Trial Plan Best for SIU," *Southern Illinoisan*, 15 June 1949, 1.

5. Robert G. Crisenberry Papers, Morris Library, SIU, biographical information, 1882–1965, box 1, folder 1.

6. "Sub-Committee to Propose Separate SIU Board Try," *Southern Illinoisan*, 14 June 1949. The article explains the existing lineup of schools under direction of the State Teachers College Board, 1. The name change to Southern Illinois University in 1947 occurred with passage of Senate Bill 13, Illinois State Archives.

7. O. T. Banton, "Separate Board May Help Answer School 'Politics,'" *Southern Illinoisan*, 29 Dec. 1948, 1.

8. Ibid.

9. "One Board for All State Schools Is Proposed," *Southern Illinoisan*, 21 Feb. 1949.

10. "Powell Says Budget Group Will Visit Campus," *Southern Illinoisan*, 24 Mar. 1949, 1.

11. "Dillavou Presents Bill to Put SIU Under UI Board," *Southern Illinoisan*, 19 May 1949, 1.

12. "Crisenberry Thinks 2-Year Trial Plan Best for SIU."

13. "Governor Signs SIU Bills," *Southern Illinoisan*, 6 July 1949, 1.

14. "Seven Members Named by Governor on SIU Board," *Southern Illinoisan*, 8 July 1949, 1.

15. Clayton, *Illinois Fact Book*, 445–46. Illinois horse racing history is featured. Also, Illinois Racing Board, letter to author, 27 June 1997.

16. Paul Powell, testimony at hearing of Illinois Harness Racing Commission, Springfield, IL, 29 Jan. 1952. PP Papers. Also, Illinois Association of Agricultural Fairs, 19 Sept. 1951. PP Papers.

17. House Bill 1044 and House Bill 756, 66th General Assembly, 1949, Illinois State Archives. HB 1104 provided amendments to the 1945 harness racing act.

18. John W. Fribley, *Memoir* (Springfield: Sangamon State University, 1981), 195, 120, 121. Also testimony 29 Jan. 1952, at hearing of Illinois Harness Racing Commission. PP Papers.

19. William (Smokey) Downey, *Memoir* (Springfield: Sangamon State University, 1982), 51.

20. Adlai E. Stevenson, Illinois State Budget Report, 1949, Illinois State Archives.

21. "State's Attorney to Investigate Deals in Stock of Chicago Track," *St. Louis Post-Dispatch*, 24 Aug. 1951; "Track Stock Paid 1650% in 2 Yrs; Owners Listed," *Chicago Daily News*, 22 Aug. 1951.

22. News articles about Irwin S. (Big Sam) Wiedrick appeared in many newspapers from 1949 to 1969. In addition to articles in Chicago newspapers, Wiedrick's business affairs and legal troubles were included in Charles O. Stewart, "Ex-Convict Was Original Cahokia Downs Promoter," *East St. Louis Journal*, 24 July 1963, and "This Is Sam Wiedrick," *Metro-East Journal*, 23 June 1965.

23. "Complete Roster of Stock Holders," *Chicago Daily News*, 22 Aug. 1951, 1.

24. Lee, *Memoir*, 137.

25. Clayton, *Illinois Fact Book*, 447.

26. Ibid., 448–49.

27. James E. Sprehe, "Origin of the Cahokia Empire," *St. Louis Post-Dispatch*, 12 Sept. 1971. Bowen Archives.

28. Clayton, *Illinois Fact Book,* 287–96.

29. Daniel McGlynn, biographical notes from files of *East St. Louis Journal,* n.d. Bowen Archives.

30. Carl Baldwin, "Dan McGlynn Retires from Politics," *St. Louis Post-Dispatch,* 8 Mar. 1959. Baldwin wrote at length about McGlynn's history in East St. Louis. Bowen Archives.

31. "McGlynn Ends His Silence," *East St. Louis Journal,* 31 Oct. 1934. Bowen Archives.

32. Baldwin, "Dan McGlynn Retires."

33. Ibid. Also, Dixon, *The Gentleman from Illinois,* 104. He wrote, "Many powerful political leaders have come along in my region, but none have displayed the strongly bipartisan aptitude of McGlynn."

34. "McGlynn Is GOP Boy Here, Green Tells 300 Workers," *East St. Louis Journal,* 13 Oct. 1940. Bowen Archives.

35. "Too Early to Discuss Jobs," *East St. Louis Journal,* 8 Nov. 1940. Bowen Archives.

36. Howard W. Allen and Vincent A. Lacey, eds., *Illinois Elections 1818–1990: Candidates and County Returns for President, Governor, Senate and House of Representatives* (Carbondale: Southern Illinois University Press, 1992), 61.

37. Ibid.

38. Harry Barnes, "Will McGlynn Become New Political Boss?" *East St. Louis Journal,* 7 Nov. 1940. Bowen Archives.

39. Theodore C. Link, "Gamblers Again Raising Green Campaign Funds, Gave Him $100,000 in 1944," *St. Louis Post-Dispatch,* 1 Sept. 1948.

40. Sprehe, "Origin of the Cahokia Empire."

41. "Shareholder List in Cahokia Trust," *St. Louis Post-Dispatch,* 12 Sept. 1971. Bowen Archives.

42. James Sprehe, "East St. Louis Mayor Survives 20-Year Reign," *St. Louis Post-Dispatch,* 4 May 1971; Alvin George Fields, "Biography," *East St. Louis Evening and Sunday Journal.* Bowen Archives.

43. State Sen. Alan J. Dixon to House Speaker John P. Touhy, 14 Apr. 1965, asking for support of legislation for East St. Louis. State Sen. Paul Simon, speech to Springfield press club, 28 May 1967, mentions his support "of greater revenue opportunities in this session of the legislature for cities." Bowen Archives.

44. Paul Powell, letter to Mayor Fields, 28 Sept. 1954. Bowen Archives.

45. U.S. Sen. Dixon, interview with the author, 18 Sept. 1990, in Washington, DC. Dixon said he never was offered Cahokia Downs racetrack stock: "As I look back on it now, they probably thought I was crazy for not wanting to get in on things."

46. Dixon, *The Gentleman from Illinois*, 151–53. Dixon told of Fields's help in getting slated for state treasurer in 1970.

47. Powell to Fields, 30 Nov. 1954. Bowen Archives.

48. Robert E. Hartley, "Dick Mudge: Maverick Democrat Against Bossism, Crime and Dishonesty." Paper presented at Illinois Historic Preservation Agency history conference, Oct. 2012. Mudge's fight with Fields for the state central committee in 1958 and 1962 includes background on Fields's elections. He served 20 years on the state Democratic committee.

49. Charles O. Stewart, "Politics Is Sure Winner at Cahokia Downs Track," *East St. Louis Journal*, 2 July 1962, 1. Bowen Archives.

50. Affidavit, 14 July 1966, attests to purchase of land trust units and common stock shares. PP Papers; Taylor Pensoneau, "Powell Had Cahokia Shares," *St. Louis Post-Dispatch*, 14 Jan. 1971, 1; Taylor Pensoneau, "Powell Put Turf Stock in Other Names," *St. Louis Post-Dispatch*, 12 Jan. 1971, 1.

51. Paul Powell, federal tax returns, 1954–69. PP Papers.

52. Gale Williams to George E. Day, 6 Mar. 1961; Charles W. Clabaugh to George E. Day, 8 Mar. 1961; Powell to William S. Miller (Illinois Racing Board), 6 June 1953. PP Papers.

53. Charles O. Stewart, "Director Asked Questions; Now He's Not a Director," *East St. Louis Journal*, 23 July 1963.

54. George Edward Day, Andrew Ryan, John A. Stelle, Schaefer O'Neill, and Dan McGlynn, letter to owners of Cahokia Voting Trust Certificates, 2 Aug. 1962. PP Papers.

55. "Trot Meet Set Here This Fall," *St. Louis Globe-Democrat*, 14 July 1957; "Cahokia Opens Season Tonight," *St. Louis Globe-Democrat*, 14 Oct. 1957. Bowen Archives.

56. Egyptian Trotting Association, Inc., list of stockholders, 1 Jan. 1962. PP Papers.

57. Paul Powell, federal tax returns, 1961–69.

58. Ibid.

59. Clyde Lee to Powell, 21 Dec. 1963. Lee reported Egyptian Trotting profits for 1963, adding, "When we were struggling at Cahokia Downs in 1957 I never thought it would be possible to put $430,000 in a surplus account in the next six years." PP Papers.

60. Stewart, "Ex-convict Was Original Cahokia Downs Promoter," *East St. Louis Journal*, 24 July 1963. Bowen Archives. Stewart's article provided a chronicle of Wiedrick's involvement with racetracks.

61. Paul Powell, federal tax returns, 1949–69.

62. Jim Wiggs, "Powell Says Dealing with Ex-con Race Track Promoter 'Honorable,'" *Metro-East Journal*, 23 June 1965. Bowen Archives.

4. Glory Years for Downstate

1. Clayton, *Illinois Fact Book*, 189. The commission included members from the House and Senate. While recommendations could be adjusted during the budget process, most of the financial issues were resolved in proceedings of the commission. Paul Powell and Everett Peters, once appointed, served on the commission until retired.

2. John S. Rendleman, southern Illinois native, graduated with a bachelor's degree from SIU and earned a degree from the University of Illinois College of Law. Upon returning to his home region he was hired by President Morris as university counsel and lobbyist. The appointment had the blessing of Powell. Dr. Leo Brown said of Rendleman and Powell, "They were partners in crime," working together in behalf of SIU, interview with author. Also, Rep. James Holloway said it was Morris who set things in motion, "but John carried them forward to completion," *Memoir*, 153. Rendleman eventually became chancellor of the SIU-Edwardsville campus.

3. Enrollment figures fluctuated, depending on many factors, including part-time students and those taking courses at distant locations. The 1949 figure is from Pete Goldman, "How Big Can SIU Get?" *St. Louis Globe-Democrat*, 7 July 1957, 1. The 1957 figure is from Carl Mayhew, "1957 Was a Year of Growth and Increased Stature for SIU," *East St. Louis Journal*, 30 Dec. 1957. Bowen Archives.

4. "SIU Potential: 27,000," *East St. Louis Journal*, 27 May 1958. Bowen Archives. The article used a figure of 16,000 for the Carbondale campus by 1970. The Edwardsville campus had not been built. Also, O. T. Banton, "Will Our State Universities Have to Turn Students Away," *Southern Illinoisan*, 9 Oct. 1960, 21. The Illinois Commission of Higher Education projected Carbondale enrollment by 1970 at 16,000.

5. Paul Powell, as cited in "State Rep. Paul Powell Reports on Record in Legislature."

6. Laws of Illinois, 1949–1961, Illinois State Archives.

7. Senate Bill 682, 1949 General Assembly, Laws of Illinois, 313. State Archives; Powell, "State Rep. Paul Powell Reports."

8. Holloway, *Memoir*.

9. Everett Peters, of St. Joseph, served in the Illinois House 1935–1941, and in the state Senate 1941–1970, according to Clayton, *Illinois Fact Book*, legislative members listings. In the Senate, Peters was a longtime member and chairman of the budgetary commission and also as chairman of the appropriations committee. Alan J. Dixon called Peters and Powell "kin folks" and said they made tons of deals for policies. On appropriations, Peters said, "In the legislature only two things amount to a damn: the amount you

spend and where it comes from," George Tagge column, *Chicago Tribune*, 28 Dec. 1968.

10. Mitchell, *Delyte Morris of SIU*, 9.

11. *Laws of the State of Illinois*, 1943. Senate Bill 6, signed 15 July 1943, amended sections of the 1869 law establishing Southern Illinois Normal University. Section 2 of the amendment bill stated, "No professional courses culminating in degrees in law, medicine, dentistry, pharmacy, engineering, or agriculture may be offered by such university."

12. "Bill Asks Ag, Engineering Degrees at SIU," *Southern Illinoisan*, 7 May 1955.

13. "Senate Education Committee Vetoes SIU Plea for Agriculture, Engineering," *Southern Illinoisan*, 28 May 1953.

14. Ibid.

15. Ibid.

16. "Union Backs Ag Building," *Southern Illinoisan*, 11 Mar. 1954; "Agriculture Building to Be Built at SIU," *Southern Illinoisan*, 16 June 1955.

17. "SIU Agriculture Program Vital, Governor Says," *Southern Illinoisan*, 18 June 1956; "New SIU Ag Building Fine for Research," *Southern Illinoisan*, 20 Feb. 1957.

18. *Laws of the State of Illinois*, 1955 session. The General Assembly passed an act creating a higher education commission to study the need for oversight. *Laws of the State of Illinois*, 1957 session, the General Assembly created an Illinois Commission of Higher Education, with advisory responsibilities. A State Board of Higher Education with more specific oversight was approved by the 1961 General Assembly. Passage was part of the deal for SIU to offer engineering degrees.

19. Stephen Kerber, "From Aesthetic Integration to Applying Art: Arnold H. Maremont, the EPEC Seminar and the Planning of SIU Edwardsville," *Journal of the Illinois State Historical Society* 97, no. 1 (2004): 43. Also, Pete Goldman, "SIU Seeking to Establish 4-Year Branch on East Side," *St. Louis Globe-Democrat*, 9 July 1957, 11A.

20. O. T. Banton, "SIU Engineering School Bill Meets Roadblock," *Southern Illinoisan*, 2 May 1957; "How Big Can SIU Get?"

21. "How Big Can SIU Get?"

22. Banton, "SIU Engineering School Bill Meets Roadblock."

23. "How Big Can SIU Get?"

24. Ibid.

25. Ibid.

26. Ibid.

27. Jacob Blechisen to David D. Henry, "Protest Aimed at U of I Chief," *Southern Illinoisan*, 7 June 1957. A copy was sent to the newspaper.

28. Holloway, *Memoir*, 157.

29. Cohen and Taylor, *American Pharaoh*, 224–25. Office of the Historian, University of Illinois at Chicago, "Permanent Campus Site Situation, 1958–1963," www.uic.edu/uichistory.

30. *Illinois Blue Book 1959–1960*, Springfield, 938–39. Illinois State Archives.

31. *Laws of the State of Illinois*, 1959 Session, Senate Bill 823; Governor's Bill Records, executive action, 23 July 1959. The act provided authority to issue bonds subject to approval in a public vote. Illinois State Archives.

32. "SIU President Tells Need for Bond Issue," *Champaign News-Gazette*, 3 Oct. 1960, 36; "Colleges Need Room for 85,000 in Year 1967," *Southern Illinoisan*, 30 Oct. 1960, 5; Banton, "Will Our State Universities Have to Turn Students Away?" This article appeared also in Lindsay-Schaub newspapers of East St. Louis, Decatur, and Champaign-Urbana, 9 Oct. 1960.

33. *Illinois Blue Book 1961–62*, Springfield, 964–65. Official vote of the State of Illinois cast at the General Election, 8 Nov. 1960, compiled by Charles F. Carpentier, secretary of state, 33–34. Illinois State Archives. "Bond Issue Passed," *The Egyptian*, 13 Jan. 1961.

34. *Illinois Blue Book*.

35. "SIU to Get $53,200,000 Share of $195,000,000 Bond Issue," *St. Louis Post-Dispatch*, 8 May 1961, 4B; "Bills for $73.2 Million SIU Bonds Signed by Governor," *Edwardsville Intelligencer*, 31 July 1961. Bowen Archives.

36. "Six Major Buildings Set at SIU," *Southern Illinoisan*, 7 May 1961; "Huge Building Program at SIU," *Southern Illinoisan*, 6 Aug. 1961. Bowen Archives.

37. Robert Howard, "Downstaters Back Powell for Speaker," *Chicago Tribune*, 1 Jan. 1959; George Tagge, "Powell Seen as Speaker in Legislature," *Chicago Tribune*, 7 Jan. 1959.

38. Holloway, *Memoir*, 58–60.

39. Tagge, "Powell Beats Daley Choice for Speaker," *Chicago Tribune*, 8 Jan. 1959; "Speaker Powell and Mayor Daley," editorial, *Chicago Tribune*, 10 Jan. 1959.

40. Green, "Legislative Redistricting in Illinois 1871–1982: A Study of Geopolitical Survival," in *Redistricting*, 1982. Population Breakdown 1870–1980.

41. Ibid.

42. "Powell Blasts Plan for State Remapping," *Illinois State Register*, 17 Oct. 1954, 5.

43. Johnson Kanady, "Democrat Hits Blue Ballot as Chicago Plot," *Chicago Tribune*, 19 Oct. 1954, 10; "Powell Says Amendment Would Give Cook Co. Control," *Illinois State Register*, 1 Oct. 1954, 7.

44. Alan J. Dixon, "Dixon Supports Remap," *East St. Louis Journal*, 22 Aug. 1954. Bowen Archives.

45. "Remap Plan Supported by 5–1 Margin," *Illinois State Register*, 4 Nov. 1954, 4.

46. Green, "Legislative Redistricting in Illinois 1871–1982."

47. Samuel K. Gove, "Reapportionment and Illinois Public Policy," *Illinois Business Review* 23 (March 1966): 6.

48. Kenney, *A Political Passage*, 131.

49. Robert Howard, "House Passes ½ Cent Boost in Sales Tax," *Chicago Tribune*, 27 June 1959; "Legislature OK's Boost in Sales Tax," *Chicago American*, 27 June 1959.

50. "How House Voted on Sales Tax," *Chicago Daily News*, 27 June 1959.

51. "Governor's Budget Inadequate, Morris Says," *Southern Illinoisan*, 24 April 1959.

52. "No New SIU Buildings This Year," *Southern Illinoisan*, 28 May 1959.

53. O. T. Banton, "Powell, Wood Contest Seen for Speaker," *East St. Louis Journal*, 11 Dec. 1960; "Powell Says He'll Be Speaker Again," *St. Louis Globe-Democrat*, 25 Nov. 1960. Bowen Archives.

54. George Tagge, "5 Absentees Smash GOP House Hopes," *Chicago Tribune*, 4 Jan. 1961, 1; "Illinois Assembly Adjourns in Uproar," *St. Louis Globe-Democrat*, 5 Jan. 1961. Bowen Archives.

55. William L. Grindle, *Memoir* (Springfield: Sangamon State University, 1986) vol. 1, 119.

56. "Engineering Bill Wins Senate, House Approval," *Southern Illinoisan*, 22 Mar. 1961; "SIU Engineering Bill Gets Easy OK in House," *East St. Louis Journal*, 29 Mar. 1961.

57. "Engineering Bill Signed by Governor," *East St. Louis Journal*, 25 Apr. 1961. Bowen Archives.

58. O. T. Banton, "Move Tied to Plan for Super Board," *Southern Illinoisan*, 8 Mar. 1961.

59. "Industrialists Applaud Engineering Bill," *Southern Illinoisan*, 3 May 1961.

60. Grindle, *Memoir*, vol. 1, 122.

61. Hartley, *Paul Simon*, 198–99. After a close call in the 1980 election for Congress, Simon commissioned a poll that revealed voters considered him weak on bringing federal projects to southern Illinois.

62. Gene Callahan, interview with author, 4 Jan. 2007. He said of Simon's approach as U.S. senator: "Simon did his share on Illinois issues, but he had a great interest in national and international issues."

63. Paul Simon and Alfred Balk, "The Illinois Legislature: A Study in Corruption," *Harper's*, Sept. 1964, 74–78. ALPL, Simon Papers, box 95, folder 35.

64. Simon interview, 20 Feb. 1998.

65. Simon, "Study in Corruption."

66. Simon interview.

67. Ibid.

68. Simon, "The $248 Million Bond Issue," *Troy Tribune*, 2 Oct. 1958, 2. Simon opposed the bond issue, saying, "The best way is the cheapest way: Pay-as-you-go."

69. Holloway, *Memoir*, 50–57.

70. Ibid.

71. Simon to William Boyne, *Southern Illinoisan*, 14 Apr. 1958, ALPL, Simon Papers, box 16, folder 7. Simon sent a list of suggested questions for Boyne to ask Powell.

72. "Powell Calls Steve Mitchell a 'Cry Baby,'" *St. Louis Globe-Democrat*, 27 July 1959. Bowen Archives.

73. Robert D. Reid, "Corruption: Legislators Say It's There, But Differ on Degree," Lindsay-Schaub newspapers, 24 June 1965.

74. Ken Watson, "Demo Slate Cheers GOP," *Illinois State Journal*, 29 Feb. 1968.

75. Callahan, interview, 4 Jan. 2007.

76. 72nd General Assembly, 1961, House Bill 601, introduced by Clyde L. Choate, passed House May 17, passed Senate June 28. Senate Appropriations Committee approved 36 to 0. Illinois State Archives.

77. 72nd General Assembly, 1961, House Bill 1616, introduced by Choate, Powell, and Clyde Lee, passed House 21 June. Illinois State Archives.

78. 73rd General Assembly, 1963, House Bill 236, introduced 14 Feb. by Choate and Powell, passed House Mar. 14, passed Senate Apr. 3. State Archives.

79. Abner Mikva, interview with author, 27 Dec. 1997.

80. Simon, interview, 20 Feb. 1998.

81. Scariano, *Memoir*, 1988.

82. Dixon, *Gentleman from Illinois*, 45–50.

83. Choate was a pallbearer at the Powell funeral. His comment was made at the service and was widely quoted.

5. Clyde Choate's Leadership Legacy

1. John G. Gilbert, *Memoir* (Springfield: Sangamon State University, 1981), preface.

2. Green, "Legislative Redistricting," Table 1, Population Breakdown Comparison.

3. Ibid., 13; "Kerner Vetoes House Remap," *Chicago Tribune*, 2 July 1963, 1; "GOP Bill to Remap House Pushed Through," *Chicago Tribune*, 28 June 1963, 1; "Court Asked to Void Kerner Remap Veto," *Illinois State Register*, 5 July 1963, 1.

4. Green, "Legislative Redistricting," 14.

5. Howard, *Illinois: A History of the Prairie State*, 555.

6. Green, "Legislative Redistricting," 15–16.

7. "Fields Terms House Remap Fair for Both Sides," *Metro-East Journal*, 5 Dec. 1965. Bowen Archives.

8. Pensoneau, *Powerhouse: Arrington from Illinois*, 306. The author places Arrington at the top of Ogilvie's work list for getting a state income tax.

9. Until the tax issue was settled, Ogilvie and Arrington accepted the 1870 constitutional language. This is clear in Pensoneau, *Governor Richard Ogilvie*.

10. Thomas A. McGloon, *Memoir* (Springfield: Sangamon State University, 1981), Preface.

11. Kenney and Hartley, *The Heroic and the Notorious*, 172.

12. John Reinhardt, Illinois State Archives, information to author, 26 Nov. 2013.

13. Pensoneau, *Governor Richard Ogilvie*, 103–04; "Details Bared in Big Tax Deal," *Chicago Daily News*, 14 June 1969, 5.

14. Pensoneau, *Governor Richard Ogilvie*, 95.

15. "Daley-Ogilvie Tax Deal Facts!" *Chicago Daily News*, 14 June 1969, 1. Pensoneau, *Richard Ogilvie*, 99. See also "The 'Inside' of Ogilvie, Daley Deal," *Chicago Daily News*, 16 June 1969, 1.

16. "Downstate Threatens Ogilvie-Daley Pact," *Chicago Daily News*, 14 June 1969, 5.

17. Ibid.

18. Henry Hanson, "Income Tax Deal Collapses," *Chicago Daily News*, 16 June 1969, 1; Pensoneau, *Powerhouse: Arrington from Illinois*, 314.

19. "Downstate Threatens," *Chicago Daily News*, 14 June 1969.

20. "Democrats Plan: 2% Tax," *Chicago Daily News*, 18 June 1969.

21. Hanson, "Income Tax Deal Collapses," 8; "Arrington Stands Firm on 3pct," *Chicago Daily News*, 23 June 1969, 3.

22. "Arrington: No Tax Compromise," *Chicago Daily New*, 23 June 1969, 1.

23. Charles Nicodemus, "Last-ditch Plea for Tax by Ogilvie," *Chicago Daily News*, 24 June 1969, 3.

24. Charles Nicodemus, "How Governor Decided to OK Tax Compromise," *Chicago Daily*, 28 June 1969, 4.

25. Pensoneau, *Governor Richard Ogilvie*, 104.

26. Ibid., 105.

27. "How Gov. Ogilvie Reached His Income Tax Decision," *Chicago Daily News*, 28 June 1969, 6.

28. Taylor Pensoneau, "Mudge's Demand for Slating of McCarthy Bloc Rejected," *St. Louis Post-Dispatch*, 29 June 1968, 3; "Mudge Offers 2nd Slate of Convention Delegates," *St. Louis Globe-Democrat*, 29–30 June 1968, 17.

29. Charles O. Stewart, "Mudge: Mayor Daley Is a Humiliating Experience," *Metro-East Journal*, 8 Sept. 1968, 1.

30. Lewis Chester, Godfrey Hodgson, and Bruce Page, *An American Melodrama: The Presidential Campaign of 1968* (New York: Viking Press, 1969). It remains the standard campaign story.

31. "Democratic National Political Conventions, 1832–2008," *The National Journal*, 23 (Aug. 1980); Robert E. Hartley, "Political Reform: Parties Try New Math on Convention Delegates Count," *Decatur Herald and Review*, 13 July 1971. Hartley (author) covered the 1972 Democratic convention for Lindsay-Schaub newspapers in Illinois.

32. Wall communicated with author by telephone and email in Aug. and Sept. 2013, and Wall shared his personal background. Also, William Schneider, "An Insider's View of the Election," *Atlantic Monthly*, July 1988. A major portion of the article dealt with Wall and the Illinois delegation.

33. Wall, communication with author, 20 Aug. 2013.

34. Wall, communication with author, 5 Sept. 2013.

35. Robert E. Hartley, "Sorting Out Walker and McGovern," *Decatur Herald and Review*, 2 July 1972.

36. Robert E. Hartley, "Turmoil Marks Illinois 170-member Democratic Delegation," *Southern Illinoisan*, 7 May 1972, 30.

37. Wall, communication with author, 20 Aug. 2013.

38. Ibid.

39. Robert E. Hartley, "Daley and Jackson Not Really There," *Decatur Herald and Review*, 23 July 1972.

40. Robert E. Hartley, "Illinois Squabble Causes Apprehension," *Decatur Review*, 10 July 1972, 1.

41. Robert E. Hartley, "Choate Keeps Lid on Illinois Stew," *Southern Illinoisan*, 11 July 1972, 1.

42. Robert E. Hartley, "McGovern's Coming Up Roses," *Champaign-Urbana Courier*, 11 July 1972.

43. Wall, communication with author, 20 Aug. 2013; Hartley, "Choate Keeps Lid On"; Robert E. Hartley, "Choate Named Delegation Chairman," *Decatur Herald*, 12 July 1972.

44. "Choate Heads Illinois Delegates," *Decatur Herald*, 12 July 1972, 1.

45. Wall, communication with author, 5 Sept. 2013.

46. Ibid.

47. Ibid.

48. Wall, communication with author, 23 Aug. 2013.

6. The Fight for Speaker—and Beyond

1. Clayton, *Illinois Fact Book*. The only exception was in 1965 after the "bed-sheet ballot" election when Democrats outnumbered Republicans 118 to 59.

2. Pensoneau and Ellis, *Dan Walker*, 220.

3. Ibid., 208.

4. Richard Icen, "Clyde Choate at Center of Contest," *Decatur Herald and Review*, 27 Dec. 1974; "Hot Battle for House Speaker," *Chicago Daily News*, 19 Nov. 1974.

5. Sink, "Clyde Choate Could Be House Speaker If . . ." *Decatur Herald and Review*, 16 Apr. 1972.

6. Ibid.

7. Richard Icen, "Speaker? 'It'd Be an Honor,'" *Southern Illinoisan*, 22 Sept. 1974.

8. Clyde Choate, interview with author, 1998.

9. Pensoneau and Ellis, *Glory and Tragedy*, 214; "Walker Puts Illinois First," *Decatur Herald and Review*, 17 Mar. 1973.

10. Nowlan, Gove, and Winkel Jr., *Illinois Politics*, 126.

11. "Blair, Choate Get Job Done without Niceties," *Chicago Daily News*, 26 Feb. 1973, 7.

12. Ibid.

13. "Democrats Organize to Encourage Choate to Stay On," *Southern Illinoisan*, 9 Dec. 1973.

14. "Choate Decides to Run," *Decatur Herald and Review*, 17 Dec. 1973; "Whatever His Reason, Choate's Return Helps," editorial, *Southern Illinoisan*, 19 Dec. 1973.

15. "Hot Battle for House Speaker," *Chicago Daily News*, 19 Nov. 1974.

16. Ibid.

17. Icen, "Speaker? 'It'd Be an Honor.'"

18. Icen, "Clyde Choate at Center of Contest."

19. Gov. Dan Walker, interview with author, 27 Nov. 1974.

20. "Retire? Not Clyde Choate," Anna *Gazette-Democrat*, 11 Oct. 2001. This article contained excerpts from stories written for the paper in 1988.

21. Icen, "Clyde Choate at Center of Contest."

22. Clyde L. Choate, candidate's statement, 7 Jan. 1975.

23. "Walker Moved to Block Choate as Speaker," *Chicago Tribune*, 1 Jan. 1975, 1.

24. Icen, "Clyde Choate at Center of Contest."

25. "Walker Moved to Block Choate as Speaker."

26. "No Need for Choate," editorial, *Chicago Tribune*, 2 Jan. 1975.

27. "Choate Attacked by Anonymous Governor," editorial, *Southern Illinoisan*, 6 Jan. 1975.

28. "Patronage Jobs Lost in Speaker Battle," *Metro-East Journal*, 7 Jan. 1975. Bowen Archives.

29. "Walker Asks Daley: Stop Choate," *Chicago Daily News*, 7 Jan. 1975, 1.

30. "Walker Visits Daley, Fails on Choate Appeal," *Chicago Sun-Times*, 8 Jan. 1975, 2.

31. Richard Icen, "Choate Finds His Strength Diminished," *Metro-East Journal*, 8 Jan. 1975, 1. Bowen Archives.

32. Ibid.

33. Taylor Pensoneau, "Chance Fades for Choate to Be Speaker," *St. Louis Post-Dispatch*, 9 Jan. 1975, 3A.

34. "Race for House Speaker Stalls House," *Metro-East Journal*, 12 Jan. 1975. Bowen Archives.

35. "Choate Defies Foes and Then Leaves Town," *Chicago Daily News*, 14 Jan. 1975, 1. "Choate Says His Fight 'Matter of Principle,'" *Metro-East Journal*, 14 Jan. 1975. Bowen Archives.

36. "Top Panel Fails to End Deadlock on Speaker," *Chicago Daily News*, 21 Jan. 1975, 1.

37. "Redmond Becomes Speaker in Illinois," *St. Louis Post-Dispatch*, 22 Jan. 1975, 1.

38. "Redmond's 7 GOP Votes Finally Make Him Speaker," *Metro-East Journal*, 22 Jan. 1975. Bowen Archives.

39. "How House Voted on the Final Ballot," *Chicago Daily News*, 22 Jan. 1975, 12.

40. Paul Ingrassia, "Choate Hurt, but Not Bitter," *Metro-East Journal*, 24 Jan. 1975, 1. Bowen Archives; "Choate's Outlook Commendable," *Decatur Herald and Review*, 27 Jan. 1975.

41. 1975 Illinois House of Representatives Journal, Senate Bill 1250, "Reapportionment: 24 Congressional Districts, redistricts state, repeals old act. SB passed, but did not go beyond second reading in House." Illinois State Archives, John Reinhardt, email 8 Nov. 2013.

42. "'Gentleman from Union' Battles Partisan Politics of Redistricting," Anna *Gazette-Democrat*, 15 June 1995, reprint of article from *Chicago Sun-Times*, 8 June 1975.

43. Ibid.

44. 1975 Illinois House of Representatives Journal.

45. Jim Getz and Patrick E. Gauen, "Could the South Rise Again," *Illinois Issues*, May 2001.

46. "Choate Quits to Join SIU-C," *Metro-East Journal*, 9 Jan. 1977. Bowen Archives.

47. Journal of the House of Representatives of the 79th General Assembly, vol. 4, 17 June 1975–29 June 1975, House Resolution 1111, 5457.

48. "Choate Quits to Join SIU-C."

49. Southern Illinois University salary books, from Walter D. Ray, archivist, SIU Political Papers, given to author.

50. Ted Lechowicz, "A Tribute to Clyde Choate," Anna *Gazette-Democrat*, 15 June 1995, special section, 6.

7. Good Times in Small Places

1. Taylor Pensoneau to author, 10 Feb. 2014, told the story of his visit to the nightclub. Also, mentioned by Choate in interview with Richard Icen, "Maneuvering Raises Names," *Southern Illinoisan*, 22 Sept. 1974.

2. Munsell, "A History of Hamilton County," 114.

3. Ibid.

4. "Johnson County Honors Speaker Paul Powell," *Vienna Times*, 30 Mar. 1961, 1.

5. Ibid.

6. Anna *Gazette-Democrat*, 15 June 1995, special section devoted largely to articles about Clyde Choate.

7. "Members of Renowned World War II 601st Tank Destroyer Battalion Reunite," Anna *Gazette-Democrat*, 15 June 1995, special section.

8. Ibid.

9. Mike McCormick, oral history, 8 July 2010, ALPL.

Bibliography

*Included here are sections listing manuscript sources, books
and selected sources, and newspapers and other periodicals.*

Manuscript Sources

Alvin G. Fields Papers. Louisa H. Bowen University Archives and Special Collections, Lovejoy Library, Southern Illinois University, Edwardsville.

Metro-East Journal Files. Louisa H. Bowen University Archives and Special Collections, Southern Illinois University, Edwardsville.

Paul Powell Papers. Abraham Lincoln Presidential Library, Springfield, Illinois.

Paul Simon Papers. Abraham Lincoln Presidential Library, Springfield, Illinois.

Scott W. Lucas Collection. Abraham Lincoln Presidential Library, Springfield, Illinois.

Special Collections Research Center, Morris Library, Southern Illinois University, Carbondale.

William G. Stratton Collections. Abraham Lincoln Presidential Library, Springfield, Illinois.

Books and Selected Sources

Angle, Paul M. *Bloody Williamson: A Chapter in American Lawlessness.* New York: Alfred A. Knopf, 1969.

Atkinson, Rick. *An Army at Dawn: The War in North Africa, 1942–1943*. Vol. 1 of *The Liberation Trilogy*. New York: Henry Holt, 2007.

———. *The Guns at Last Light: The War in Western Europe*. Vol. 3 of *The Liberation Trilogy*. New York: Henry Holt, 2013.

Baldwin, Carl R. "East St. Louis." *Journal of the St. Clair County Historical Society* 3, no. 8 (1983). 8–18.

———. "East St. Louis." Pt. 2. *Journal of the St. Clair County Historical Society* 3, no. 9 (1984): 19–25.

Barnhart, Bill, and Gene Schlickman. *Kerner: The Conflict of Intangible Rights*. Urbana: University of Illinois Press, 1999.

Biles, Roger. *Big City Boss in Depression and War: Mayor Edward J. Kelly of Chicago*. DeKalb: Northern Illinois University Press, 1984.

Buck, Solon J. *Illinois in 1818*. Urbana: University of Illinois Press, 1967.

Callahan, Gene. Interview, oral history program, 6 July 2011. Abraham Lincoln Presidential Library.

Camelon, David. "How the First GI Bill Was Written." *American Legion Magazine*, January and February 1969.

Clarke, Jeffrey J., and Robert Ross Smith. *Riviera to the Rhine*. Washington: Center of Military History, 1993.

Clayton, John, compiler. *The Illinois Fact Book and Historical Almanac, 1673–1968*. Carbondale: Southern Illinois University Press, 1970.

Cohen, Adam, and Elizabeth Taylor. *American Pharaoh: Mayor Richard J. Daley: His Battle for Chicago and the Nation*. Boston: Little, Brown, 2000.

DePue, Mark R. "The Cutback Amendment of 1980: Unintended Consequences of Pat Quinn's Reform Zeal." Paper presented at annual history conference of the Illinois Historic Preservation Agency, Springfield, IL, 2013.

Dixon, Alan J. *The Gentleman from Illinois: Stories from Forty Years of Elective Public Service*. Carbondale: Southern Illinois University Press, 2013.

Egyptian Trotting Association. "Amount of Stock and Debentures Owned by Each Stockholder." 1 January 1962. Paul Powell Papers. Abraham Lincoln Presidential Library.

Gabel, Christopher R. "Seek, Strike, and Destroy: U.S. Army Tank Destroyer Doctrine in World War II." Leavenworth Papers. Combat Studies Institute. Leavenworth: U.S. Army Command and General Staff College, 1985.

Gottfried, Alex. *Boss Cermak of Chicago*. Seattle: University of Washington Press, 1962.

Gove, Samuel K., and James D. Nowlan. *Illinois Politics and Government: The Expanding Metropolitan Frontier*. Lincoln: University of Nebraska Press, 1996.

Green, Paul M. "Legislative Redistricting in Illinois 1871–1982: A Study of Geopolitical Survival." In *Redistricting: An Exercise in Prophecy*, edited by Anna J. Merritt. Chicago: Institute of Government and Public Affairs, 1982.

Hartley, Robert E. "Dick Mudge: Maverick Democrat Against Bossism, Crime, and Dishonesty." *Journal of Illinois History* 15 (Autumn 2012): 177–96.

———. "'I worked for my friends': John H. Stelle's Life as a Political Operator." Paper presented at annual history conference of the Illinois Historic Preservation Agency, Springfield, IL, 2010.

———. *Paul Powell of Illinois: A Lifelong Democrat*. Carbondale: Southern Illinois University Press, 1999.

———. *Paul Simon: The Political Journey of an Illinois Original*. Carbondale: Southern Illinois University Press, 2009.

Hartley, Robert E., and David Kenney. *Death Underground: The Centralia and West Frankfort Mine Disasters*. Carbondale: Southern Illinois University Press, 2006.

Holloway, James. *Memoir*. 2 vols. Springfield: Sangamon State University, 1981.

Howard, Robert P. *Illinois: A History of the Prairie State*. Grand Rapids: William B. Eerdmans, 1972.

———. *Memoir*. Springfield: Sangamon State University, 1982.

———. *Mostly Good and Competent Men: Illinois Governors 1818 to 1988*. Springfield: Illinois Issues, Sangamon State University, Illinois State Historical Society, 1988.

Illinois Blue Book. Springfield: State of Illinois.

Josowitz, Edward L. "An Informal History of the 601st Tank Destroyer Battalion." (unpublished manuscript, Salzburg, Austria, 1945). U.S. Army Heritage and Education Center, Carlisle, PA.

Judd, Dennis R., and Robert E. Mendelson. *The Politics of Urban Planning: The East St. Louis Experience*. Urbana: University of Illinois Press, 1973.

Kenney, David. *A Political Passage: The Career of Stratton of Illinois*. Carbondale: Southern Illinois University Press, 1990.

Kenney, David, and Robert E. Hartley. *The Heroic and the Notorious: U.S. Senators from Illinois*. Carbondale: Southern Illinois University Press, 2012.

Lee, Clyde. *Memoir*. Springfield: Sangamon State University, 1988.

Littlewood, Thomas B. *Horner of Illinois*. Evanston: Northwestern University Press, 1969.

———. *Soldiers Back Home: The American Legion in Illinois, 1919–1939*. Carbondale: Southern Illinois University Press, 2004.

Lockard, Melvin. . . . *and even the stump is gone: Reminiscences of a Southern Illinois Banker.* Tucson: Pepper Publishing, 1995.

Martin, John Bartlow. *Adlai Stevenson of Illinois.* Garden City: Doubleday, 1976.

Masters, Charles J. *Governor Henry Horner, Chicago Politics, and the Great Depression.* Carbondale: Southern Illinois University Press, 2007.

McCann, Kevin. "Kitty League 101." *The Bull Pen Kitty League Newsletter,* June–July 2005.

McCormick, Michael. Interview, oral history program, 8 July 2010. Abraham Lincoln Presidential Library.

Mitchell, Betty. *Delyte Morris of SIU.* Carbondale: Southern Illinois University Press, 1988.

Moore, Debra H., and Andrew F. Theising. "The Hollow Prize of East St. Louis: Institutional Function and Institutional Culture Limited a City's Future." *Journal of Illinois History* 11, no. 1 (2008): 17–38.

Munsell, Malinda L. "A History of Hamilton County." (unpublished manuscript, May 31, 1966). Copy from McCoy Municipal Library, McLeansboro, IL.

National Archives Personnel Records Center. "Choate, Clyde L., Enlisted record and report of separation, honorable discharge," 23 May 1945. Final payment roll, 26 May 1945. National Archives, St. Louis, MO.

National Archives Trust Fund. Unit journals and operations reports, October 1944, 601st Battalion, College Park, Maryland.

Nowlan, James D., Samuel K. Gove, and Richard J. Winkel Jr. *Illinois Politics: A Citizen's Guide.* Urbana: University of Illinois Press, 2010.

Pensoneau, Taylor. *Governor Richard Ogilvie: In the Interest of the State.* Carbondale: Southern Illinois University Press, 1997.

———. *Powerhouse: Arrington from Illinois.* Baltimore: American Literary Press, 2006.

Pensoneau, Taylor, and Bob Ellis. *Dan Walker: The Glory and the Tragedy.* Evansville: Smith Collins, 1993.

Rakove, Milton L. "Some Dissidents/Abner Mikva." In *We Don't Want Nobody Nobody Sent: An Oral History of the Daley Years.* Bloomington: Indiana University Press, 1979.

Redmond, William A. *Memoir.* 2 vols. Springfield: Sangamon State University, 1986.

Reynolds, John. *The Pioneer History of Illinois.* Belleville: N. A. Randall, 1852.

Scariano, Anthony. *Memoir.* 2 vols. Springfield: Sangamon State University, 1988.

Schapsmeier, Edward L., and Frederick H. Schapsmeier. "Scott W. Lucas of Havana: His Rise and Fall as Majority Leader in the United States Senate." *Journal of the Illinois State Historical Society* 70 (November 1977): 302–19.

Smith, George W. *History of Illinois and Her People*. Chicago: American Historical Society, 1927.

Sprehe, James E. "Origin of the Cahokia Empire." *St. Louis Post-Dispatch*, 12 September 1971.

Stelle, John H. Press release endorsing Everett Dirksen, 4 November 1949. Scott W. Lucas Collection, Abraham Lincoln Presidential Library.

Stelle, Russell. Interviews with author, 21 April 2010, 22 April 2010, and 18 May 2010.

Taggart, Donald G., ed. *History of the Third Infantry Division in World War II*. Compiled by the Third Infantry Division Office, Historical Section. Washington: Infantry Journal Press, 1947.

Theising, Andrew J. *East St. Louis: Made in USA, The Rise and Fall of an Industrial River Town*. St. Louis: Virginia Publishing, 2003.

U.S. Congress. Senate. Special Committee to Investigate Organized Crime in Interstate Commerce. 81st Cong., 2nd sess. Proceedings of hearings, 23–24 February 1951 in St. Louis, MO, parts 4, 4A, exhibit 5. Washington: Government Printing Office, 1952.

U.S. Department of Veterans Affairs. "History Born of Controversy: The GI Bill of Rights." (10 February 2010). http://www.va.gov/opa/publications/celebrate/gi-bill.pdf.

U.S. Tank Destroyer School. *TD Combat in Tunisia*. (unpublished manuscript, 1944).

Watters, Mary. *Illinois in the Second World War: The Production Front*. Vol. 2. Springfield: Illinois State Historical Society, 1952.

Yeide, Harry. *The Tank Killers: A History of America's World War II Tank Destroyer Force*. Philadelphia: Casemate Publishers, 2013.

Zaloga, Steven J. *Operation Dragoon 1944: France's Other D-Day*. Long Island City: Osprey Publishing, 2009.

Newspapers and Other Periodicals

Anna (IL) *Gazette-Democrat*
Brazil (IN) Times
Carbondale (IL) *Southern Illinoisan*
Chicago Daily News

Chicago Sun and *Sun-Times*
Chicago Times
Chicago Tribune
Decatur (IL) Herald and Review
East St. Louis Journal (Metro-East Journal)
Eldorado (IL) Daily Journal
Illinois Blue Book
Illinois State Journal
Illinois State Register
McLeansboro (IL) Times-Leader
St. Louis Globe-Democrat
St. Louis Post-Dispatch

Index

ROBERT E. HARTLEY is the author of several books for Southern Illinois University Press, including *Battleground 1948: Truman, Stevenson, Douglas, and the Most Surprising Election in Illinois History*; *Paul Powell of Illinois: A Lifelong Democrat*; and *Paul Simon: The Political Journey of an Illinois Original*. Hartley was a journalist in Idaho, Illinois, Ohio, and Washington State from 1959 to 1986.